The Evening of Life

(Compensations of Old Age)

TRANSLATED AND CONDENSED
FROM THE ORIGINAL FRENCH
OF MONSIGNOR BAUNARD
BY JOHN L. STODDARD

Louis Baunard.
b 24 August 1828
d 9 November 1919 ⟩ 91

THE BRUCE PUBLISHING COMPANY
MILWAUKEE

Nihil obstat

H. B. RIES,

Censor Librorum

Imprimatur

✠ S. G. MESSMER,

Archiepiscopus Milwauchiensis

July 9, 1930

AUTHOR'S PREFACE

An old man who has reached a very advanced age has, in his hours of solitude, gathered up in retrospect his impressions of the principal religious, moral, scientific, and political questions and events that, during the century of which he formed a part, chiefly contributed to the guidance of his mind and the conduct of his life. From these, he derives a new and clearer light with which to illumine the last stage of his journey, and in this volume he transmits it, as a modest heritage, to those whom he leaves behind and who, like him, will also reach old age. He presupposes in this book the presence of one of his contemporaries, whom he calls his brother, and this will explain the familiar, conversational tone found throughout its pages. Yet it does not exclude from the style a certain warmth, such as can still remain upon an old hearth now covered by the ashes of many years; nor does it lack a certain beauty that colors and consoles us for the coming of life's sunset.

Though largely made up of the author's personal recollections and experiences, this book consists still more of the memories of others. It calls upon the most illustrious of our contemporaries in literature, in the sciences, in the State, in the

AUTHOR'S PREFACE

Church, and in society, to give us—especially in the confidences of private letters—their views concerning things both human and divine, fortunate and unfortunate, which occurred in their time and were for them a light, an example, or a useful lesson.

The recollection of so many venerable landmarks and so many treasured names has given the author much joy, for has it not been said that "to remember is almost to begin again"? But above all, he has considered the writing of this book to be the supreme duty of his closing life. He has, therefore, made it the object of his constant meditation during some years of retirement, which, however, have been hardly sufficient for this review of more than three quarters of a century. It is his wish that this should be an offering of thanksgiving to the divine Master of life, Who has prolonged his existence till he could render Him this final act of homage. It is a service to which could be applied these words from the Book of Wisdom: "My course grows longer and the river of my days draws nearer to the sea. Therefore, will I now make true doctrine shine forth to all, and will enlighten all that hope in the Lord. Behold, I have not labored for myself alone, but for all who seek the truth."

Perhaps it will seem to some readers that, in order to speak competently and authoritatively on the

AUTHOR'S PREFACE

subject of old age and of old people, the author should not only be one of them, but should occupy, in point of years, an exalted rank. He will, therefore, disclose the fact that he attained several years ago, the limit of fourscore. May this advantage, which surely will not make him envied, entitle him at least to the fraternal confidence of the old, the compassionate indulgence of the young, and the prayers of all!

THE AUTHOR

TRANSLATOR'S PREFACE

Is there such a thing in the world now as old age? Are there any "old" people left? One is inclined to doubt it, when one sees white-haired women going about in public with short skirts, sleeveless dresses, and bobbed hair; and septuagenarian men skipping through fox trots with jaunty self-complacency. Many from whom we turn with averted eyes appear to be reincarnations of the old court fools with cap and bells. Such sights usually excite ridicule or pity, for nothing totally conceals, and little can retard, the inevitable touch of time. Since the silent, sandal-footed years that make us old are unavoidable, they should rather be welcomed than ignored. Goethe compared them to the Sibylline Books, whose value augmented in proportion as their number lessened. To grow old gracefully and with dignity is almost a lost art.

What causes this modern mania to avoid the thought and mention of old age? There was a time—and not so long ago—when it was honored in both man and matron. It had a dignity peculiarly its own, which every land and every century—till ours—had respected. How foolish of us moderns to treat it with frivolity! A wise French writer has aptly said: "Not to do honor to old age is to demolish in the morning the home wherein we are to sleep at night."

The greatest minds of antiquity and the loftiest spirits of the Christian world have always occupied themselves with this stupendous theme, as part of their spiritual education. It is a mistake to suppose that only the old can calmly meditate upon old age and death. One of the finest poems in the English language is Bryant's "Thanatopsis," which, though conceived from a purely pagan standpoint, is so noble and uplifting that it might daily be read with profit. Yet this was the work of a young man not yet twenty years of age. To shun the contemplation of eternity and the approach to it, is like lingering in a lighted ballroom, and refusing to survey the glittering stars and the vast heights of interstellar space.

God knows, we receive warnings enough to consider what life means and what death may mean. Cyclones, floods, and earthquakes follow one another with appalling frequency. "Humanity," say the Orientals, "is a caravan on the way to death." Every now and then a comrade falls out of line; but generally, we refuse to think about it, regard it as exceptional, close up the ranks, and the caravan moves on. Yet Seneca truthfully said: "Nothing reconciles us so quickly to the thought of our own death as the sight of one friend after another disappearing from our midst." But it is usually only late in life that we realize this.

x

TRANSLATOR'S PREFACE

It is our modern craze for sport, speed, luxury, sensual excesses, and the unbridled pursuit of pleasure that makes of us such triflers. But there is still another reason why so many banish old age from their thoughts. It is the fact that *they no longer believe it to be a period of preparation for another world.* They have become materialists, hedonists, and practically atheists, who treat the prevalent loss of faith in the supernatural as a joke, dance on the ruins of religion, find no other immortality for man than that of fertilizing the soil, and boast that they have banished the Creator from His universe. The materialist's god is man; his distant forbear was a beast; his family tree, a growth of the African jungle; his soul, a secretion of the brain. "The lights of heaven are put out," shouts Viviani gleefully. What a sad achievement —if true!

Although old age is unquestionably near the end of life, its outlook is not necessarily gloomy. Its standpoint might be likened to a strand between two seas—the sea of memory and that of hope. Whether it looks backward over one, or forward over the other, it finds a reason for serenity and cause for joy. Moreover, as life wanes, the desire to live on—often alone or misunderstood by the rising generation—grows less intense, till it becomes merely a wistful waiting for the end. The cords that bind us to this world are loosened one by one,

to be caught up by unseen hands and fastened elsewhere. We find ourselves at last fearlessly facing
and tranquilly expecting a world whose details are
unknown, but whose existence is undoubted. Nor
do we fear the passage.

Meanwhile, we sit beside still waters or linger in
the peaceful solitude of pleasant fields of intellectual reading and spiritual experience. We no
longer care to mingle with noisy crowds, to be
buffeted in the maelstrom of the world, or to throw
spotted bits of pasteboard on a table in tourna-
ments for pennies or for prizes. But with a few
congenial friends, in perfect sympathy of mind and
soul, we watch the sun sink toward the western
horizon.

For somehow we have come at last to know
    Of other shores beyond the sunset sea,
Where these poor, human lives shall further grow
    Toward something, vastly nobler, yet to be;
And where already, ere our sun be gone,
    The stars are heralding another dawn!

The book I have translated is one of the most
beautiful on this theme that I have ever read. The
author's preface fully explains its scope and character. I desire to make only the further statement
that the original volume seemed to me too long,
and here and there too exclusively national in sen-

timent, to reproduce in its entirety; but in my opinion the best of the book is here.

I hope that it will give to others the pleasure, hope, and consolation it has given me. For it admirably represents the *Christian* standpoint on old age. Philosophy can render old age bearable, as many writers of antiquity have proved; but Christian faith alone can make it desirable, beautiful, and hopeful. Old age without the consolations of religion is moonlight as compared to sunlight. Our century largely lacks these consolations, and hence is restless and unhappy. Its infidelity brings dissoluteness to the young, discouragement to the mature, and despair to the old. Its cynicism makes men look unmoved upon the present tragedy of the world. Great principles are wanting and great men are rare. Life has become almost unbearable—especially to the old—through the machines we have created, the speed at which we move, and the amusements we have invented as narcotics. Desire and discontent keep pace with our achievements. We who are old are the worst sufferers, for boisterous youth guffaws at our preference for decency and quiet, and decimates us with its automobiles. We dare not confide our melancholy to anyone, but it is there, and sometimes, without seeming cause, our eyes grow dim with tears. The saddest part of it is, that it is symptomatic of an orphaned, soul-starved race seeking unconsciously its Father. I hope that this translation of a noble work may help some weary souls to find Him. For, on the day when all that is immortal in us shall go forth empty-handed into eternity, all the acquired money of this world and all the fleeting pleasures purchased by it, will be a worthless passport at the gate of heaven, compared to such faith and hope as inspired Whittier, in his poem, "At Last," to write:

When on my day of life the night is falling,
  And in the wind from unsunned spaces blown,
I hear far voices out of darkness calling
  My feet to paths unknown.

Thou Who hast made my house of life so pleasant,
  Leave not its tenant when its walls decay;
O Love Divine, O Helper ever present,
  Be Thou my strength and stay.

Be near me when all else is from me drifting;
  Earth, sky, home's pictures, days of shade and
    shine,
And kindly faces to my own uplifting
  The love which answers mine.

I have but Thee, my Father, let Thy spirit
  Be with me then to comfort and uphold;

TRANSLATOR'S PREFACE

No gate of pearl, no branch of palm I merit,
    Nor street of shining gold.

Suffice it if—my good and ill unreckoned,
    And both forgiven through Thy abounding
        grace—
I find myself by hands familiar beckoned
    Unto my fitting place.

There, from the music round about me stealing,
    I fain would learn the new and holy song,
And find at last, beneath Thy trees of healing,
    The life for which I long.

CONTENTS

CHAPTER   PAGE

AUTHOR'S PREFACE v
TRANSLATOR'S PREFACE ix
1. OLD AGE—THE ASCENDING LIFE . . . 1
2. THANKSGIVING 17
3. THE CENTURY—PROGRESS AND SUFFER-
   ING 31
4. APPREHENSION: "WHERE IS LIFE
   GOING?" 48
5. SCIENCE AND BELIEF—OUR GREAT
   MASTERS 71
6. SCIENCE AND SOPHISM—BANKRUPTCY . 85
7. GOD EVERYWHERE—THE WORLD AND
   THE SOUL 107
8. THE GOSPEL—A TORCH 125
9. THE CHURCH—AUTHORITY 146
10. BEREAVEMENTS — CONSOLATIONS . . . 166
11. SHADOWS—MISTAKES—REGRETS 178
12. RETIREMENT—REPOSE—THE FIELDS . . 191
13. BOOKS—LAST PAGES 210
14. OLD AGE AND THE BETTER LIFE 223
15. EXPIATION—REPARATION 235
16. IMMORTALITY—HOPE 254
17. PREPARATION—THE END 272
    BIBLIOGRAPHY 285

CHAPTER
ONE

Old Age — The Ascending Life

My conception of old age is this: It is not a decline, it is progress; it is not a descent, it is an ascent. It is, therefore, of the benefit, the grandeur, the lofty revelations, the intimate joys, the solemn duties, and the supreme hope of this ascending life that I wish to speak in this book.

My brother, you are now about seventy years old, perhaps a little more, perhaps a little less. At all events, the evening of your life has come. You feel its shadow darkening your eyes; its chill penetrates your frame. Seating yourself wearily beside the dusty road, you say to yourself, as you contemplate the setting sun: "I, too, am going down!"

Yes, brother, we are going down; you speak the truth. But, when you say this, of what are you thinking? Of the body, are you not? Of the old invalid, worn out by sixty years of work in the service of that immortal sovereign—your soul. But it is with this august sovereign herself, not with her subaltern, the body, that you have to do. Ask her —your soul—about her lofty desires, her noble aspirations, her views and dreams of what is beyond

1

the grave. Then listen silently to what the spreading of her ample wings, preparatory to her flight on the supreme voyage, says to your mind. "I feel myself borne upward," said the aged Dufaure, as he breathed his last sigh to God.

Alfred de Vigny, in half a dozen lines of a note in his "Journal d'un Poète," sketches the following scene in Iceland. "In the polar nights, which are six months long, a traveler is climbing a mountain. From its summit the sun, which has long been invisible, appears to him in the distant east. Already the peaks are illumined, although the darkness of the night still shrouds the valley at his feet. Such a traveler, is the poet," says De Vigny. Such a traveler, *we* say, is also the old man. It is by the breadth and the depth of the perspectives which disclose themselves in the light thus awakened, and by the glittering summits soon to be crowned with a radiant sun that will never more sink below the horizon, that the traveler through life is able to measure the altitude to which the years have brought him. He has ascended, he is still ascending. There is in this comparison more than mere imagery and poetry. It is something which has been seen and experienced by thousands. In proportion as I advance in age, I feel in my mind and heart the impression of an upward progress toward scenes and toward horizons ever grander, more vast; while, reciprocally, everything that is below me grows smaller and more insignificant.

Recently I passed a few days in my native town. How grand those places which I knew in childhood once seemed to me! My father's fields, where, as a little boy, I disappeared from sight in the deep furrows of tall grain; the great woods, whose exit opened into a distant point of light; an ancient church, whose arches seemed to meet in the sky; and an old feudal dungeon, whose lofty towers I measured with my gaze from the threshold of my father's little home. All this was then infinitely great! Can it be possible that today that is, to my maturer eyes, only one of the varieties of the infinitely little? It is the effect of perspective; for the things of today reveal themselves to me from the height of that lofty terrace called old age, to which my eighty years, like so many rounds of a ladder, have brought me.

The truth is, life is an ascent; and time may be compared prosaically to an elevator. Old age is the last landing place but one; after it, I shall be left upon the threshold of my Father's house. Imperceptibly I have been ascending, and I am still ascending. Even the events of last year (great events at the time) have already become small, and what a tiny place they occupy among the countless years and deeds! And the personages of the past! They remind me of the heroes of Gulliver's Travels; giants yesterday, they seem to me today nothing but pigmies; village chanticleers, which as a child I naïvely took for eagles, because they flapped their wings, erected their combs, and crowed! And the impressions of those days; the joys and sorrows, griefs and enthusiasm, for example, of my college life! How all those dark or roseate clouds, which passed above my timid or exultant heart, have been dissolved, scattered by the breath of years! How grateful I am to age for having brought me thus insensibly to the region of pure realities, where, at last, things are judged for what they are, and men for their real worth! For it is a fact, my brother, that everything on this earth is only relative; the Absolute exists in God alone. And if the elevation of my present point of view has already corrected the errors and exaggerations of my earthly vision, what will it be when I shall have reached the superelevation of the heavenly vision? What shall we think of man and his deeds, when, having ascended to God and having been absorbed in Him, we shall behold Him and all things in the light of glory? *In lumine tuo videbimus lumen!*

In the *Chaumière Indienne* of Bernardin de Saint-Pierre, the pariah thus consoles himself for his miserable existence: "My unhappy life resembles the black mountain at the extremity of the torrid kingdom of Lahore. While you are ascending it, you see before you only sterile rocks; but

when you reach the summit, you perceive the
boundless sky above you and at your feet the entire
kingdom of Cashmire." Thus did the saints console themselves for this world and for this life.
"How small the earth appears to one who sees
heaven!" exclaims the poet. Thus also does the
soul excuse the incapacities of the body. "If I get
out of breath," said Henri Lasserre at seventy years
of age, "it is because I am ascending." And Father
Lacordaire, three years before his death, exclaimed:
"I feel myself growing old. The body is changing,
wrinkles are deepening, the hair is whitening, and
the senses grow feebler. But the soul floats above
the incipient ruins, as the light of day illumines
and transforms to gold the columns of a fallen
temple."

"Alas! Postumus, Postumus, the fleeting years
glide swiftly by. No piety prevents the coming
of either wrinkles, approaching age, or invincible
death." These lines of Horace present a different
conception of old age. It is that of the swift passing of time. Art has often portrayed Father Time
with wings. He is not supposed to walk, but to
fly. Yet it is especially in the last lap that his course
is not only accelerated, but becomes precipitate.
The wheel of the chariot now turns so rapidly that
still more of reckoning the number of its spokes.

Tell me truly, brother: Have the years still really
the eye despairs of counting its revolutions and

twelve months, the months thirty days, and the days twenty-four hours? For evening treads upon the heels of morning, the sunset follows close upon the dawn; and between the two, the moments which remain melt in the fire of our latest suns, like a snowball in the hand of a child.

Where now is the time when to me, a happy, artless boy, a year seemed like a century? Life then flowed on as slowly as the newborn rivulet trickles from its source. But the cares, the undertakings, the eagerly formed plans, and all the impetuous streams of life which come to swell its current, have made of it a rapid, leaping torrent. And now, how fast it hurries on, my brother, how fast it hurries on! "Alas, Postumus, Postumus!"

"You see, my son," the good old priest who was my childhood teacher said to me one day, "it is the law of spiritual gravitation which is working on our souls, like that of physical attraction on our bodies. The intensity of its speed is in direct proportion to the proximity of the body that attracts. The center of attraction for our souls is God. We who are old now hasten to Him, not only because we are asked by Him to come, but because He is so near!"

Let me mention another phenomenon, which is no less perceptible in those who have reached our age. It is the reversion of memory to the most distant shores past which our stream of life has flown. We, who are old, well know this magical revival of our youth and childhood, when memory beguiles us with the fancy that those youthful scenes can live again. Yet at the same time, singularly enough, our memory no longer registers recent events. Nothing new cuts its image deeply on this old and worn-out photographic plate, which resists every impression of today's solar rays, whether they are those of places, dates, names, writings, or objects which I look for and even touch, yet can no longer find! But, while I impatiently strike my poor old forehead, vainly seeking everything recent that has slipped away, a "distant" ray of light whose sudden arrival lingers in my mind and illumines it, without my having summoned it, appears. It has leaped forth, like a flash of lightning, from the black, subconscious depths of an abyss, in which I had thought it forever lost; and it unearths to my astonished gaze a fossil world I had not sought. Do I call it a "fossil" world? No, it is a living world. It is my youth, my early childhood, that is thus restored to me, vivid, smiling, charming, and pictured in the same old frame of places, persons, and actions, with a fidelity and vivacity which revive the old emotions simultaneously with the vision.

O sweet mirage, which, by repeopling them, can make so beautiful and consoling the arid deserts of the last stage of our journey! And you, unhoped-

for visitors from the past, who come to ease the
sorrows of farewell to earth, what do you wish
from me? "Dear phantoms," asks Maxime du
Camp in his *Crépuscule*, "whence come you? What
do you bring me? What do you desire to say to
me? For these beloved spirits address and answer
me. In spite of the tone of sadness with which
their voices appear veiled, how harmoniously they
speak to my heart! They have the sweetness of
the melodies that lulled my infancy to sleep, and
that one hears with tear-dimmed eyes." They
come from the depths of the valley, and usually
ascend from it in the hush of evening. The old
man on the icy summit bends forward and listens
to them eagerly. How penetrating is their tone!

What is this sentiment, my brother, and why do
we feel it? I have reflected on it, and this is my
conclusion: It is part of the consummation of life.
The two ends of the chain are being reunited; the
two poles of existence meet by means of some mag-
netic current which makes itself felt in the soul.
Not, however, without a quivering and trembling
of the nerves. The circle is about to be completed;
the globe has been circumnavigated, and life has
rounded itself into an entirety.

And to what end? Why am I given this mental recapitulation of the whole course of my existence? Is it a preparation for the speedy rendering
of my account? I prefer to say, O my Creator and

Father, what Thou revealest thus before my eyes is a long résumé of all Thy benefits, gifts, and graces to me in the past. It is to remind me of the general offering of thanksgiving, due to Thee from me, and which Thou hast a right to look for from my love. Accept, then, my supreme, spontaneous rendering of gratitude. It is the evening sacrifice spoken of in the Ancient Law, of which the old man in his suffering body is the victim, and at the same time, in his sanctified and consecrated soul, the priest!

How far we are here from the pagan concept of old age! The ancient world considered the passing of the old man, as of one descending a hill, staff in hand, his white head shaking in the evening wind. Seeing him journeying thus, bent over toward the ground, antiquity saluted him compassionately and respectfully. He was returning to the earth, and that salutation was an essential farewell.

The Christian world, on the contrary, views the passing of such a man, as of one ascending tranquilly toward a mountain summit, which, though invisible, is near. It is the last stage of his long journey; and his bared head is raised to seek and salute the wished-for crest. He reaches it. The clouds roll far beneath his feet; a light, descending from on high, illumines his forehead; the heavens open. From the celestial side, loved voices call him toward them: "Come to us"; while, on the earthly side, other loved voices whisper to him: "Farewell, till we meet again." No, our type of an old man is not a mortal who is finishing his course— he is an immortal who is beginning it.

*   *   *

But not only our recollections group themselves together in old age; our thoughts do the same. Memory has reawakened the former; intelligence unifies the latter. It is at eventide that the reaper gathers the ears of corn to bind them into sheaves. "When I was a child," wrote St. Paul, "I thought as a child, I spoke as a child." How small and infantile were my own childish perceptions! I had then merely isolated, incomplete, and fragmentary ideas—points, not lines; grains, not ears of corn! As a child, I could only spell out laboriously the books of men and the Book of God. Now I can read them; the letters form words, the words make phrases, the phrases fill pages. Fórms of knowledge and ideas approach one another and group themselves together, making unity in the midst of universality.

Who has opened to me this field of broad and fruitful generalizations? Ask the tourist of the Alps or Pyrenees how it happens that, as he nears the summit, the mighty mountain mass, instead of presenting, as it did a while ago from the depths

of the valley, only chaotic disorder, now displays
to his admiring gaze the majestic harmony of a
stately edifice? It is because it towers on high,
just as the old man's spirit soars above the plains
of existence. Edgar Quinet, at the end of his life,
experienced the truth of this. "I had looked forward to old age," he says, "as to an icy, narrow
peak, concealed in mists. On the contrary, I now
perceive, encircling me, a vast horizon which had
never before been visible to my gaze. I understand
myself and everything more clearly."

Life ascends, life concentrates itself, life becomes
broader and more luminous; but that is not all.
Life purifies itself. Upon the heights the air is
pure. The tranquil chastity of age, freed from
the tyranny of the senses, loves only with the soul,
and in fact loves only souls. "Sooner or later,"
wrote Vauvenargues, "we enjoy only souls." Beneath the bodily exterior, it is souls that we seek
in books, in art, and in life itself. It is the highest
form of enjoyment. But what an elevated heart
one must have to appreciate it! Joubert understood this. He, the Platonist—Platone platonior,
as he called himself—having reached the age of
seventy, wrote, on the third of May, 1821: "Old
age makes happy only the old priest and those who
resemble him." To which Sainte-Beuve adds:
"Yet Monsieur Joubert rose to those loftier heights,
as he advanced in life and entered that state of

happiness. Old age appeared to him as something purified from the body and near to God; and he heard distinctly that voice of wisdom, which is of neither sex; the voice of Fénelon and that of Plato, which he knew so well. Wisdom is repose in light and virtue."

Finally, old age is the age of peace! This altitude is above the region of storms. In the mind there are fewer violent opinions, less professional obstinacy, fewer aggressive disputes. In the heart, also, is an indulgent goodness, born from a long experience of men and life; born also from the feeling of one's own intrinsic poverty and frailty.

In the character, also, there is now more tolerance. Père Lacordaire wrote, shortly before his death: "We are growing old, my friend, but without losing anything of real youth, which is that of truth and love. I confess to you, I have never felt inwardly more serene than now. When one is young, one has a multitude of ideas which are not yet clearly defined. One looks, one hesitates. Moreover, the character is not yet formed. It is either too inflexible or too yielding. But at our age the soul of a man is fully molded. He has now only to live as he really is, tranquilly yet resolutely, awaiting the hour of rest."

*   *   *

I will, therefore, exclaim with Father Gratry: "O my God, give to me the supreme serenity of a soul which has survived its passions, but not its strength; and which, in the final period of calm, conceives the origin and apprehends the principle of eternal life!"

"It is the *autumn*," writes the same author in his admirable book on the *Knowledge of the Soul*— the autumn of life, whose mists and waning beauty he at first compares to a "chant of death." But when the author reaches the last page, he perceives that all the time he has been singing not of death, but of life, and he writes: "I cannot help seeing that the more I wish to describe the beginning of my decline, the more I find that, after all, it is progress that I am recording. This autumn is not the season of the fall of leaves, it is only that of the fall of flowers, necessary for the coming of fruits."

Old age, like autumn, has its own poetry; the tender, melancholy poetry of the season most beloved by painters and poets, when nature decks herself in her richest hues, the leaves are turned to gold, evenings are tinged with purple, migratory birds depart for sunnier lands, and seeds bury themselves in the ground to become impregnated with life. This is the poetry of outward things; but there is an inward poetry which is better still. It is composed of those songs which the soul of

the old man repeats to itself; songs which are made
up of souvenirs and hopes, of sadness and of smiles.
It is the poetry of solitude and of great, eloquent
silences; the poetry of the highest love, the poetry
of purity, of penitence, of tender farewells, and of
promised reunions that shall never end.

It is this supreme poetry—the most beautiful of
all—that has been called the swan's song. It is that
of Scipio's heavenly "Dream." It is that which
inspired those venerable bards, whom antiquity
represents to us as chanting, to an accompaniment
of harps of gold, the praises of the heroes and the
gods. Better than that, I find this poetry accompanied by the harps of the Hebrew prophets. It
is the canticle of Hezekiah: "By the rivers of
Babylon   .   .   ." and the Psalmist's "How amiable
are Thy tabernacles, O Lord of hosts!" Does not
Saint Augustine also tell us that the last stage of
the Christian's journey will end in the chant of
Alleluia?

A modern poet, Sully Prudhomme, confides to
us in verse the fact that he hopes at last to seat
himself in contemplation on those peaceful heights.
He says:

Let the years come! I long for that wise age,
  When through the veins the blood more calmly
      flows,
When earthly passions no more fret the sage,
  And one bears cheerfully the ills one knows;

Oh, may I sit, at last, upon life's crest,
  And contemplate the past, exempt from pain,
As from some lofty peak, with soul at rest,
  One views the routes and rivers of the plain.

But to contemplate one's life is to look backward
and downward. Should we not rather direct our
gaze forward and upward? "Lift up your eyes to
heaven," says our Savior, Who awaits us there.
He, Himself, comes to meet us, as our days draw
near their end; and the evening which I hope for,
at the close of my day, and of yours, my brother,
is like that mysterious, sacred one, when Jesus,
having risen from the tomb, rejoins the two disciples on the road to Emmaus. The divine Con-
querer of death does not overwhelm them by His
majesty, or dazzle them by His glory; He merely
revives their hope which had been well-nigh lost,
and rekindles their love by the secret ardor of His
presence.

"Lord, abide with us," said the two pilgrims,
"for the day is far spent"; and this we, too, shall
say to the divine Companion of the evening of our
life. Like those two pilgrims to Emmaus, we also
shall entreat Him not to go on, but to enter our
abode, to seat Himself near us, and to break bread
with us. He Himself is the Viaticum; we are the
travelers. We shall recognize Him in His supreme
act of love under the symbols, in which He veils
Himself. And even if, in that hour dark with

earth-born shadows, He shall still conceal Himself from our clear vision, we shall find Him, on the morrow, face to face in all His peace and glory.

> Abide with us and never, Lord, depart!
> Celestial phantom, aid our failing heart!
> The mighty mountains shroud the vales below,
> The century closes, with a world in woe;
> We fear the deadly cold, the waning light,
> We love Thee, Lord; abide with us tonight.*

---

*From the French of Jean Aicard.

CHAPTER
TWO

Thanksgiving

Our whole life, but especially that part of it known as old age, ought to be a song of thanksgiving. The last combat then is ending, the battle is won, the crown awaits us: *Vixisti, Victor, vicisti!* (O Victor, thou hast lived and conquered.) It is the hour in which to bend the knee, to salute the sword, to lift up our eyes, and to say to the Lord of hosts: *"Te Deum Laudamus."*

In all the literatures of the world, old age is called a crown; *corona dignitatis,* says the Holy Bible. True, it is the crown of a conqueror, yet it is a crown of laurel interlaced with thorns; and those who gain it, although kings among men, must receive it on their knees, in thanksgiving, as a gift from heaven.

For what blessings, then, are we to give thanks? First of all, for old age itself. If life in general is a benefit, old age is an exceptional favor. Very small, indeed, is the sacred battalion of life's veterans. According to statistics, the average limit of human life is about forty years. If, then, you are sixty, seventy, or eighty years old, you have seen a third or a half of your generation disembark in the course of this voyage, while you, a more fortunate passenger, have prolonged it into oceans, the farther shores of which you do not yet perceive. It is a rare and precious gift. For if "time is money," what a treasure old age must be, rich as it is with the accumulation of past years, of which it can make eternal years the reward!

During even sixty years, that is, during nearly 22,000 days and nights, we have been, as it were, carried in the motherly arms of that Providence, of which a philosopher has written: "Has not God placed man on the earth, like an infant in its cradle? He proportions to his strength the length of the day which He gives him; and, when the hours of wakefulness are ended, He draws the curtain on the world and imposes silence upon nature, in order that everyone and everything may sleep and recuperate its forces. Thus does He carry us from sleep to wakefulness and from wakefulness to sleep, and, like a nurse, cradle His child between night and day." Again: "Who has thanked God sufficiently for all the joy He puts into our hearts by the light of day, and for all the mysterious sentiments inspired in us by the influence of the night? Who remembers to thank Him for the sweet hope which the morning awakens in us, and for the tender melancholy that the sight of the setting sun imparts to us?"

Is all this nothing, my brother? Is it nothing that we have had these thousands of daily reawakenings to life for more than three quarters of a century, during which morning caused light to flow into our minds as well as into our eyes, and brought to our hearts a blood fresher for new work and more responsive to new pleasures? Is it nothing that we have enjoyed this continued gift of health, that is to say, an uninterrupted succession of victories over the thousands of visible and invisible enemies of our existence? And what shall we say of the blessings of the family, home, school, friendship, education, and the joys of mind and heart?

Must not this munificence of earth and heaven, multiplied by the almost incalculable hours of our existence, lift our hearts today in gratitude toward the eternal Heart? And do you not feel inclined, my brother, in this evening of life, to bind together into sheaves all these collected benefits and to offer them to God, like those which the Hebrews, after the harvest, were wont to lay as an oblation before the altar of Jehovah with an accompaniment of sacred songs?

The following would be my hymn of praise tonight, my brother; would it not be, more or less, yours, also? "For all the gifts Thy hand has scattered over each and all the seasons of my life—childhood, boyhood, youth, and manhood, even to my present advanced age, I bless Thee, Lord! For the good and humble father and mother Thou didst give me, for my brothers and sisters, for our modest home where Thou wast prayed to, loved, and served, and where, thanks to Thee, we lived together retired, united, and happy, I bless Thee, Lord! For the daily bread, which Thou hast never denied me, for the ample life of the fields, with which Thou hast nourished me, for the first awakenings of my intelligence, when it caught its earliest glimpse of Thee and apprehended Thee in the light of Thy works, I bless Thee, Lord! For the little school, where my first book was put into my hand, and the first pen between my fingers; for the church, where the priest, who loved me, taught me to weep before the crucifix, to exult before the Gospel, and to worship before Thine altar, I bless Thee, Lord! For the friendships I have found and for those that I have kept, for the kindnesses that have been shown me, for the heaven-vouchsafed ignorance of many things by which I was surrounded, for the indulgent goodness which has pardoned my faults, and for all the strong and tender hands which have been extended to me on the road that leads to Thee, Who art Goodness Itself, I bless Thee, Lord! For the poetical love of the beautiful which Thou hast inspired in me, for the light of truth which Thou hast deigned to give me, for the way of righteousness in which Thou hast caused loving guides to walk before me, providing thus illustrious examples to illumine my path, I bless Thee, Lord! For the perils and pitfalls which I have escaped, for the pernicious currents of evil from which Thou hast preserved or rescued me, from the maladies of which Thou hast cured me, for the vigor which I gained in my youth, in order still to serve Thy purposes in the post Thou hadst prepared for me; for all these mercies, I thank Thee, Lord, I thank Thee, Lord!"

*   *   *

Service, work, duty. In the last analysis, that which constitutes the worth of life is not existence itself, but the use we make of it and what we make it yield us. In the last poem of Ibsen, which the old poet entitled: "When We Shall Awake Among the Dead," the final words of his heroine, Irene, are these: "When we awake among the dead, we shall perceive that we have never lived!" She says this of useless existences, of lives that were direct failures. But what shall we say, my brother, of the world's merely obscure and simple lives?

No doubt those who have really lived are those who have accomplished great things, because they themselves were great men—the founders of nations, the liberators of peoples, the explorers of oceans and continents, inventors, scientists, poets, writers, artists of genius and talent; and *their* thanksgiving was the dedication of their work to the Eternal.

But how about the little ones, the very little ones —the innumerable multitudes who did no works and left no name? A fine offering, truly, to lay at the foot of Thy throne, great King, would be the clod of earth that I have turned, the iron bar I have hammered, the piece of wood I have carved, or the stone I have polished, and the bit of woolen I have spun or cotton I have woven! What a sorry figure I should thus present in Thy sight! And how much should I then weigh in Thy eternal balance, I a poor atom, lost in the whirlwind of universal existence?

But it is not thus that our Father judges us; for in the Gospel, He says to the humblest and poorest laborer, who brings to Him the very small, but conscientiously acquired fruit of his efforts: "Well done, good and faithful servant. Thou hast been faithful over a few things, I will make thee ruler over many things." How much encouragement this word "well done" contains! And how much consolation is in that phrase "a few things" (*in modico*) and how many promises are indicated in the "over many things" (*super multa*)!

Well done! Good laborer who every day are accustomed to bow your forehead over the few acres of earth which, during sixty years, you have opened, turned, improved, sown, and reaped *in modico;* yet who, on every Sunday, raise your fore-head heavenward, presenting to God the living homage of two generations of your sons and daughters, who have learned from you to walk uprightly before Him. Come, I will make thee ruler *super multa!* Well done, good artisan, good workman, good maidservant, who come to me after the duty you have long fulfilled in the weari-some and obscure post to which I assigned you! Is not the smoke that rises from the factory, from the locomotive, the forge, the farmer's chimney, the home of the poor widow, and the stove of the humble servant also an agreeable incense to Me?

There is not a single station in life, a single con-dition of fortune, birth, or rank which does not furnish to a noble soul both the occasion and the obligation of blessing God for His gifts; and whether we have carried the sword or the trowel, handled a pen or a brush, held a compass or a pickax, a scalpel or a hatchet, it is equally our duty, at the close of day, to lay our instruments of labor with thanksgiving at God's feet. But what, you may ask, is the best way of expressing and showing our gratitude? I find it in a sincere and joyous con-tentment with my lot. Listen, my brother, to the following conversation of two men whom a storm once compelled to seek shelter together under an oak tree. One was a gentleman of the court of Louis XIII, the illustrious De Rancé, the other a poor old shepherd who knew nothing but his flock. "Noticing in this man," relates De Rancé, "an unusual air of serenity and peace, I began to converse with him. He told me he was sixty years old, and I asked him if he found pleasure in the occupation in which he passed his days. He replied that he found in it profound tranquillity; that there was something so consoling in caring for these simple innocent animals, that the days seemed to him only like moments; that he found so much quiet sweetness in his condition that he preferred it to all else in the world; that kings were not so happy and contented as he; that nothing was lacking to complete his happiness; and that he would not wish to leave this earth to go to heaven, if he did not think he should find there, also, pastures and flocks of sheep to tend." De Rancé declares that the naïve contentment of this humble peasant revealed to him the source of true happiness: "Admiring this man's simplicity, . . . I understood that it is not the possession of the good things of this world that constitutes happiness, but the innocence of our morals, the simplicity and moderation of our desires, the absence of things which one can do without, a joyful submission to the will of God, and a love and appreciation of the state of life into which it has pleased God to place us." I have spoken thus of the thanksgiving of the humble; but what is the thanksgiving of the great, when they are no longer so, but have been deprived of their power and fallen from the summit of their grandeur?

After the tale of a shepherd, let us consider the case of a queen driven from her throne, banished from her kingdom, the widow of a husband who had been beheaded (Charles I). Around the coffin of Henriette of France, daughter of Henry IV and Queen Marie of England, is gathered the entire court of Louis XIV, to weep over her misfortunes. But she herself had not wept over them; and from the pulpit, Bossuet testified that "the unfortunate princess always thanked God every day"—for what? "Not for having made her a queen, but for having made her an unhappy queen!"

From the dungeon which he was to leave on the morrow to ascend the scaffold, the High Chancellor of England, Sir Thomas More, wrote a farewell letter to his daughter. His lines breathe more than contentment; they express tender joy. He writes: "It seems to me that God holds me on His knees and rocks me gently, as His child." If we linger in that same country, we shall also one day hear the poet Milton, old and blind, blessing and thanking God—for what? Actually for his blindness! He writes: "In the night which envelops me, the light of the Divine Presence shines with greater brilliancy. God looks upon me with more tenderness, because henceforth *I can see only Him!*"

In reviewing, therefore, my long life, I bless my God for all that I am, and for all that I have done, or rather, for all that He has done through me. In spite of my cowardice and numberless failures, He has mercifully deigned to keep me in His service, and I bless Him for His patience and His pardons. He has allowed the labors of His servant not always to remain unfruitful nor his work entirely lost; and I bless Him for His munificence. He has given to me, more than to others, length of days and the complete circle of life's seasons, so that I can reap where I have sown; I bless Him, therefore, for His merciful forbearance.

I have had my days of sadness, as well as my days of joy. I have also met proud and wicked men; but, more than many others perhaps, I have known intimately saints, sages, and heroes. On the whole, life has been good to me; and now, at last, at the end of my journey, when I have been obliged to stop, I have found beneath the open sky a mossy stone. Here I may rest my weary limbs while waiting for the heavenly hand which will assuredly be stretched out to me when the hour shall come for me to depart. Thus, taken all in all, the best thing for me to do, will be to cling unceasingly to that hand. Without it, O my God, what should I do? For it is not enough to recognize the fact that I have been aided, supported, and led throughout my life; the real truth, the adorable truth, is that I am *carried*.

*   *   *

"Carried by God." What sort of statement is this? Is it merely a vague proclamation of a universal Providence, extended to all human beings? Is it a recognition of that guidance, as applied to the government of every one of us and to every act of our existence? Yes, certainly; for I read that truth everywhere in the Holy Scriptures. But there is another book which gives me a *personal* revelation of that constant, sovereign, and divine intervention which I have experienced, and which impresses me in an entirely different manner; this is *the history of my own life.* I read from one end of it to the other, on every page and in every line, that I at the same time am both free and—carried. Impenetrable mystery of the harmonious action of free will and grace! But it is a mystery which I have verified in my life, and which is interpreted and justified for me by a daily experience of three quarters of a century. It is none other than an experience of the direct action of God.

Innumerable memories confirm this, reminding me of circumstances in which, groping blindly, I could not see my way; times when, inert and helpless, I could not rise from where I lay; or when, rebellious and refractory, I refused to walk. It was then that, suddenly, I felt myself not only enlightened, incited, and restored inwardly, but assisted and supported by Someone Who, dominating me by

His strength yet enveloping me with His tenderness, took me and carried me in His arms. At times I cried, and even struggled on His breast, like a sick or threatened child, whom his father bears away and saves, despite his resistance, in the night. But now the night is passed; the day has come; my eyes are opened, and I recognize my Savior! He it was, then, Who carried me, in spite of everything, to heights of wisdom and happiness on which I had turned my back. He, better than I, knew the way to those pure altitudes; for was it not He Who created us for our destinies, whose secret He withholds, and of which He is the Master? And Who but He enabled me gently yet firmly to reach the desired goal, smoothed the pathway to it, and lowered all the intervening barriers? How many errors were made clear by Him, how many illusions dissipated! How many mistakes corrected! How many hours of anguish soothed! Who else has caused the obstacle at last to become a means of attainment, the byway to become a highway, and a hitherto unseen door to open, through which has passed out, not my will, O my God, but Thine, while through it have come back to me perfect security, peace, and joy?

It is precisely when human reason sees itself compelled to abdicate before the unknown and the impenetrable, and the powerless will is forced to face the seemingly impossible, that some unexpected dénouement comes to reveal the presence of an invisible but all-powerful factor in the problem, to which alone the result is due. Certain signs infallibly betray its presence; but to determine just how many times it intervenes, requires a constant, thoughtful, and delicate attention of both mind and heart. This instrument of observation is within the reach of all, but how few make use of it! And yet it would reveal to us unsuspected marvels. A recognition, based upon experience, of the part which divine intervention plays in each of our acts, would be the assignment to its proper place of the supernatural element in the history of every one of us. Old age renders us peculiarly well adapted for this work, since it permits us to perceive, from the height we have attained, the unity of the direction of our life-course, above the apparent divergence of the paths. Order at last discloses itself, where before we had seen only confusion. It is the same with the goodness, beauty, and grandeur that are now recognized. This view, which dazzles us by its clarity, at the same time overwhelms us with gratitude and love for our immortal Leader, in anticipation of the time when this celestial guidance, now so evident, will be the object of our eternal thankfulness.

The Talmud tells us, "There will come a day, when every prayer will die away into silence on the lips of men, except the prayer of thanksgiving." And in his prophetic vision, St. John represents to us the "four and twenty Elders prostrate before Him, Who is seated on the throne of heaven. They are clad in white robes, and on their heads are crowns of gold. And there, casting down their crowns at His feet, they sing to Him continually the song of gratitude: Blessing, glory, wisdom, honor, and thanksgiving be to our God, Who liveth forever and ever.   Amen!"

CHAPTER
THREE

The Century
Progress and Suffering

When we old men of a former generation meet,
it is usually to sing in a duet or chorus the pathetic
old song, "Do you remember?" This song has some
ninety-nine couplets and invariably ends in a minor
key with the plaintive words: "How changed
everything is! But are we on that account better
and happier today?" What is your opinion on this
point, brother? A modern writer says: "If,
through the caprice of some moralizing or jesting
divinity, we were suddenly carried back over seventy years to a metropolis of muddy, ill-paved
streets, devoid of sidewalks and electric lights; to
cities without busses or street cars, and traversed
by an insufficient number of wretched taxis; to a
country not yet crossed by railroads or airways,
. . . if we found there merely a few newspapers, existing only through precarious privileges,
likely to be recalled; if mail was irregular, inter-
mittent, and expensive; if telegraphic communication was not even suspected; if ether had not yet
deadened the agony of the surgeon's knife; if Pas-

teur had not yet muzzled hydrophobia; if our
motor ships were not yet churning up the oceans;
if the isthmuses of Suez and Panama were still
impediments separating worlds; and if, on the high-
ways of France, one could still see long lines of
galley slaves tramping to their hideous fate; should
we not have a right to exclaim: "When was all this
to be seen? And who could live in such an age?"

But that was seen only yesterday, and those who
lived in those times were ourselves—the grand-
fathers and great-uncles of today! The mocking
fairy who takes us back there is our memory, which
could recall to us, also, many other things quite as
marvelous as these; but fortunately, also, better
ones; for of all the results of progress, the one we
old men value most is that which reveals itself in
the greater amount of good brought to the mass
of mankind, especially to children.

I hasten, therefore, to say for my sake and for
yours, my brother, let us think back to the time
when the peasant woman and the workman ate
only black bread, almost never meat; wore only
gingham or overalls, slept on straw, and lived in
a hut in the village or in a cellar in the town. Read
again the description which La Bruyère gives "of
certain savage male and female animals with human
faces, scattered over the country . . . retiring
at night into dens, where they live on black bread,
water, and roots." Compare those times with to-

day. Tell me if, now, the dwelling of the laborer
has become better ventilated, better lighted, and
more healthful; if his food is more substantial, his
wife better clad, his children cleaner, his day's work
better paid, his hours of toil shortened, his weekly
day of rest assured, his old age cared for, and his
life prolonged, why should not we Christians who
are his brothers, not only be happy over it as an
evidence of true progress, but grateful for it, as a
wonderful blessing?

Still livelier is the impression of progress which
our old age receives from the extension over the
world of easy communication, now established
between all branches of the human family which
but yesterday were widely separated. There are no
more great distances. From one end of the globe
to the other, intercourse is universal, and all things
are brought near to one another. Above the moun-
tains, over the seas, and through the air, humanity
circulates and mingles in ever-increasing rapidity,
uniting continents and peoples. Hundreds of thousands of miles of railroads now exist, traversed at
a speed of from forty to fifty miles an hour.
Motor ships, like floating cities, plow the ocean with
a speed of thirty-four knots and more. Surpassing
all this, we have the marvels of electricity, the telegraph, the telephone, the submarine cable, the
radio; that is to say, the thought, the word, and
even the voice of man are now transmitted to an

almost limitless extent and with the velocity of light itself. What is this, in the last analysis, but the realization of the grand dream of *one humanity*, yesterday dispersed, today assembled, and tomorrow, let us hope, fused into unity, to become eventually one great and happy family, whose members will embrace one another in a harmony of universal peace?

It is a transformed world, as I have said; a unified world, as I have ventured to hope; and an extended, amplified world, as I must still add. For I have not spoken, nor can I here speak fully, of those explorations, discoveries, and conquests of new continents, which have brought about the examination of the entire globe and for the first time put man into possession of the whole of his earthly heritage. Nor have I spoken of the astronomical researches into the remotest regions of the firmament, by means of the adaptation of photography to the scientific observation of the heavenly bodies, and by the use of the spectroscope in the intimate investigation of their chemical composition. The contemplation of these marvels transports the mind to sublimity and overwhelms it by immensity. It would seem, at first, as if there were now no more secrets hidden from observation, as there are no more limits to the work of creation; and our little orb is lost in infinity.

Now, who would believe it possible that *old men*

are not only the most astonished, but also the most sympathetic, admirers of this progress? There is a good reason for this. In the first place, we are still the contemporary survivors of nearly the whole of this progressive movement, and are carried back by our recollections to its beginning. Yet, at the same time, we are witnesses today of the height it has attained; consequently, we are in a better position than young people to judge it all objectively and to measure properly the distance traversed.

Remember, brother, we are among the steadily lessening few who have seen the first electric lights brighten our streets, the first locomotive run, the first ship motor turn, and the first electric telegraph register the death sentence of those old, obsolete semaphores, whose arms I fancy I can still see waving wildly in the air. "Undoubtedly," said Michelet, "we are living in an age of miracles. We must be a part of it." And we old men do this the more willingly because, in the midst of all these great inventions and discoveries, we have not looked on idly, but have been to some extent associated with them and employed by them, have even added to them our modest contributions. We are the veterans of this campaign of conquest, and consider these discoveries as a part of ourselves. Accordingly, when someone speaks in our presence of the onward march of the century, it really seems as if we were being congratulated on having marched so well! And when we hear men boasting of our latest triumphs—wireless telegraphy, aviation, radium, radiography, and many more—there is not one of us who does not thank God for having prolonged his days until the coming of these discoveries and benefits. There is none whose heart is not thrilled by the names of their inventors, whose head is not lifted with a feeling of pride in the age and land in which he lives.

Does this, however, mean that we belong to those who think, on that account, that the world dates only from today? No; among men of our age, is not our admiration more discriminating because of a calm reflection, which tempers our enthusiasm without cooling it? Shall we go further? There are moments when these discoveries and inventions, which seem to be the instantaneous intuitions of yesterday, appear to have been late in coming in the general evolution of humanity! Take, for example, the discovery of the interior of the African continent, which lies at the very door of France. It was not made until three thousand years after the Carthaginian, Hanno, had ascertained its contours; while the recent discoveries in the heavens were made more than two thousands years after Hipparchus and Ptolemy had already determined and predicted eclipses. And how slow has the world's progress been in the sphere of electricity, when we consider that the ancient Egyptians pointed out the power of attraction possessed by amber! Finally, how many centuries were necessary for man to discover those latent forces of nature, the sources of which were, nevertheless, the most simple, ordinary elements—water, fire, iron, and so forth, all of them things within his reach or under his hand!

Ought not the admiration of our progress, as a whole, to be wisely tempered with a little modesty? Moreover, what are these marvels of human intelligence and power, compared with those which nature so quietly causes to issue from her breast in each of her kingdoms? How narrow is the territory at present conquered, compared to the immensity of conquests yet to be achieved! How strangely *backward* we, who today call ourselves so *advanced*, may appear to the conquerors who are to come! Poor human intellect, be not too proud! "O youthful Alcibiades, handsome Athenian," exclaimed Socrates, "you are proud of the few plethrons of earth which you possess in Attica; yet, in reality, they constitute merely a point. Behold, on the map of Greece, of Europe, and of the world gigantic areas, the very names of which you do not know!"

*   *   *

What is progress? Is it merely a blind movement forward, wherever it may lead; or is it an advance toward a goal of perfection, either moral or material, the former alone being worthy of the name? Another question: Has this century's march forward given us a happier existence, and has the progress which created wealth, speed, and power, also created by the same act happiness and virtue?

Let us first speak of happiness. Do you, my brother, like most men, understand by this grand word mere comfort and well-being? If happiness means only that, I grant you, in general, we are better nourished than our fathers, better warmed, better clothed, better informed, better and more rapidly transported, better cared for in illness, and better armed for our defense. All these constitute well-being, as I have said; but they no more constitute happiness, than matter and the body constitute the soul. Happiness is made up of a more immaterial essence than those things. But again, does the happiness which is born of progress consist in the facilities which industrial inventions have obtained for men, whereby they can correspond, see one another, become acquainted, unite in groups, and live in a constant intercourse of interests and thoughts from one end of the earth to the other? Augustin Cochin has amused himself by picturing the lament of a modern country gentleman who complains of his insufficient postal service: "See how I am treated!" he exclaims. "I receive my letters only twice a day. Only six trains daily pass my door, going at the rate of only fifty miles an hour. I am three miles from a telegraph station. This is unbearable. I am going to protest. Other men of my social position are better treated. My needs of correspondence and knowledge are not sufficiently provided for." But, a few years ago letters arrived only twice a week, the railroad was nine miles away, and the train traveled at the rate of thirty miles an hour. "No matter," the man continues, "I am ill treated. Things ought to be better in this century of progress!" Cochin is jesting, but what he says is perfectly true. The habitual possession of comforts deadens our enjoyment of them and, far from satisfying it, only stimulates the desire for more. This is not happiness.

I will go even further. I am not the first to think that our material progress has, *in the moral order,* done more harm than good, because it has been diverted from its proper ends. This fact, which is as general as it is painful, is evident in each of the principal fields of human activity; and I will attempt to show this, if the young, and those who are dazzled and carried away by everything modern, will bear with me. The swiftness and ease of communication by means of railroads is certainly a mode of progress. But what harm has this not done to the home? It has scattered sons and daughters, ruined the family spirit, and broken the intimate family life—the only happy one—whose fragments it has carried away and dropped at scores of railroad stations and chance meeting places, often to the everlasting regret of the survivors.

Machinery is also a form of progress. Yet see how the rural country life is now deserted for the city with its factory, mine, mill, and department stores! And when, at evening, those dark pits disgorge their endless lines of men and women, who rush to pack themselves, like animals, into subways, can we call those whom they bear away, *happy?* Only yesterday, I witnessed this spectacle and asked myself: Are these feverish, overtired, and unnerved beings bringing back to their meager supper tables happiness, goodness, refinement, peace, and joy? An economist has said: "Iron ore, when it has once passed into the process of manufacture, emerges from it polished, brilliant, and molded into shape; but the loving and intelligent men who have been toiling in the work of its production come out of it coarse and brutalized."

The press is a proof of progress. It is supposed to stand for enlightened opinion, widespread instruction, and public power controlled. But does it not also frequently stand for armed falsehood, exploitation of the masses, and a perversion and violation of the conscience? What, after all, generally speaking, is the press? According to the hands that manipulate it, it is either an illuminating beacon, or an incendiary torch.

"Big business" is perhaps the most conspicuous form of modern progress. But big business is born of industrialism—a vast system of production which knows no limits or restraints, crushes mankind under the weight of machinery, arms capital and labor against each other, and gives rise to that excessive concentration of humanity in monster cities, where pauperism on the one hand, and exaggerated luxury on the other, rise ominously, like giants, to confront and spy on each other. Between the two are envy, rage, and a multitude of artificial needs, easily acquired pleasures, and vices; while behind them are the vestiges of tainted lives, a brutalized race, and ruined health. This is not progress; it is still less happiness.

Come with me into the factory, my brother. Manufacturing there is in full swing. It is the work of genius. Watt imprisons steam and stores up movement; Arkwright, Crompton, and Hargreaves invent weaving and spinning machines; the old spindle and shuttle are driven from the cottages; the great factory is opened, and handicrafts are systematized and prolonged indefinitely. But this new work requires the massing together of men. Farewell fields, villages, and streams! Manufacturing is an established fact, and the spindle is vanquished. But in the conflict that ensues, a new generation is sacrificed, body and soul; and among our inventions of genius move legions of pale-faced women and children, clothed in rags.

Consider also military progress, especially the facility of mobilization by utilizing the speed of trains. But what if this possibility of the rapid concentration of peoples should result only in making them, at first, distrustful of one another, and finally, in bringing them more quickly to the field of carnage? Much is said, too, of progress in armaments. But what if this also should express itself only in the most frightful expenditure of intelligence and money for the purpose of mass-extermination; or should finally end in the universal maintenance of entire countries on a war footing, which, under the euphemism of "an armed nation," conceals the retrogression of civilization to the madness of barbarism?

*   *   *

Let me say it frankly: There were formerly more dignity and certainly more happiness in life. There was more poetry in men's souls, more politeness in their manners, more charm in their relations, more enthusiasm in their hearts. Do you remember, my brother, how much more enjoyable life was, before it was carried away by the whirlwinds and shaken by the convulsions and terrors of today? And oh, the disenchantment of this

modern life and the accompanying dissatisfaction
with oneself! I allow another to depict it: Everyone is struggling feverishly in the pursuit of pleasure, yet everyone is bored. The modern man flees
from solitude and silence. When, having no more
faith, man now beholds reality in all its nakedness,
it terrifies him. Whether he drives in his motor
car at the rate of sixty miles an hour, or is present
at the first-night performances of all the fashion-
able plays, he has only one wish, and that is to be
somewhere else and to escape from himself. It is
a kind of self-fear which impels everyone to nar-
cotize himself, that he may no longer see himself
as he is. If such is the modern man, what is modern
society? The appalling increase in criminality, ex-
cused by the fatalistic doctrines of Behaviorism,
and encouraged by the constant lightening of the
penal law; the homicidal lowering of the birth rate;
the war between classes; the incessant strikes; the
financial and economical crises; the political revolutions; the clash of arms, which from time to time
makes frontiers tremble and chills the blood of
nations; and the ever-threatening instability of
human society—do all these things, which charac-
terize our modern world, make for human *happiness?**

Will you listen to a more eloquent speaker on

---

*These words were written before the world war. What would the
author say now?—J. L. S.

this subject? This time the warning does not issue
from the pulpit, but from the Institute of France.
"Man by his labor of the last hundred years," writes
M. Devenel, "has produced factories, docks, ships,
telegraphs, schools, and theaters. He has created
wealth, pleasures, philanthropy, insurance companies, political constitutions, and even systems of
philosophy; but he creates neither love nor joy,
and above all, no resignation, ideality, peace, or
hope." All our modern conquests of the elements,
all our victories over matter, have *in the sphere of
morals* led to nothing. The mass of intelligent people still remains irritated and exasperated, with
senses more acute, but with the mind bent on at-
taining some impossible goal, while the soul is
always sad and disappointed. By overproduction
we have evoked the spirit of force and unloosed the
spirit of speed, and they are now devouring our
work. We must, however, keep on going, for our
slave-producing machines drag us on. Soon there
will be no more spare room on the habitable earth,
and no more leisure left in life.

But even were our pleasures multiplied a hun-
dredfold, mankind would still be the victim of that
terrible ennui, inspired by the sight of cities without more evidences of religion, which is a thing of
primary necessity for society. Since all workmen
and peasants have now become "bourgeois," in the
sense we give to this word today, and since they

have become thinkers as well, they will, on that account, finally experience a suffering of which they formerly knew nothing—the suffering of thought; and they will be tormented by the fact that, while they are still in this world, they have lost the certainty of finding a better one when they leave this. "Then will the people reject with loathing all the man-made religions they have so laboriously acquired; and they will beg with tears to have again a soul and to have their God given back to them."[1] For in this work of man, God has been disowned and outraged. Man had been overwhelmed by Him with favors, yet from those very favors he has made weapons to dethrone Him, "waging war against Him with His own gifts."

Meanwhile, in this mighty industry which is almost exclusively expended for the material improvement of life to the detriment of its moral perfection, the soul has been forgotten and sacrificed. The whole force of scientific and industrial energy has been exerted on the material side alone; the equilibrium has been displaced, and the balance lost. To this fact are due our contradictions, our sufferings, the creaking and grinding of the machine, and, for want of any controlling power, the violent use of the brake. The predominating force, acquiring headlong speed, has dragged off every-

[1] Vicomte S' Avenel. "Le Mechanisme et la Vie Moderne," in *Revue des Deux Mondes*, Nov., 1908.

thing precipitately. The rapid train of modern life, rushing along in search of nothing but a cheap and common realization of sense pleasures, has traveled over immense distances, scattering along the route, as if it were worn-out, cumbersome luggage, all that constitutes the supreme good of humanity— religion, morality, purity, faith, high ideals, pity, conscience, and hope. Numberless have been the regions thus traversed, but not one place for restful happiness has been found. Through the blindness of some, the infatuation of others, and the fever and frenzy of most, the wrong route has been taken. If, then, the train has left the rails and failed to reach its destination, and if innumerable unfor- tunates have, for this reason, been crushed to death, whose fault is it? It is the fault of its officials, its teachers, its rulers.

But it will be said: Even if no more happiness is left us, there remains at least pleasure; and, in fact, it is to the vile service of this brutal master that the prodigal son, called Progress, has enslaved himself. What has he gained by it? And what is the last word of the philosophy of pleasure?

On that point, let us listen to the Danish poet and philosopher, Johannes Joergensen, in his *Le Néant et la Vie*. He asks of the Hedonists: "With what are you finally going to make the world happy?" The voice of Heinrich Heine answers: "With champagne, roses, and the dance of smiling nymphs." "Yes, but when you intellectuals reveal the depths of your souls to us in your books, it is quite another thing. Then life seems to you no longer worth living, and I find you sad, bitter, and despairing. Well, after all, so be it! You wanted pleasure, and that is your affair. But here you are, although skeptical and despairing in regard to yourselves, pretending to be guides for other human beings, in order, you say, to make them as happy as you are! What, then, have you got in reserve to do that with? As a compensation for all your crises of despair, and as something open to everyone, to the peasant in the country as well as to the workman of the towns, you recommend— music and the dance hall! Well, certainly, in such a hall life will have many charms. It will offer free gratification of the passions and the stimulus of a contact with multitudes of whirling human atoms, petrified with selfishness. As for the man who cannot pay for the wine, the roses, and the nymphs, he must retire to a little distance (far enough not to spoil the joy of the others) and put the barrel of a revolver to his temple. One more man gone. One less atom alive. No matter! Nature is eternal, and the chaos of human bodies will continue its joyous dance, like a whirlwind of dust in a ray of sunshine."

CHAPTER
FOUR

Apprehension:
"Where Is Life Going?"

"Where is life going? Where is *my* life going?"
This question, which presents itself at every period
of our existence, appeals most powerfully to old
age. For the old, transition to the other world is
always possible . . . tomorrow! The old are
already in sight of the port. If they miss the entrance to the channel, it means for them shipwreck
and irremediable loss. Who will solve this supreme
question? My mind, my heart, my conscience—
my entire being is dependent on the answer. This
explains man's apprehension. It is at once his grandeur and his torment. By turns it makes him either
tremble with fear or thrill with joy. All the philosophies have sought for a reply to it and clamored
for its settlement, and I have inquired of them,
one after another. What have they replied to me?
What said the philosophies of yesterday? What say
those of today?

In my youth, we addressed this question to the
spiritualistic (as distinguished from the materialis-
tic) philosophy of that time—a mode of reasoning

which was eloquent and vibrant with feeling, because it was plainly uneasy, tormented, and suffering. And yet, in spite of this, its spirituality—sincere, but incomplete, indefinite, and veiled in clouds—refused to accept the torch of Revelation. Our teachers told us that they envied us our simple but happy faith; and we young men of that time were troubled to see them suffering from a malady which we thought very noble, yet at the same time cruel.

May I be pardoned, if I here recall the fact that it was from this sincere feeling my first attempt at apologetics was born, perhaps prematurely? It was a tender, plaintive book, characterized by youthful enthusiasm and bearing the title: *Doubt and Its Victims*. At that time, I cherished the dream of recounting, in a series of monographic studies, what I called *The Combat of Faith*. First, I wrote of *Doubt and Its Wounded*. This was completed. Then came *Faith and Its Victories; the Conquerors*. This was begun. Finally, *The Vanquished; the Slaves and Captives of Infidelity and Falsehood*. Here I stopped; not only because God then opened before me unexpectedly another path to follow and another life to embrace; but because I hesitated to go on, doubting my strength and my leisure for new studies, at an age when usually one does not begin them again. The truth is, another philosophy was just then taking men's minds by storm, and was attacking precisely this yearning of mine for the Infinite. It denounced as a childish chimera and morbid hallucination the faith with which Christianity had inoculated us, and declared it was weakening our powers and filling our heads with dreams of a future where we should find neither truth nor happiness.

After that, we heard Quinet pour forth against the philosophy of hope, his eloquent, but arrogant and bitter, complaint: "Why did Christianity ever come, to awaken man, asleep upon a bed of roses, and to arouse within him a limitless ambition? Ever since that hour, man has looked upon the earth disdainfully. The vale of Tempe has become a vale of tears; and man has made a conquest of the infinite at the price of infinite pain."

We also heard Taine, then a young man, attack in his turn, "the great disorder which, since the downfall of the ancient civilization, has been introduced into the human machine; and the destruction of the primitive equilibrium of healthy races." "Man," he said, "has assumed duties which are beyond his powers, which carry away his heart beyond the natural desires of his senses and the curiosity of his mind. It is the great *Beyond* that he now desires. For eighty years, music and poetry have been busy portraying the *sickness of the century;* and the feverish tumult in our cerebral life tends to irritate the wound, rather than to heal it."

We also heard Renan protest against "supernatural ideas, which no longer conceive of life except in terms of sadness"; and heard him sigh for the sensual paganism of "those little houses of Pompeii, where everything was gay and perfect, and everywhere were forms of happiness and pleasure!" Pleasure! It was, then, really paganism with its voluptuous sensualism, which in Renan's time, returning offensively to the present, aspired to raise again its idols of flesh and blood upon the gothic ruins of our churches, on the summit of which the Cross, uplifted toward the sky, would be superfluous! There would be no more thoughts of the Beyond! For, after the freethinkers, came the free livers. "Let us crown ourselves with flowers, for tomorrow we die! O smiling, joyous little houses of Pompeii! O vale of Tempe! It is there that pleasure is to be found, and, therefore, peace and happiness will be found there also. That, *that* is life's goal!"

From this theory, an entire philosophy has been created; for from such "principles," philosophies are often born. Henceforth, there will be room for that system only; then spiritual philosophy and Christianity will lie crushed by the same blow. This new philosophy of materialism will be only a gigantic system of radical negations, including the negation of reason itself.

Have you a taste for beautiful ruins, my brother?

Let us see a few. First, as a principle, there will be no more science worthy of the name, except the science of phenomena, derived from observation, or that of truths found in the domain of the exact sciences. Hence, there will be no more search for the Absolute, no hope of a future, no concern about the supernatural and suprasensible. This is the *positivism* of Comte and Littré. Consequently, there will be no God as Conserver, Providence, Lawgiver, Rewarder, or Avenger; and this is *deism*. Nor will there be any longer a spiritual and immortal soul; no future life, no hope, no Beyond; and this is *materialism*. There will be also no more supernatural, no divine intervention, no revealed religion, no transcendental Cause of things; and this is *naturalism*. No longer will free will exist, the moral world being governed, like the physical world, only by necessity and fatality; hence, no more duty, merit, or demerit; and that is *determinism*. There will be no absolute truth, no more assured certainty, no immutable principles; the "yes or no," the "to be and not to be," the thesis and antithesis, all become identified in a new logic; and that is *skepticism* and *Hegelianism*. Moreover, ideas, like things, will go on transforming themselves indefinitely through their own force, subject inevitably to the law of progress, and moving always in a vortex of eternal transformation; and this is *evolutionism*.

But even this is not enough. There appear upon the scene pitiless logicians who draw from these academic theories the practical concept of a new society, proclaiming that there is no longer any authority, superiority, God, or even any master. And this is *anarchism, born from deism.* When heaven is closed and the earth reduced to a uniform level, when there is no society, will there still be any humanity? All, however, will be well as soon as there is nothing of the past left! This is *nihilism. Nihil!*

I do not wish to exaggerate; I have a horror of declaiming. But I must ask myself: In such doctrines, what allowance is made for the human soul, its faculties, its aspirations, its inspired flights of genius, and its destiny? And what becomes of our original question: "Where is life going?" It must be going somewhere, my brother; and would it be worth while for us to have lived, inspired by lofty aspirations, hopes, and love, and to have grown old in the sublime expectation of a better world, if finally we must lay our heads down on the cold, hard earth, without the hope of reawakening, and lie there through eternal night?

The poetry of nihilism corresponds to its philosophy. The latter proclaimed the grandeur of free thought; the former sings the raptures of free living. Paganism has found once more its poets among us. For I recognize the ancient songs of the age of Horace and Tibullus and the Evoé of the bacchante in the erotic stanzas of Théodore de Banville, who mingles with his peals of laughter and his words of blasphemy the hiccoughs of a drunken orgy.

"We, who have no fear of God—
    As the monk has, whom we pity—
Gayly greet the bright blue sky
    Far above the giant city.
We shall die; but mother dear,
    Nature, sovereign and serene,
Thou wilt turn our lifeless clay,
    Into trees of glistening green,
    Into flowers of brilliant sheen.

Drink to problems still unsolved!
    Drink to beauty's glowing cheek!
As the gardens yield their flowers,
    We yield love to all who seek;
Some day we shall see the slave
    Smile at his discarded chain,
And—his limbs at last unbound—
    In a peace devoid of pain
And a world with roses crowned,
    Drink, a careless, happy child,
    To the Gods, then reconciled."*

---

*From the French of Théo. de Banville.

This, then, is the universal peace, whose reign such happy days will typify! Meanwhile, of what will you, who "have no fear of God," be afraid? Of men, of laws, of conscience, of a sense of shame? These old words have a hollow sound, as soon as they no longer contain the idea of God. Well, well! But, on the other hand, there has come upon the world such a flood of depravity and criminality, and such increasing demoralization, that we begin to see what one *can really fear from a civilization which has freed itself of that great primal fear.* O you, who have no fear of God, how great is my fear of you!

But when you say you have no fear of God, is it quite true? Do you always "greet the sky gayly," for example, in a thunderstorm? And are you sure that everything will end for you in universal tranquillity and a "peace, devoid of pain"? At the foot of those flowery gardens you describe, what do you show me? Some lifeless clay—*yours!* Resplendent "flowers with brilliant sheen" bloom on the border of a grave—*your grave!* Is this the paradise of poets? "A wind, as from the graveyard, has blown over our literature of today," someone wrote recently. But if you who have no fear of God proclaim the fact so loudly, may it not be because you feel some secret need of reassuring yourselves against that fear? To hear you boasting thus in your darkness reminds me of a certain character who, having lost his way in the forest, looked about him in terror with haggard eyes, and began to whistle nonchalantly to the moon, so as to make himself believe, though trembling in every limb, that he was not a man to be frightened by the wind and ghosts.

One of these braggarts—the notorious Gustave Flaubert—wrote in one of his latest letters, "It seems to me that I am passing through an interminable solitude, going *I know not where*. . . . Nothing more sustains me on this planet save the hope of leaving it soon, and of *not going to one that might be worse*." Notice what a "peace, devoid of pain," they have at last! Observe this Bohemian's way of making us believe that he is not afraid of God! Yet there are today millions who have adopted that religion and that kind of happiness. Is it to this that life is tending? Is this the outcome of men's apprehension? Are these "the healthy and happy races," that were promised us?

*   *   *

But let us leave the poets and turn to the sages, or to those who at least have assumed that name— the philosophers. Here we are no longer confronted by the Epicureans, but by serious stoics who, like those of ancient Rome, claim the honor of cultivating virtue and of explaining the world without God. I will question, therefore, four or five of these about the aim and meaning of life.

And I shall address myself to the greatest masters
of contemporaneous free thought; less, however,
to their printed works and published teachings,
than to their private life and correspondence; less
to their days of pride, than to their hours of calmness and final meditations, when, as Lucretius says,
"*true words* at last spring from the heart that soon
will cease to beat": "*Tunc verae voces imo de pec-
tore tandem eliciuntur.*"

"Where is life going?" If you had asked this of
Hippolyte Taine before his fortieth year, he would
have shown you, as he did his friend Guillaume
Guizot, the beautiful red and green ferns of Barbi-
zon, near Fontainebleau, which one day, when his
body should have been committed to the earth, he
thought he was to nourish and color with his
hydrogen, oxygen, and nitrogen. This was, at that
time, his fairest hope and his entire conception of
immortality. (Letter of October 19, 1855.) If
you had spoken to him then of morality and re-
sponsibility, he would have defined virtue and vice
as "chemical products, like sugar and vitriol." If
you had pronounced before him—that man of
thought, pure and simple—the name of his country, France, or spoken of the French, he would
have answered: "Have I a country, when I am
thinking? Am I a Frenchman, when I write? Are
there any Frenchmen? I know nothing of them.
What is thought itself? A secretion of the brain.

What is life? The vibration of the atom swept along in the eternal whirlwind of entities!" How sure he was of himself, then!

But wait till the national catastrophe of 1870 had awakened in him the sentiment of patriotism; wait till the influence of the Christian virtues of Madame Taine had aroused in him his moral sense and caused him to comprehend—as Paul Bourget assures us—that "those who live nobly, end by finding faith through their merits." Wait till "the spectacle of contemporaneous France had opened his eyes to the moral and social virtues, of which Christianity is the source; and lo! he himself is now frightened at the profound nihilism of his philosophy and the pernicious conclusions that could be drawn from it." In his second-last letter, published August 25, 1892, speaking of the state of soul of a believing Christian, whose name is not given, he says to M. Boutmy: "I am entirely of your opinion about Mr. X, his beliefs, his virtue, and his happiness. It is possible that scientific truth is, fundamentally, injurious to the human animal, as he is constituted." But does not this pernicious fruit condemn the tree that bore it? You will say, Taine did not repudiate his infidelity. I know it; but he nevertheless finally appealed to Christianity, *as the only possible remedy for the condition of dissolution from which society was dying.* He saw in it especially the only means to check the pas-

sionate outbursts of our present democracy. Taine's
life ended in discouragement. He wrote: "These
scientific researches darken my old age. From a
practical point of view, they are of no use. A vast
and rapid torrent is sweeping us away; what is the
good of making a report on the depth and swiftness of the current?" (July 23, 1892.) Finally,
we have those decisive words of his to Monsignor
d'Hulst, when returning some documents relating
to the state of the Church in France: "If the
Church, by some miracle of zeal, does not succeed
in regaining these pagan masses to make them believers, it is all over with French civilization." Such
was the last word of the leader of determinism.
Verae voces. Was he not apprehensive, my brother?

The Abbé Barnave, a comrade of Taine at normal school, having gone to visit him in his solitude
at Menton-Saint Bernard, brought back this hope:
"Taine is advancing toward the light. Let us pray
for him!" My brother, did you pray for Taine on
learning of his death? I did. We were of exactly
the same age. He said of himself in a letter, "I
know that I am bringing only a pebble into a
beaten path; but 10,000 cartloads of pebbles, well
laid and well beaten down, finally make a good
road." We, also, my brother, have to contribute
our pebble to a well-worn path: *"Prepare the way
of the Lord!"* God be thanked that it is not the
same path as Taine's!

"Where is our life tending? If you had asked this of Littré when, in 1861, he wrote the life of *Auguste Comte,* or when he was translating Frederic Strauss, or was philosophizing on *Revolution and Positivism* in 1873, he would have answered you with his inexorable formula of the unknowable: "Whatever lies beyond positive science, whether materially, in the depths of limitless space or, intellectually, in the infinite chain of causes, is absolutely inaccessible to the human intellect." But wait; already the formula of the agnostic contains an express reservation: "Inaccessible," he explains, "does not mean that it is absolutely worthless. It is an ocean which beats upon our shore, and for which we have neither shallop nor sail; but the clear vision of it is as salutary as it is awe-inspiring." Yet, as something awe-inspiring, the vision makes him apprehensive; and as something salutary, it will save him. His return to faith began with the respect which he professed and demanded for the beliefs of others: "I have become too well aware of the moral sufferings and difficulties of human life," he said, "to desire to take away from anyone convictions which sustain him in the hour of trial. And I ask myself by virtue of what new discovery, either philosophical or scientific, should one wrest from the human soul those lofty preoccupations? They seem to me part of the eternal essence, because the mystery which envelops the

universe is, by its nature, eternal." And it is actually the leading agnostic of the age, whom the solemn preoccupation with eternal things makes thus
apprehensive!

It was in 1872 that he was forced to confront
the eternal verities by the cruel and inexorable disease which held him in its grip for nearly ten years,
while, at the same time, the sight of the charity
and piety of his wife and daughter showed him the
lofty paths of light and love. These paths he entered, and rose ever higher in their pursuit. For
the conversion of Littré, it should be remembered,
was not, as some would like to make us believe, an
affair of receiving baptism, conferred upon an
almost unconscious, dying man. He had already
entered the path of repentance: "I would prefer
never to have existed, rather than have sinned,"
he said. "Are you weeping?" his confessor asked
him. "Yes," he replied; "I weep because I have
sinned, and I have not known of whom to ask forgiveness." Finally, he entered the path of light.
And this profound scholar read and meditated on
the Church's catechism, perused eagerly the
writings of Lacordaire, and enjoyed the biography
of Père Olivaint. "Decidedly," he said, "such men
are of far greater worth than we." Concerning
his progress in the way of charitable works, we
shall speak later. While treading the path of humility, he said: "If I had died four years ago, I should

have left life well satisfied with myself; but now I
die dissatisfied with myself."

As for the path of prayer—when the Sister who
was attending him read to him those words of the
Ave Maria "pray for us, poor sinners," the sick
man, striking his breast, repeated: "Yes, indeed,
poor sinners!" and added, "The Blessed Virgin represents to me the two things that I most value in
this life, tenderness and purity. Blessed are the
clean of heart!" And one day, contemplating a
picture of the Son of God on the way to His cruci-
fixion, with his own heart following Him, Littré
exclaimed: "It is there that He imparted to us the
secret of His life." Final words! Words of faith!
Verae voces! Thus, on the 11th of June, 1881,
died the former high priest of positivism.

*   *   *

Vacherot is another type of individual. He is
an idealist. He retains the idea of God, but only
the idea. His God is merely a mental abstraction,
a being of the reason, without any actual or possible reality; it has not, and it cannot have, any
objective existence outside of the mind that conceives it. If, then, you ask him, "Where is life
going?" the idealist will reply, "It is going to the
ideal!" And he sings to it his hymn: "Sublime
Ideal, thou art not only divine, thou art God; for
before thy face all beauty pales, all virtue bows,

all power prostrates itself. The universe is great and thou alone art God!" This is the poor, pantheistic god of Hegel, and the unreal, vague ideal of Renan. It was concerning this hollow creation of Vacherot's imagination that his friend, Ernest Havet, wrote him wittily in these terms: "What you, in your learned book, call the *God-idea*, I call simply *the idea*. What you call *God-nature*, I call merely *nature*. Did you ever hear of the tyrant who wished that, when he was not present, the people should do homage to his hat, placed on the end of a pike? I am one of those who think that there is no longer any God in your system, but only the hat which you want to make us worship."

It was this same phantom that Vacherot, in 1885, brought upon the stage in his last work, entitled *Le Nouveau Spiritualisme*. But by that time the worthy man had lived a long while. He, himself, had inhaled, close beside him at his own fireside, the penetrating perfume of Christianity; and on the other hand, had shuddered at the ravages of impiety and immorality in his own country. If the chimera of the God-idea still deluded his pensive mind, atheism no longer satisfied his religious soul. His intellect was on one side, his heart and conscience were on the other. Although an atheist, he wished to retain the cult of the divine, while still remaining the prisoner of a doctrine which concealed from him the face of God.

His book ends with this indignant complaint
against the foolish and insipid impiety of his time:
"To ridicule noble things is nothing new, and to
ridicule sacred things is more common today than
ever before. But to laugh at God, Himself, and
in such a way as is now the fashion, one must have
a sort of mind that brings disgrace upon mentality." At last, however, the Gospel conquered
even him. In 1892, recalling the words of Christ:
"Heaven and earth shall pass away, but my words
shall not pass away," he replied: "No, divine Master, not as long as there shall remain sons of Adam
to receive them!" Every year, during Holy Week,
he read the Passion, and meditated upon it, "in
order to be penetrated with its spirit." Moreover,
he said and wrote that Christ, Whose crucified
figure he had with him and before him, should
receive his last conscious glance!

Shall I mention Berthelot, his companion and
twin soul? He also was proud, and said willingly
of his own versatile personality: "In order that
science may not crumble piecemeal into specialties,
there must exist at least one brain capable of com-
prehending it in its entirety. I think I have such
a brain; but I fear I shall be the last to have one."
Who was ever more sure of himself? It is, therefore, not of him that I intend to ask: "Where is
life going?" In his opinion, the answer is to be
found in his chemical apparatus. He was a great

chemist, but a very inferior thinker, and never
had any uneasiness about eternal things. Not he!
And yet, like Taine, as he neared the end, he was
apprehensive as to what would be the fruit of the
tree which he had planted. He asks himself how
this world, which he had promised to reconstruct
scientifically, was going to get on; and what, after
all, materialism had done for the moral progress
and happiness of the race. To that, his reply is
not only one of apprehension, but of despair.

On the 7th of January, 1909, at the French
Academy, Francis Charmes and Henry Houssaye
—appointed to deliver a eulogy on Berthelot—
portrayed to us, one after the other, a gloomy,
pessimistic, and discouraged old man, breathing out
a long complaint of the inefficacy, if not the ultimate injurious effect, of his work. In this complaint, one hears the man, himself, casting bitter
doubts on the pretended services of that science
of which he had emphatically crowned himself
king. I quote his words: "When man shall have
reached the farthest limits of material progress,
will the *human soul* also be progressing? Will
moral ideas, conscience, self-denials, self-sacrifice,
and the love of the good and the beautiful be proportionate to man's scientific discoveries and the
comforts and conveniences of existence?" Upon
those vital questions, Berthelot had doubts which
disturbed his haughty self-complacency to the

point of causing him to write: "The triumph of
reason and justice will never be seen." When he
wrote this, Berthelot had just been cruelly wounded
in his intimate family relations, and the reaction
had shaken his confidence, in what he calls "the
perpetual illusion of life." Moreover, he had then
reached that time of life of which he says: "As
for old age, its dreams are ended. It sees every one,
whom it loves, dying; it is surrounded by the ruins
of its affections; it finds consolation only in the
noble feeling of having done its duty toward other
men, and meanwhile, it smiles kindly on innocent
childhood, and aids youth with its sympathy in
the eternal effort of humanity to reach the true,
the good, and the ideal."

But the discourse of Henry Houssaye informs us
that even this consolation, founded on the chimerical theory of mankind's continuous progress, at
last crumbled completely away. "And when," he
adds, "the scientist, leaving his laboratory, found
himself before the spectacle of the world, and saw
in it so much moral misery, so many errors in the
ideas of men, so much power in accumulated
money, so many monstrous or imbecile theories, so
many characters debased, and consciousness betrayed, he was compelled to believe rather in the
continuous progress of human weakness." The last
word concerning the state of his soul reveals him in
despair. The complaint of Job is not more bitter.

He says, "My life, full of doubts and irreparable vicissitudes, has left upon me an impression of sadness and apprehension. . . . In proportion as my personal consciousness has developed, it has only increased my apprehensions. That is why I have always taken refuge in action, in order better to struggle against *despair*." This is his final word: "*Verae voces.*"

Who next? We pass to Herbert Spencer, who ends his thick and heavy autobiography in two volumes with the confession that he has no longer in regard to religion the same beliefs that his books express. Spencer also interrogated his soul, and wrote: "I have perceived that religious doctrines have and still retain a precious moral efficacy; moreover, that the object of these doctrines is to fill in men's souls a sphere which certainly will never consent to remain unfilled." And he concludes: "I, therefore, have come to regard with increasing sympathy the religious beliefs which occupy the sphere that a rationalistic interpretation seeks in vain to fill; the more it tries, the more certain it is to fail." It was two years before his death, in 1893, that the old man made this declaration as an epilogue to his life and to his book (*An Autobiography*, Vol. II, p. 468). Thus ended the father of evolution. *Verae voces.*

Accordingly, along the whole line, at one or another stage of free thought, we hear the cry of

Scripture: *Ergo erravimus a via veritatis.* We have
strayed from the way of truth! Yet these men
were its masters, and its greatest masters; for concerning these high matters, only the sovereigns
must be consulted. But how unstable are their
thrones, and how their crowns waver under the
breath of the passing years!

*   *   *

I must close, my brother. Yet I will not do so
without presenting, after these philosophers, the
figure of a poet, a poet of yesterday, who thought
himself also a philosopher, and who naïvely mis-
took for philosophy the empty reveries which had
taken the place of the ardent beliefs of his youth.
I speak of Sully Prudhomme. Listen to this ending,
recounted recently at the Académie Française by
Frédéric Masson: "Four years ago," he said, "I
went with Coppée and some other friends to visit
Sully Prudhomme, who could no longer leave his
home at Châtenay. How horrible his physical sufferings were, was evident from the agony revealed
in his noble face, from the continual agitation of
his feeble body, from the contractions of his feet,
and from the length of time it took him to speak
with panting breath. But his soul seemed even
more wretched than his body. Regardless of our
efforts to direct the conversation to subjects which
had formerly interested him, he constantly re-

turned to that of death and what lay beyond it. He told us how he had once known peace in the Christian faith, and how he had found in it happy promises. Then he related how he had gone away from it, and had wandered ever since in the path of doubt, without succeeding in finding anywhere a certainty that satisfied both his imagination and his reason. He asked us, and even urged us to reply, since he wished to know, if we, too, had the same wound in our hearts. And when Coppée, who until then had tried by gayety to enliven him, suddenly became very serious, and answered in a tone of absolute conviction: *As for me, I believe,* the poet turned and looked at him. In his beautiful eyes was visible a jealous admiration, and, raising his poor hands, he said only, 'Ah, Coppée, you do not know how fortunate you are!' . . . We left the house and garden without exchanging a word, so deeply had we been moved by this double martyrdom. When we found ourselves again on the road, Coppée, gazing about him at the trees, the flowers, the blue sky, and the joyous life of nature on that bright spring day, said, as if he were continuing the conversation: 'And then, it is so much more simple!' "

Who was the simpler, wiser, truer, and happier man, Coppée who said contentedly, "I am trying to end my journey as a Christian," or Prudhomme who cried, suffering and tormented, "I abandon myself to the laws of the universe, as their prey"? Everywhere, therefore, over and over again, we find, under the laurel that encircles these heads, apprehension and doubt! Thus, my brother, I am brought back, at the end of my career, to the picture of intellectual and moral suffering which I presented to the public in that first book of mine. It is often said, however, that modern unbelief is more sure of itself than the unbelief of sixty years ago, and that its negation is brutal and violent, rather than grieving and complaining. But, fundamentally, is it any less unhappy and apprehensive than it was then? Could not a sympathetic writer today, although dealing with different errors and new forms of suffering, if he used other names, utter again the eternal lament of my "Victims of Doubt"?

"Where is life going? Where is *my* life going?" When, in my turn, I have asked this not of men, but of God, a voice from on high has replied: "I am the Way, the Truth, and the Life." I bless Thee, therefore, O my God, for I know where my life is going, and I know its meaning and its reward. I have been walking in the right way, as Thou didst open it before me in the days of my youth; and now, dear Lord, vouchsafe to make the trembling steps of my old age secure in that same path! The distance I still have to travel is, perhaps, only the brief interval of a single evening. This is the final stage of my pilgrimage; but I know that I shall find Thee at its end.

CHAPTER
FIVE

Science and Belief
Our Great Masters

Our own generation, or that part of it which has long since passed its sixtieth year, has been able to know all, or nearly all, the great masters and promoters of scientific progress in the nineteenth century. They formed a dynasty, whose members succeeded one another to the crown, without a break. It was a royal dynasty, for these masters were truly kings and princes in the realm of the exact and natural sciences, which they founded or enlarged. It was also a sacred dynasty, for they reverently lowered their scepters before Almighty God.

Would you like, my brother, to recall with me the features of these noble men and the souvenirs of their reign down to our own day? It seems to me that those who were then incontestably first in the domain of science can tell us, better than all others, where life is going. As in ancient times there were Fathers of the Church, so we have had in our time fathers of science. At the head of this company marches Volta.

When we octogenarians were born, Volta, an Italian by birth, who, however, became a French subject under Napoleon, as well as a member of the Institute and a senator, had just died in 1827. His great invention of the Voltaic pile had opened up measureless horizons to the researches of science, as well as to the destinies of the human race. When, in 1924, the city of Como celebrated the centenary of Volta's wonderful invention, the force of electricity, which he had known how to capture and tame, was already lighting all the cities of the world, and linking together all the notable points of our planet. Francis Arago has described the great discoverer, as he saw him in Paris, "with his white hair, his erect carriage, his broad forehead furrowed by meditation, and his penetrating gaze, in which were mirrored the clearness of his intellect and the serenity of his soul."

In order to place him in the circle to which he belonged, I imagine him, as a painter has portrayed him, surrounded by his friends of "Young Italy," and seated between electrical instruments on one side and an open Bible on the other, on the first page of which are seen the words: "*Let there be light!*" Before him is his friend Silvio Pellico, who had been converted by him, and whom he called his son, engaged in that conversation, which the grateful poet thus commemorated: "In old age, O Volta, Providence placed me in your path, a young man who had gone astray. I said to you: 'You, who have penetrated further than others into the secrets of the Creator, show me the paths that lead to light.' And the old man answered me: 'I, too, have doubted; I, too, have searched. The great misfortune of my youth was to have seen the teachers of that time arming themselves with science in order to attack religion. As for me, *I see today everywhere only God.*' "

More explicit still is the profession of faith which Volta solemnly made and wished to have universally known. It is as follows: "I have always held, and still hold, our holy Catholic religion to be unique, true, and infallible; and I thank God infinitely for having endowed me with this supernatural faith. I have not, however, neglected the means of confirming my belief and of dissipating all doubts, through the reading of numerous books both hostile and favorable to it. Having thus learned the reasons for and against it, I have deduced from them arguments which prove it to be conformable to human reason and such as every enlightened mind cannot but embrace and love. May this declaration—which I desire to be known to everyone, for I do not blush for the Gospel— bear fruits everywhere!" With these sentiments this great man died on March 5, 1827, at the age of 82.*

*Footnote by the Translator. The vocabulary of science crowns Volta

Another of those fathers of science was Ampère. He was destined to survive Volta by nine years, and even surpassed him in the elevation of his genius and faith. Physician, naturalist, chemist, astronomer, mathematician, writer, and even poet, this versatile character, wholly absorbed in spiritual meditations, had no equal since Pascal, with whom he has more than one trait of resemblance. Even if he did for a moment experience painful doubts, he soon recovered and retained a tranquil, ardent, and tender faith. This humble and sincere disciple of Him Who called Himself "the Light of the world," was a mystic, and I admire him as much as it is given me to comprehend him. But in the scientific depths in which electrodynamics and electromagnetism revealed to him the secret of their laws, I also listen reverently and in silence to the soliloquies of this sublime mystic, kneeling before the adored Master, Whom he called his heavenly Friend. Among his utterances on religious subjects are the following: "What are all these sciences, all these reasonings, all these discoveries, and vast conceptions which everyone admires? Only the truth of God remains eternal. If you are nourished by it, you will be immortal like it. Meanwhile, work and study, but do so in a spirit

with immortality. The scientific language of the world continually uses words connected with his name. Among these are *volts, voltage, volto-graphy, volto-electrometer,* etc., and especially the adjective *voltaic,* which appears in *voltaic-arc, voltaic-current,* etc.

of prayer. Study the sciences of this world, but regard them only with one eye; let your other eye be constantly fixed upon the eternal Light. Listen to learned men, but do so only with one ear; let the other be always ready to receive the words of your heavenly Friend. Write with one hand only; with the other hold fast to the garment of God, as a child clings to the cloak of his father. . . . May my soul, from this day forward, remain always united to God and Jesus Christ! Give me Thy blessing, O my God!"

Another of our kings of science was Augustin Cauchy, who retained the crown of sovereignty till his death in 1857. Of him, Renan wrote in his *Souvenirs de Jeunesse*: "The Academy still possesses, in our day, a large number of Christian believers; for example, Augustin Cauchy, whose prodigious discoveries in the realm of the unseen, more and more confirmed in the half century since his death, are continually giving birth to other discoveries." Cauchy must have been a believer, for in 1844, he wrote and addressed to all the Friends of Science the following precise and powerful profession of faith: "I am a Christian; that is, I believe in the divinity of Christ, as did Tycho Brahé, Copernicus, Descartes, Newton, Leibnitz, Pascal, Euler, Boscovich, and Gerdil; and as did the great astronomers, physicians, and geometers of the past centuries. Moreover, I am, like most of them, a

Catholic; and if anyone should ask me why, he would see that my convictions are the result, not of the prejudices of my birth, but of profound examination. He would also see that verities, more incontestable, in my opinion, than the square of the hypothenuse, have engraved themselves forever on my mind and in my heart."

One day in the month of May, 1857, we learned that Cauchy had just expired, leaving science, faith, and charity to mourn him profoundly. His last words to the priest who attended him had been these: "Father, men pass away, works remain." He had, himself, founded and presided over the work of oriental schools, and, a year before his death, this ardent defender of Christian truth had had the joy of bringing to its fold his greatest pupil and neophyte, L'Hermite.

Another of our Christian princes of science was Jean Baptiste Biot. In his youth, he had passed through a period of skepticism, but did not remain there long. He was not only a geometer, a physician, and a chemist, but also a man of letters, a moralist, and a member of both the French Academy and the Academy of Sciences. His noble mind instinctively revolted against that gross materialism, of which Horace Walpole had said: "Of all the gods which have ever been invented, the most absurd is that old, dull, heavy divinity of the Greek Sophists, whom modern men of letters wish to restore to a place of honor, the god of matter."

SCIENCE AND BELIEF   77

Biot found truth upon those heights of study, of which, as director of the French Academy, in 1860, he spoke as follows: "The sciences are beautiful when one is able to penetrate their spirit, but very injurious when one does not go as far as that. For if they do not elevate man to heaven, they lower him to the earth. Much study is necessary in order to comprehend and admire matter; but much more study, in order to comprehend that it is, in itself, nothing." Biot died as a devout and believing Catholic, after receiving the Blessed Sacrament and the Church's absolution and benediction.

We come now to Jean Baptiste Dumas, who was made perpetual secretary of the Academy of Sciences in 1868, and subsequently, a minister of France. Here is an utterance of his before his fellow academicians, which might be called his profession of faith: "Where does life come from, gentlemen? Science does not know. Whither does life go? Science is ignorant of this also. There are those who wish to explain the origin of life and the production of consciousness by mere transformation of forces. They would like to prove that life and consciousness, after death, lose themselves in the vast vibratory movements which pulsate through the universe. But to be born without a cause, to live without an aim, and to die without a future: is that our destiny? No!" Speaking, then, of Christian and spiritual doctrines, he added: "The passing fever of scientific thought which is now in the process of rebirth, at present menaces these strong Christian doctrines, although it has nothing to substitute for them. But the fever will be subdued, as it often has been before." Dumas formulated his faith briefly in the following words: "I believe in the God of revelation, as I do in the God of nature and of reason. He is the same God."

While the star of this scientist was setting in splendor, that of Pasteur was at its zenith. There remains nothing more to be said of this great servant of humanity and truth that is not already known. The entire world admires his genius, his discoveries, his character, his patriotism, and his services. Pasteur was one of those rare men who, with the greatest ease, cause their generation to make gigantic strides in the scientific study of the profoundest mysteries of nature and of life. But the same penetrating gaze that plunged into the depths of the infinitely little, rose religiously toward the sublimities of the infinitely great, to that uncreated, yet creative Infinite, which is the scientific name he used for God. The Christian world was proud of the splendid profession of faith which he made under the dome of the Institute, on the 28th day of April, 1882, at the solemn session of his reception into the French Academy. Replying to Renan, he let that systematic doubter of everything transcendental hear a lesson on the supernatural, which has been equalled by few others. It ended thus: "Through the notion of the Infinite, the supernatural finds itself already in the depths of the heart, and so long as the mystery of the Infinite shall impress itself on human thought, so long will temples be reared in its worship, and on the pavement of those temples men will be seen, kneeling or prostrate, completely absorbed in contemplation of the Infinite." Pasteur was one of these men. Bowing in reverence before him, Joseph Bertrand, secretary of the Academy of Sciences, said of him: "Faith is for Pasteur a torch, and his science radiates light everywhere." It was the study of the natural sciences themselves, through his perception of their inability to satisfy man's spiritual aspirations, that led Pasteur to a childlike faith and trust in God, and he recited unequivocally every article of the Credo. He once said: "When one has studied much, one returns to the faith of the Breton peasant. If I had studied still more, I should have the faith of the Breton peasant woman." This was a familiar repetition of what he had uttered formally on March 2, 1875, before the faculty of medicine. He then said: "In view of the great problems of the beginning and the end of things, only two states of mind are possible: either faith in a solution given by a direct revelation; or torment of the soul, expressing itself by absolute silence, or—what amounts to the same thing—by the avowal of the impossibility of thoroughly understanding anything."

Pasteur's religious belief was not aggressive. It was as serene and humble as it was solid and clear. He exercised exquisite delicacy in speaking of it before scientists of less breadth of vision, who had the misfortune not to share his faith. Thus, one evening in 1882, he met a young physician, Dr. Coudereau, who, in the previous year, had taken an active part in an international congress of atheists. Pasteur spoke to him of the congress, and asked him if he was very sure that religion was born of ignorance and fear. "Certainly," replied Dr. Coudereau, "in proportion as a man becomes educated and loses his fear through knowledge of science, he ceases to be religious."

"There are some exceptions to that," replied Pasteur. "There are still some men who have studied all the elements of life, and for whom life, in its origin and destination, would remain a mystery, if they consented to receive no other light than that of the laboratory. Such men, in proportion as the domain of their knowledge increased, have felt the religious idea vibrating ever more strongly within them. God has appeared to them at the highest point of their researches, and they have believed."

"What is yet unexplained today," replied the

young doctor, "will be explained later, and you, yourself, dear master, will contribute to that result." "That 'later,'" answered Pasteur, "will perhaps not be in my time. I may die today, and I need to know today. Therefore, I believe; and 'I believe' means I know."

Pasteur, who had been ill for a year, had no illusions regarding the gravity of his condition. Knowing that he was to die soon, he prepared himself for it religiously and fearlessly. A little sadness, nevertheless, mingled with his Christian resignation. "I am sorry to die," he said; "I should have liked to render more services to my country." Sometime before, on New Year's Day, as he was receiving the visit of the most distinguished scientists who flocked to his dwelling, Madame Pasteur appeared with an opened telegram in her hand. "It is," she said, "from the Holy Father, who sends you his blessing for the new year." Pasteur at once checked all conversation, and two tears dropped upon the paper which he held in his hands.

In the month of July, 1895, the great, yet humble, Pasteur died, as Volta, Ampère, Cauchy, Biot, and Dumas had also died. Joining in the last prayers, his hand in that of his wife, the crucifix upon his lips, he directed his gaze toward the heaven where, we may well believe, he has found that supreme blessedness, of which he, himself, said: "Happy is he, who carries his God within him, as the ideal of beauty and goodness, and who obeys Him. That is the living source of all great thoughts and great actions." Until his tomb was built in the Pasteur Institute, his body remained for some time in the crypt of Notre Dame—a resting place of which he was eminently worthy. Maxime du Camp writes of him: "Whenever I meet Pasteur, I have a desire to prostrate myself before him, and I am surprised that his head is not surrounded by an aureole." And Prof. Granchet said of him: "When, a thousand years from now, a doctor shall speak to youthful generations of the progress and evolution of medicine, he will mention, before all others, the two immortal names: Hippocrates and Pasteur."

Of this brilliant galaxy of devout scientists, the last whom I shall mention is the great astronomer Leverrier, the discoverer of the planet Neptune. Of this astronomical genius, Sully Prudhomme, on learning of his decease, wrote, "What universal mourning this death has caused! Since Newton, there has not been a more powerful mathematical genius, even if there may have been a more inventive one. His work is colossal, and so exalted that it moves one to tears." Leverrier, indeed, looked into the "Beyond." One day, after his discovery of our outermost planet, Monsignor de Coutances said to him graciously: "Dear master, you are now carried to the stars." "I expect, Monsignor," replied Leverrier, "to mount still higher; I hope to go to heaven."

To Jean Baptiste Dumas, who had just vindicated spiritual, as opposed to material, science at the French Academy, his colleague, Leverrier, gave hearty support in the Academy of Sciences. On June 5, 1876, he expressed himself in the following terms: "During our long work together, continued for 35 years, we were sustained by the spectacle of one of the grandest works of creation, and by the thought that it was always the imperishable truths of religion that we were studying. It was, therefore, with emotion that, at our last session, we heard our illustrious secretary affirm those great principles which are the very source of purest science. That lofty declaration of his faith will remain an honor and a source of strength for French science, and I esteem myself happy that the occasion has presented itself for me to refer to it in the midst of our own academy and to give to it my hearty approval."

Leverrier also caused a crucifix to be placed in the hall of the observatory; and even when ill, he would often walk painfully to the Cross and bow with reverence before it. It was on the 23rd day of September, 1877, the anniversary of the discovery of his planet, that Leverrier, who has been called "the giant of modern astronomy," expired as a believing Christian, comforted by the prayers of his parish priest, as he desired; "for," he said, "I am not only a Catholic, I am also a parishioner."

Such were our masters; such was our school—
the truly Christian school, to which we are still
faithful. These men had been the teachers of our
teachers; and the lessons which we did not hear
directly from their lips, we gleaned indirectly from
their books. Illumined by the twin beacon lights
of science and of faith, what wonder that these
masters seemed to us inspired from on high? Nor
could we doubt that antiquity would have called
them demigods, as it did Prometheus, who was believed to have stolen fire from heaven.

CHAPTER
SIX

Science and Sophism
Bankruptcy

We have seen that our age has known a lofty, sound, and, above all, a very liberal science. It had, also, the honor of being associated with the greatest names of our epoch.

But there is another kind of science, in the name of which everything that mankind had hitherto believed and affirmed, is denied. In its ranks are found evil minds, corrupt morals, and bad laws. It certainly has some famous names among its advocates, and the masses acclaim them; but the world suffers from them. "O Liberty, Liberty!" said Madame Roland, as she ascended the scaffold, "How many crimes are committed in thy name!" Can I not also say: "O Science, how much ignorance and how many follies and misfortunes shelter themselves today under thy standard!" What, then, has happened? Whence does this disorder come? What is the origin of this confused mingling of unbelief with science, since it does not necessarily issue from science itself?

The evil proceeds from the fact that a godless

philosophy has grafted itself on contemporary science, as a parasitic plant fastens itself upon a tree, which it grasps and strangles, enveloping it in such a way that it seems to identify itself with it. It is a case of the conquest, exploitation, and confiscation of science by philosophy. Science furnished the facts, as was proper in her own domain; but the prevailing philosophy at once seized upon these facts, in order to interpret them according to preconceived ideas. Then, when they had thus been adulterated, they were presented in their new form, always under the fascinating name of genuine science, of which they wore merely the mask. It was a secular science, that is to say, a science without God; but it was announced that this was to be thenceforth the only science. In fact, for the past thirty years, we have seen her despotically exploiting her monopoly, pronouncing oracles, declaring excommunicated any science proclaiming opposite views, and overthrowing all dogmas, in order to impose her own. Do you recollect, my brother, the declaration of war which was made on everything divine and supernatural in two celebrated speeches of Ernest Renan and Marcellin Berthelot? These men, in their respective intellectual specialties, seem to represent perfectly the atheistic philosophy and science of their time; and their arrogant threats were like the bloody javelin which the Roman priest hurled into the enemy's territory with the cry, "To arms!"

Renan and Berthelot rivaled each other in their predictions. "The day will come," said Renan, "when humanity will no longer believe; *it will know*. It will know the moral and metaphysical world, as it already knows the physical world. For myself, I see only one result for science to achieve, and that is to solve the riddle of the universe, to explain man to himself, and, in the name of the only authority that exists, which is that of human nature in its entirety, to give him a substitute for the creeds formerly imposed upon him by religions, but which he can no longer accept."

Berthelot, taking up the same theme, emphasizes the value of science to philosophy in the following astounding terms: "The world today is without mystery! The rational conception of it claims to be able to make all things clear; to comprehend *everything*, to give a *scientific explanation* of everything, to extend its inexorable determinism to the realm of morals, and *to overthrow forever the notion of miracles and the supernatural*." Is this piece of pretentiousness a serious scientific program, or is it not rather a piece of bravado, a provocation, a challenge? It is certainly a declaration of war. To overthrow God—what a victory that would be! And to replace God—what a future it suggests!

At the command of free thought, however, science undertook to do this; but as free thought

reserved to itself the supreme management of the
contest and its conclusions, and as it practically
professes atheism, it is to atheism that science, thus
directed, will necessarily lead men. Everything will
furnish science with material for this deduction,
everything will provide premises for this conclusion, and everything will have to give way to this
preconceived idea. Science is only the pretext; the
name of science is the flag; the victory to be gained
is the defeat and dethronement of God. By these
learned gentlemen, science will be called truth only
when it shall be a negation of divinity; and, in the
last practical analysis, it will be merely *the way to
get along without God*.

But is this really science? Certainly not, my
brother. That which is no longer the work of calm
reason, but only the result of prejudice and irra-
tionality—and, moreover, an outcome of the most
disturbing and blinding of all passions, the hatred
of God—is not the work of science. It is the result
of the *a priori* form of reasoning, which is thought
to be the invincible method of insuring victory to
preconceived ideas. Now, among the various kinds
of sophisms, there is not one more antiphilosophical
and antiscientific than this. Bossuet thus describes
it in a maxim which Pasteur was fond of quoting
to his pupils: "The greatest error of the mind is
to believe beforehand that things are so, because
one wishes that they should be so." Let us examine

this still more thoroughly. Does not the prejudice from which this great error proceeds, often itself proceed from another kind of error? Undoubtedly many deniers of the Divine have lived pure and moral lives. Yet, Augustin Cochin knew what he was saying when he wrote the following lines: "Do not use the word "ascetic" in regard to those men. It perhaps applies to two or three of them who are alchemists of negation, buried in their investigations, wholly devoted to their subterranean labors, saddened by the ruins they make and the amputations they perform. But most of them fold their wings only to put their feet on the ground. Denying what annoys them, and freed, by their philosophic principles, from every duty which puts them under moral obligations, they know very well how, in practical life, to slip from their ascetic *abstractions* into less austere *distractions*."

Who does not know the truth of this? Who does not see it? My brother, I can assure you that I have often had occasion to probe to the bottom in more than one of these learned minds, consumed and devastated by this mania. In every case, I started out in search of the microbe of atheism; but when I did not find it in the head or the brain, I sought it in the conscience, in the heart, in the senses; *and it was there.*

Yes, it is by this doorway, and certainly not by that of scientific knowledge, that the masters of the modern school have made their way into the souls of the people, to overthrow there the thrice-holy altar of God. The masses understand absolutely nothing of the mysterious secrets of science. What they really long for, on the lower side of their nature, is their beloved *"liberty"*; that is, moral emancipation, unrestrained concupiscence, and limitless enjoyment. And if, in addition to that, they see the flag of science floating in the breeze at the head of this popular movement, then these poor, big children completely lose their heads, and shout: "Long live science! Now, at last, we, the people, are instructed. Now, we know what to depend on." And their heads are raised in hostility toward heaven.

Look at them when, every ten years, above the enormous panorama of the International Exposition, built by them, furnished and resplendent with the products of their hands, these crowds of workingmen survey the Eiffel Tower, which they have been able to raise higher than the towers of Notre Dame! What do you think the humble steeple of their little village church looks like to them, beside that? "Long live science!" shout the workmen, as they clink their glasses. And if, near by, some impostor in the green coat of an academician comes to tell them triumphantly: "The world is without mystery," those simpletons are very much inclined to believe it. They hear him add: "Our rational conception of things claims to be able to clear up everything, to understand everything, to give a scientific explanation of everything, to extend its inevitable determinism to the world of morals, and to overthrow forever the notion of miracles and the supernatural." They open their eyes wide before such great words, and in honor of "science" go away singing, sneering, insulting a passing priest, jeering at the tolling church bell, at the wayside cross, and at the white dress of a child going to First Communion!

My heart is filled with bitterness, my brother. They have deceived these poor people, of whom I am one. They have given them a strong concoction called "science," which has excited them to delirium and intoxicated them to brutishness. Meanwhile, they are more ignorant than ever! They now know nothing of their real selves, nothing of their duty, nothing of their life. They no longer comprehend what honor, goodness, dignity, respect, pity, and joy are. They have no idea what they are, whence they came, or where they are going. In this new school they have unlearned everything they once knew, even the name of their heavenly Father Who calls them, and that of the heavenly country that may await them. And yet, O Master, it was for them that Thou didst utter those adorable words: "This is life eternal, that they might know Thee, the only true God, and

Jesus Christ, Whom Thou hast sent!"

Let us now look at the facts in the case. What has really resulted from the wonderful promise to explain everything scientifically, that is, quite apart from, and even in opposition to, the divine and the supernatural? Beginning with the physical world, where do we stand today in regard to this attempt of science?

The work of science in our century has certainly been enormous; it has my hearty admiration. I am not the recipient of a diploma in science, but I take great interest in it. My age will have seen the entire world reëxamined minutely and subjected to the severe verification of experience. Small and weak in comparison with the immensity of creation, and fleeting in comparison with measureless time, man has not let himself be discouraged either by the weakness of his instruments or by the magnitude of his task, but has gone from what is near and known, to what is distant and unknown, and by this route has traveled over prodigious distances. He has made wonderful discoveries—geological, geographical, astronomical, physical, chemical, biological, and historical.

All this is true; and to my admiration of these discoveries is added my gratitude for the practical application of them, which science has made for the welfare of humanity and the advancement of civilization. That was all very well; *but it was not*

the work which philosophy had hired science to do.
What philosophy had expected from science was,
first, that these discoveries should give the lie to
the Bible, the Word of God; and second, that they
should furnish the requisite means for getting rid
of God, as well as plausible reasons for doing so.
The task was not an easy one. This God, this necessary Being Who was to be removed, was always
present in the mystery of causes and, finally and
fundamentally, in the mystery of the First Cause
of the universe. There were times when the relation of cause and effect revealed itself so clearly
and brilliantly, that the mind, stupefied and
troubled, was surprised to find itself driven back
to what the atheist, Lucretius, called "a certain hidden force"; and to what Claude Bernard, although
an obstinate determinist, named "the guiding idea
of forces." But this "hidden force" is really the
creative omnipotence of God, and this "guiding
idea" is that of the intelligence of God. Yet the
philosophers exclaim: "No, no; we know nothing
of a God. Find other causes for us. We will call
them all scientific, provided you do not mix them
up with that abhorrent theology."

But, as we have said, the task was not easy. All
along its route, during the last four centuries,
science had always heard, near her, voices of
authority and conviction which enthusiastically
glorified the Author of the universe; these voices

were the noblest that made themselves heard in
those centuries, and the speakers were the greatest
men of the intellectual world. They unanimously
invited mankind to join them in a chorus of
thanksgiving to the God of science. "No, no," reply the modernists; "close your ears to those old
songs. How could the teachers who sang them be
real scientists if they were believers? Today they
count for nothing. Science dates from us. In fact,
we are science." Again I say, the thing was not
easy. Sometimes, science found itself passing so
near to God, that it was necessary to make a great
detour in order not to come face to face with Him.
The hypothesis most dear to it today is that of the
universe as forming a single whole and obeying the
same laws, or rather the same common, fundamental law. It is claimed that all the organic and in-
organic world has sprung from the same primal
force, of which all phenomena, whether physical or
psychical, are only different manifestations, under
abstract, ideal expressions. In this, my brother, you
recognize monism. I should not be afraid of its
principle, if it were freed from a gross materialism.
For the recognition of unity in the universe, and of
an orderly tracing back of effects to one principle
and First Cause is a purely religious, intellectual
conception. Do we not hold that unity and simplicity are essential attributes of divinity? And is
not the application of them to the laws of the uni-

verse the signature of the supreme Workman to His work? "Nature is one because God is one." "No, no," cries atheistic monism at once: "For us, including Spinoza, Hegel, Haeckel, Taine, and Guyau, this unity of principle and law proves only the consubstantial unity of all being."

And so, in defiance of tradition, the philosophy of unity, instead of concluding logically in monotheism, its true terminus, ends, by means of a flagrant sophism, in unintelligible pantheism. Monism is broad, but it is shallow; and its insolent philosophical constructions are towers of Babel, which will never reach heaven, there to dethrone Him Who has called Himself the Alpha and Omega, the Beginning and the End. Nevertheless, monism imagines that by means of these sophistical subterfuges, it has found an escape from divine intervention in human affairs. It prefers the god Pan to our great living God. What blindness, passion, and folly!

Let us proceed still further, my brother. We were promised, "Apart from all ideas of a divine creation and in opposition to the notion of miracles and the supernatural," a rational, scientific explanation, "not only of the physical world, but also of the moral world." We were told that the inevitable determinism of compelling laws was to extend to man. Those laws, however, were laws of matter—that very matter which man himself was thought to consist of; the matter from which he comes and to which he will return entirely. What this conception of the world impatiently commanded its servant, science, to make clear, comprehend, explain, and, in a word, to materialize, was, therefore, the whole moral world, including man, his nature, origin, soul, thought, conscience, liberty, duty, and destiny! Why has science been so slow in doing it?

Nevertheless, the task was begun. It was servile work, that of a slave, if there ever was one. I picture to myself science like Samson, betrayed and sold by Delilah, as with sightless eyes, chained to a tyrannical idea, she turns her mill to the profit and pleasure of the modern Philistines. But why has no molecule of life been discovered at some outermost boundary of being, which philosophy could call the uncreated embryo of primitive humanity? All the kingdoms of nature have been questioned, the interior of the earth and the life-tenanted depths of the seas investigated. The smallest and crudest rudiments of organic matter have been examined in the hope of finding there a germ of putrefaction which could audaciously take the place of the Author of life! And there have been moments when impatient atheism thought that *at last* science was about to satisfy its desire, that the sphinx was about to solve the riddle of the world, and that the longed-for answer was to make itself heard. But silence! . . . The sphinx said nothing, or . . . said something else.

Are you acquainted with the allegorical story by Leopardi, *The Mummies of Ruysch*? Let us pause a moment, brother, to reread it. Ruysch, the great Danish anatomist, was awakened one night by an orgy of dancing in which the mummies collected in his laboratory were indulging. They had come to life again, and as they danced, they chanted a hymn to their great patroness, Death. The famous scientist, perceiving them through the cracks in his door, was for a moment, in spite of his philosophy, bathed in a cold sweat. Nevertheless, he entered the laboratory. "My children," he said, "what game are you playing? What is all this uproar? Have you forgotten that you are dead?" Then one of the mummies informed him that this revel was of no consequence, but merely the celebration of the first night of the great mathematical year which was just beginning, and that the dead could enjoy this rare periodical meeting only a quarter of an hour. Ruysch took advantage of it to ask them about affairs in the other world, of which he thought the dead should certainly know much more than the living. But a quarter of an hour is soon passed; and when, pressed by his questions, the mummies were just about to pronounce the solemn solution of the enigma, the stroke of a bell was heard. It was the moment to withdraw; it was the end. All became silent as before.

How many times, in the course of this century, have we not seen the philosophers of atheism indulge in similar follies from which they expected the revelation of the mystery of the world and of life? Yet, each time, just at the moment when they thought they were to have it, it vanished never to return. Is it necessary for me to recall to you some famous incidents of this sort?

We had, for example, the long affair about spontaneous generation. In the form in which it was conceived in advance by a learned professor of zoölogy, it was going to convict Revelation of falsehood, and bring about a dismissal of the Creator of the world, inasmuch as He has now nothing to do. Haeckel had put the question squarely in the form of this unavoidable alternative: "To admit anything except spontaneous generation for the production of life, is to admit the supernatural; you must accept either one or the other; *tertium non datur.*"

You recollect the memorable session, when, after repeated experiments made by Pasteur, the commission of the Academy of Sciences pronounced its verdict in these terms: "Organized beings, in the present state of our globe, always receive life from bodies already living; and whether great or small, they are not born without having ancestors."

That was the axiom of Cuvier: "Life is born only from life." "The experiments of Pasteur are decisive," wrote Flourens, perpetual secretary of the Academy of Sciences; "to doubt them any longer is not to comprehend the subject."

The other kind of science, the atheistic sort, had to acknowledge its defeat. Virchow wrote in the *Revue Scientifique* of December 8, 1877: "To speak frankly, we savants (materialists) would have had a slight preference for the victory of spontaneous generation, if only some proof of it could have made its appearance! But we have no proof of such a thing, and no one has ever seen a spontaneous production of organic matter. It is not the theologians, but we savants, ourselves, who reject it."

The ape-man also had its glorious days! Man, "that fallen god, who still remembers heaven," was declared to be the descendant of something similar to the gorilla and the orang-utan. This was thought to be a good joke on the old God of creation, Who claimed to have made man in His own image and likeness! But unfortunately for the advocates of this theory, they have never succeeded, however hard they tried, in establishing scientifically our simian origin. There are always yawning gaps in our quarterings of nobility. The promoter of this race evolution, Dr. Virchow, was one of the first to give up his former teaching on this point and leave his school as well. In 1892, I read in the *Revue Scientifique* of November 5, the following: "The celebrated rector of the University of Berlin, compelled by the evidence, has just proclaimed the absurdity of the fiction of the *pro-anthropos,* in the following declaration made to the prehistoric Congress of Moscow: 'In the question of the ape-man we are repulsed all along the line. All the researches, pursued in the hope of finding continuity in progressive development, have been without result. There exists no *pro-anthropos.* There exists no ape-man. The intermediate link remains a phantom.' "* Nevertheless, in support of the anti-creationist theory, science still sought some specimen of matter which would offer proof for the first appearance of spontaneous life on the globe. In 1868, Huxley believed that he had found this convincing evidence in a certain gelatinous, marine, amorphous substance, to which he gave the suggestive and thought-provoking name of *Bathybios,* or "depths of life." There was great applause. Here it was, at last! But, eleven years later, in a congress of members of the British Association, the

---

*I blush to have to expose the embryological frauds which Haeckel was recently forced to admit. Pressed by Dr. Brasse, he had to confess in the *Berliner Volks-Zeitung,* of December 29, 1908, that "a part of his embryogenic drawings were really falsified." He had, for example, placed a human head on the embryo of an ape and also added eleven vertebrae to a human embryo. Nevertheless, on leaving his professorial chair, at Jena, he declared that he was conscious of having consecrated his life "to the service of truth!" Cf. *Revue Pratique d' Apologétique,* November 15, 1909, pp. 276 and seq.

president, having thought he was acting rightly in greeting Huxley as the incomparable expositor of the beginnings of life, Huxley replied by a gesture and smile of denial. Then, rising, he invited the learned assembly to laugh with him, even if the joke were on him. And with good grace, he declared that he, himself, had finally recognized that his *Bathybios* was nothing but a precipitate of sulphate of chalk and some old bits of tar glued together, coming probably from the hulls of ships navigating in those waters! The *protoplasm* is still to be found!

But now we come to something very different. We read, at present, that the physical sciences are on the eve of seeing themselves completely revolutionized! Recent radical theories about the very nature of matter and its properties, about the atom and its energies, the radiation of bodies, imponderable fluids, etc., are about to overturn, from top to bottom, the foundations of the physics and chemistry of yesterday. Berthelot, himself, lived long enough to witness the discovery of radium, which overthrew the principles stated by him as final, and he also saw the opposing theories of Gustave Le Bon regarding the *evolution of forces*. This meant the shattering of his fundamental distinction of the ponderable and the imponderable, upon which contemporaneous materialism had built its church. But Berthelot had reached the age when one no longer revises his illusions. What, then, remains today of his aggressive provocations and his proud program? Is the world "without mystery"? Has science cleared up everything, understood everything, and explained everything? Is the moral world a slave to determinism? Is the notion of the supernatural abolished? Science has taught us much of the physical world, it is true; but what has it taught us of the moral world, of man, his beginning, nature, duties, and end? What, indeed? It will be remembered that on the day when Brunetière intended to call this negative science to account for its proceedings, he found in it, on summing it all up, only a colossal deficit, beneath which he wrote this word, which unloosed the well-known tempest of abuse against him: *"Bank-ruptcy!"*

Can it be true also that doubt has now penetrated even into the domain of the exact sciences, and that mathematics and geometry themselves "offer definitely, even in their axioms, only *conventional formulas*, or at most *hypotheses without any objective value whatever*"? Yet it is a very eminent mathematician who declared this in a profound work entitled, *Science and Hypothesis*. I do not claim to be a judge of the subject, but I have at least the right to ask myself, whether, in view of such uncertainties and weak assertions, the present time is a suitable one for the scientist to proclaim the dogma of his infallibility and to crush religion with the absolutism of his sovereignty?

The orator, who received that great mathematician, Poincaré, in the French Academy on February 3, 1909, drew from this state of things a moral lesson for the use of the present bewildered teachers of our secular schools; for he interpreted him in these terms: "By this frank assertion of your doubts, how completely you lay in ruins the chapels, around which are gathered, to celebrate the mysteries of a pretended religion of science, the crowds of rationalists and freethinkers who, by means of a certificate of having completed the primary studies, have acquired the right . . . to believe in nothing! What a massacre you make of those old demonstrations and definitions, in which you now see only conventional formulas and temporary hypotheses! . . . But what is left after all that? Nothing, or almost nothing. And the most precious idols of elementary religion disappear in the depopulated heavens, to join the extinguished stars."*

*   *   *

My first conclusion, therefore, is: *Let science be modest.* "The hour of scientific affirmation has not yet sounded," wrote recently the scientific editor of the *Temps.* "It may even be asked if it will ever

---

*Frédéric Masson.

sound. Science is, above all, made up of *little temporary judgments;* and if she be wise, the interrogation point is the only mark of punctuation that she will prefer."

My second conclusion, which I borrow from a master, is: *"Let theistic science and Christianity be reassured.* At the conclusion of the century which has just ended, Albert de Lapparent, the successor of Berthelot to the post of secretary of the Academy of Sciences, in drawing up the balance sheet between belief and unbelief, closed thus: "After one hundred years of effort to explain everything, apart from our religious beliefs or in opposition to them, the science which is free of prejudices, liberated from all *a priori* philosophy, and faithful to its method of calm observation has reached conclusions which differ little from those of our old dogmas. Let us not fear, therefore, to affirm boldly that this end of the century is *favorable to men of faith and particularly to Catholics.* The power which tried to exterminate them has doubtless grown greater, but the light which it has caused to shine has only accentuated the extreme complication of all the problems involved. Moreover, we should bear in mind that it is not merely against us believers that science has turned her weapons. Those who have been wounded worst in the fray are those philosophers whose hateful passions science has refused to serve. The applications

SCIENCE AND SOPHISM   105

of pure science have, of themselves, been sufficient
to condemn numerous assertions of our adversaries.
Accordingly, our principles remain intact, con-
fronting a world which may continue to misun-
derstand them, but will never find truth or salvation outside of their acceptance."

And here I close, my brother. I have said that
scientific and industrial progress is good, but that
the use made of it is bad. I repeat here: *True*
science is good. That which is bad, is the *atheistic*
philosophy which many wish, unlawfully and
falsely, to deduce from it. Let us give up this part-
nership of science and atheism! Let us break every
pact with impiety! Moreover, I find in the masters
of modern science less loftiness of genius and of
heart than in their predecessors. They are uncertain and, in the last analysis, are sure neither of
themselves nor of their utterances. Some of them
have, indeed, become better informed and have retracted their former statements. Can the same be
said of us? Which of our masters or of our Christian men of genius have repented being Christian
believers, as they advanced in science and in life?
God be praised, the school to which our youth belonged will also be to the end the school of our old
age. Between the spirituality of the one and the
materialism of the other, and between the serenity
of the one and the apprehension of the other, the
choice cannot be doubtful. At the end of my

career, paraphrasing the words of a dear friend, I can truly say to my beloved pupils: I began the study of these questions fifty years ago, and I have thought of them continually ever since; I have also read everything of importance that the ablest and most powerful atheists, positivists, and pantheists of every shade have written about them; and I can assure you that it has all confirmed my faith in an *absolute, personal, and creative God.*

CHAPTER
SEVEN

God Everywhere
The World and the Soul

Sir Joseph Banks* the Humboldt of England, when asked by King George III what was the most beautiful thing he had seen in his voyage around the world, replied: "The evidence of the Creator of it all." Similarly do I, at the end of my life's journey, utter the words of Volta in his later years: "I see God everywhere."

And in fact, He *is* everywhere: in the universe, in humanity, in myself, and in each of the souls akin to mine. He is everywhere as Cause and Creator, as Law and Legislator, as Exemplar and supreme Ideal. He is like the ocean, which envelops the whole earth and cleanses every shore; and whatever may be the current of ideas on which my thought embarks, it is to Him that everything finally comes, and in Him that all ends at last.

---

*Sir Joseph Banks (1743-1820), president of the Royal Society for 41 years, made a voyage to Newfoundland in 1766, collecting plants. He fitted out, at his own expense, a vessel in which he accompanied Captain Cook on his famous voyage around the world (1768-1771), after which he visited the Hebrides and Iceland. He was the first to make the island Staffa known to the world. He introduced into the West Indies the mango from Bengal, the bread-fruit tree from Tahiti, and many other fruits from Asia.

I looked at a star glittering in the firmament, and thought: To the voice of God, that called it from the depths of space, that star replied: "Lo, I come!" and rendered homage to Him with its tender light. I turned and beheld a tiny glow-worm, hiding by night beneath a blade of grass; and I seemed to hear a humble voice whispering the words: "I, too, shine for the Most High." For the infinitely little in the universe utters the same name as the infinitely great. The organ of creation has always chanted that divine name through the entire gamut of its varied tones; but today how many new motifs modern science has added to this anthem to the Creator by means of all the wonderful, freshly discovered manifestations of His attributes! It is the delight of my mind to recognize Him in all these, as being greater and more worthy of adoration than ever before, just as it is the supreme rapture of my soul to feel Him more intimately present in my life and heart. The brilliant revelation of God, peculiar to this century and age of progress, would awaken such sentiments in all men, if they would but open their eyes to its magnificence. For the profounder knowledge of the universe which we possess today brings us more than ever into the presence of a Creator, wiser, greater, diviner, and more powerful than the God our fathers knew.

I smile, when I remember what the old childish

cosmogonies of antiquity, even those of civilized
Greece, used to teach about the formation of the
world. They represented our globe as rolling
through space upon invisible rails, and the stars as
pinned, like golden nails, on an azure tapestry, or
as torches hung from the vaulted ceilings of celestial palaces. And what a very human conception they had of the stupendous nebulous expanse
of the Milky Way! Yet even then, Pythagoras was
listening to the "harmony of the spheres," which
brought him the name of God. And did not Plato
say that God was a geometer? "Knowest thou the
path of light?" asks the Lord of Job, "and the extent of its course to us? Hast thou laid the measures of the earth and the great paths of the clouds?
Where wast thou when I laid the foundations of
the earth, when I shut up the sea with doors, and
when I caused the stars to rise on the evening of
the first days? If thou knowest it, tell Me."

"Yes, Lord," we might reply to this challenge,
"we know something of these secrets of antiquity.
We know now that light travels at the rate of 186,-
000 miles a second and that it reaches us in eight
minutes and nineteen seconds from the sun, which
is nearly 93 millions of miles from our earth. We
know, also, that the earth revolves round the sun
at the rate of about 1,100 miles a minute, or sixty
times as fast as a cannon ball. We know, moreover,
that everything in this vast universe is in motion

and constantly at work, as in a machine shop, run by an invisible force and guided by a hand that never rests. The universe, as we know it today, is an immeasurable void, in which innumerable worlds sweep on through space in mutual dependence and in solemn silence—a silence which froze with fear the thought of Pascal. "Silence everywhere, movement everywhere, and in everything grandeur, order, simplicity, unity, ease, and harmony. And in this universal movement, there is not a vibration of an atom and not the wing-beat of an insect at a single point of all these worlds, that has not its repercussion on that whole immensity." Immensity, simplicity, unity, harmony, and life—how all that resembles Thee, my God!

*   *   *

"Number the stars, if thou art able," said the Lord to His servant Abraham. They are the letters of the name of God, which for a long time man was only able to spell out with difficulty. "The ancients," writes Malebranche,* "thought they had made a great advance, in saying that the sun was as large as the Peloponnesus; but today scientists tell us that it is a million times larger than the whole earth. The ancients counted 1,022 stars. Today science despairs of numbering them all." The catalog of Bonner, published from 1859 to

---

* *Entretiens Sur la Métaphysique et la Religion.*

1886, carried the number of the stars to 457,847.
At present, photography reveals more than 400,-
000,000! In this immensity, what is our tiny
earth? A grain of dust, which our sun carries with
it in its orbit, itself drawn on by other solar systems. Like innumerable stellar fleets, they move on
toward mysterious shores which continually recede
in a gigantic sea whose limits may never be known.
Vision sublime! How can our earth-clouded minds
aspire to translate a book which shows in characters
of fire the infinite power of God and the impotence of man? The power of God, do I say? Yes,
but also His infinite wisdom and supreme intelligence. The profoundest revelation of this, however, is not given us by the external spectacle of the
universe, but by an inner penetration of the laws
which govern it and which presided over its formation. In our day, more than ever before, God, by
introducing us, so to speak, into His laboratory, by
initiating us into His calculations and unfolding to
us His cosmic plan, has revealed to our admiring
gaze the innermost secrets, not only of the government of the universe, but also of the method of its
creation and its constitution. Thanks to modern
science, we can imagine ourselves present at the
formation of our planetary system; we ascertain
the movement and the shape of the celestial bodies;
we analyze their composition; we weigh their
density; we measure their respective distances. As

photography came to the aid of the telescope, so the spectroscope has come to the assistance of photography. Today, we study not merely celestial geometry and celestial mechanics, but also celestial physics and celestial chemistry. All these sciences form, however, really only one science, whose laws are applicable to the entire work of Him, Who, as our Credo states, is the "Creator of heaven and earth," of things visible and invisible.

This declaration "Creator of heaven and earth," is affirmed by Faye, the great geometer and director of the observatory of Paris. He had taken up again the astronomical calculations of Laplace, correcting his mistakes and completing his system. But the greatest mistake of Laplace had been that, in his *Mécanique Céleste*, he had left out of consideration the supreme Mechanician. Faye, however, like Tycho Brahe, Kepler, Newton, and Galileo, bowed in reverence before the Creator; and the last, impressive page of his *Origine du Monde* is a kind of apology for science, now better informed. He writes, "Today, we contemplate and know, at least in its directly discernible form, a world which Laplace did not know. We are aware now that there is something else besides our bodies to be reckoned with and something else besides the splendid stars. There is intelligence and thought. And, as our human intelligence did not create itself, there must exist in the vast universe a higher Intelligence, from which ours is derived. Henceforth, the greater our idea of this Intelligence is, the nearer will it approach the truth. We can, therefore, make no mistake in considering that Intelligence as the Creator of all things, and in attributing to the Owner of it those celestial splendors which amaze our thought. Thus we are fully prepared to comprehend and to accept the traditional formula: "Almighty God, Maker of heaven and earth."

Magnus in magnis, maximus in minimis! Great as God is in His grander works, does He not show Himself even greater in His lesser ones? After the infinitely great, let us speak of the infinitely little. Now it is the turn of the microscope to enable us to read the name of God, and never was this name so legible as it is today. I remember that, in our classes, in order to give us an idea of the infinitely little in the animal and vegetable kingdoms, our teacher made us read about the strawberry plant in the studies of nature, with its city of thousands of imperceptible tenants, which Bernardin de Saint-Pierre describes. Look at this fragile speck of mold through a microscope. It becomes a forest! Each tree there has its roots, its branches, leaves, and flowers with their organs, tissues, and canals of nourishment like those of the oak tree or the palm. Who made that fairy scene in countless specimens, so fine, so beautiful, so exact, and so adapted to its functions? "I do not know how other men are constituted," says Lamartine's *Stone Cutter;* "but, as for myself, I cannot behold, I do not say a star, but even an ant, a leaf, a grain of sand, without asking it: 'Who made you?' " "God," said Victor Hugo, "is the *obvious Invisible.*"

In the animal kingdom, the infinitely little was formerly exemplified by the cheese mite. Today, have you succeeded in counting the animalcula that swarm in a single drop of water? Yet each of those tiny creatures has its complete organs of respiration, nutrition, locomotion, and reproduction! Where, then, is the limit of life? Does any engineer know how many thousands of threads and fibers enable that wonderfully clever airplane which we call a Coleoptera bug to fly? Or that perfect submarine, the gudgeon fish, to move? Ask the name of the Inventor!

From there let us descend to the extreme manifestations of cellular life, to the ultimate organisms of living matter, and to the remotest limits of that molecular world, which resolves itself into atoms, millions of which could be located on the head of a pin. And let us picture these atoms, as they are attracted toward their center by continual vibrations, forming as many little worlds, controlled by the same laws as those which govern the orbs of infinite space. There exists today a veritable astronomy of the atomic world! Render homage to its Creator, and repeat with Maeterlinck: "The atom, itself, is a manufactured product, that bears the mark of the divine laboratory." Such a study makes the head spin; but it gives, above all, the impression of divinity. Long ago, Father Faber, of the English Oratory of St. Philip Neri, gave me the following religious avowal in a letter, part of which I here transcribe: "Without having a deeper knowledge than that which one can gain from popular manuals on the different branches of science, it seems to me that when we come to the study of chemical affinities, the doctrine of imponderable fluids, and the question of atoms, especially the theory of Boscovich, which makes matter consist, not of solid molecules, but of central, mathematical forces, it seems, I say, as if we were descending into the laboratories of creation. At every moment one expects to surprise God at work, so closely do these considerations and revelations appear to draw us to the primitive state of things and to lead us, so to speak, to the very edge of the infinite. For my part, I confess that I have trembled, and have not been able to avoid a feeling—half of fear, half of curiosity—when reading of discoveries which descend to the profoundest mysteries of being. One recognizes there the presence of God, and feels His nearness by that involuntary shiver and that beating of the heart, which tell us of the approach of someone whom we love. For a devout mind science is something eminently religious."

From the laboratory, let us pass, then, to our oratory, my brother; and with the inspired Psalmist, sing: "O Lord, my God, Thy knowledge is too wonderful for me. It is high; I cannot attain unto it. Whither shall I go from Thy spirit, or whither shall I flee from Thy presence? If I ascend into heaven, Thou art there; if I descend into hell, lo! Thou art there. . .•. Wonderful are Thy works; as my soul knoweth right well. (Ps. cxxxviii. 6-14.)

I would that every great scientific discovery and every great invention, worthy of, and profitable to, humanity, should publicly inscribe upon its brow the name of God. Utter that divine name with adoration and thanksgiving, ye forces of nature, made captive and harnessed to the service of man! Let it be brought by means of motor ships and railroads from one end of the earth to the other! Let the fleets of the air lift it into the loftiest regions of the sky! Let electricity inscribe it everywhere in characters of gleaming light! Let this name also be the first that continents, united by electric power, flash to each other, as they did on August 5, 1858. The submarine cable having been laid in the depths of the Atlantic, the American station received, at the southern extremity of Trinity Bay, Newfoundland, the following telegram, cabled by the station of Valentia in County Kerry, Ireland: "*Glory to*

God in the highest and peace on earth to men of good will! Europe and America are united."*

There had not been a greater day than that for the two worlds since Christopher Columbus landed on San Salvador, and chanted the *Te Deum* there, kneeling before the Cross.

Should not this century, to which, more than to any other, the God of heaven and earth has revealed the marvels of His power and multiplied the gifts of His munificence, be the most believing, the most reverent, of all ages? But alas! How do we act today? At present, atheism is invading us, denying everything, forgetting everything, shutting its eyes to everything divine! The impression it makes upon us is that of emptiness. One becomes dizzy on the brink of this abyss of darkness. According to this new philosophy, we comprehend nothing of the world, nothing of man, nothing of life. All is chaos; it is night. My sun is vanished from the sky. I see nothing stable either in myself, or in the world about me; no more certainty in my thought, no logical connection in my ideas, no higher ideal for my aspirations. And, around me, no trace of a First Cause, no reason for the existence of any-

---

*The same day, on his side, Mr. Hudson, the old captain of the *Niagara*, one of the two ships which had transported the cable, announced his success to his family in the following words: "God has been with us. The cable has been laid without accident. It is to God that we must ascribe the glory."

Similarly, the great exposition in the Crystal Palace bore the following inscription over its main entrance: *GLORIA IN EXCELSIS DEO.*

thing, no final authoritative word on anything. The world's activity is nothing but a senseless game played, century after century, by shadows. Life is a dream, history a series of scandals, truth a mirage, virtue folly, and humanity a whirlwind of atoms revolving aimlessly in space and time, borne onward by a movement which has had no author and has still no goal. And man? He is the latest product of a vast fermentation forever seething in that bottomless and brimless vat called nature. Carbon, oxygen, thou art my father! Putrefaction, thou art my mother! Worms, you are my brothers and my heirs!

It is also an abyss of pain and sadness. Years ago, I found this poignant sentiment in the following words of a despairing young philosopher of that time: "Atheism has begun its work and will slowly destroy, one after the other, our thoughts, our principles, our desires, and our emotions. It destroys, but it does not replace. It is negative; it is the synonym of impotence to comprehend or to explain, to believe or to act. Neither has it discovered a single principle on which two men can agree, nor laid the first stone of its new construction; it has not fixed upon its site; nor even raised the first shovelful of earth to build upon. It certainly digs deep, but only to bury all we love. Yet this new age which atheism labors to create will eventually come.

What mental anguish there will be, when all our old ideas of the good and the beautiful shall be effaced, and when the light that lighteth every man that cometh into this world, after having grown gradually fainter, shall finally be extinguished! There will be, at first, a sort of eclipse, a feeling of uneasiness, such as we experience when the shadows deepen, and the solitude of evening oppresses the heart. Yet this will not be a normal evening, followed by a normal night; for the night at present has stars and the prospect of another day. Nor will there be a normal autumn, for the yellow leaves that now fall show us the places of the buds of spring. But when God shall have disappeared, there will be nothing left except a void greater than that which a man experiences in the desolate home when, after having conveyed his loved one to the cemetery, he opens the door of his desolate house to find no one there awaiting him. Still, even there, although the object of his love is gone, *love, at least, remains*. But when love itself shall have left us, what will then console us?"

My brother, I cannot think that this will be our fate. I prefer to believe in the signs of a coming spiritual, theistic reaction, like that which was recently pointed out to me by a highly intellectual mind. He said: "All, or nearly all, that can be said against God has been said in support of the uncertain utterances of a science which can, as yet, only stammer in its speech. Materialism and mechanism are losing ground daily, and will lose more ground. You will see that the prejudice of high science to the existence of God will be compelled to yield the field to the great theistic interpretation, which is simple, natural, and satisfying alike to reason and common sense. The proof of final causes is as immovable and sublime as the cathedrals. We firmly believe that a magnificent movement, still only in its infancy, will soon bring back the great majority of scientists to these conclusive principles. Yes, in spite of the opposition to the religious idea brought from without, I have the sensation of going up stream again and the joy of seeing the light once more increasing. Thus science will finally make for herself a new and brilliant vindication, deduced from the gospel of nature, open to all eyes. In fifty or a hundred years, despite the adverse outward appearances today, a better science will have outgrown its infancy and will have reconquered its legitimate sovereignty; it is not irrational to express the hope that God will come back again, as Master of the twentieth century."

*   *   *

But I will not wait till then before adoring God Who, if He is the God of the sciences, is above all the God of my heart. Moreover, it is not from sci-

ence that I possess my certainty and hope, but from
my faith. "How good it is," wrote Cochin, "under
my poor thatched roof, during a hailstorm, to love
Thee, O my God, while others are discussing
Thee!" At this hour of a life so near eternity, instead of waiting for men to settle their disputes, I
feel myself urged to repeat my Credo to the Eternal Father, and to renew to Him the following
profession of faith which, at every turn of my long
journey, I have been called upon to lay solemnly
upon His altar:

I believe in a living God, Who is above all and
before all; I believe in a First Originator of all
movements, in a First Cause before all causes, in a
necessary Being, in a supreme Designer of all de-
signs. I believe in God, in accordance with a philosophy which, six thousand years ago, opened its
teachings with the indestructible affirmation:
Nothing exists without a cause. I believe in God
in harmony with poetry, which began with man's
first cry of admiration on beholding the order and
beauty of the universe. I believe in God in conformity to the arts which, by translating something of the ideal beauty of the world, permit us
to appreciate with ecstasy its universal unity and
eternal splendor. I believe in God in fellowship
with a holiness which, even on this earth, reflects,
in part, the complete image of His perfection.
Finally, I believe in God in unison with the whole

creation, with universal history, and with the living and the dead. In the retrospect of the vanished centuries, what a long line of thinkers, artists, legislators, poets, and scholars we behold lifting their voices in God's praise! Sermons in stones also extol His name as do the seas, the rivers, and the forests. The stars of heaven radiate it. I feel as if I were present at an ecumenical council of all God's creatures, proclaiming and—if I dare use the expression—decreeing the supreme dogma: *I believe in one God!*

In these pages, I have sought proofs of this belief from nature and from man; but I find still stronger and more irresistible proofs in the depths of my own being. If there is in man any innate idea, it is the notion of God. If there is any belief which is essentially inherent in mankind, it is that of God. There is not an idea in us which does not presuppose the idea of God and is not supported by it. There is no certainty which does not rest upon that first of certainties; *that God is, and that God does not deceive.* Intimate proofs—proofs of instinct, proofs of conscience, and fundamental and indestructible moral proofs, all confront us with the solidity of granite, the hardness of the diamond, the brilliancy of the stars. "God everywhere" was the title I wrote at the head of this chapter. But He is present nowhere more than in my own conscience and my heart. He is necessary to the life

of the world, but He is no less necessary to my
own. He is essential to my happiness and to my
hope. "We want God!" are the words uttered
today by the tearful and despairing masses, from
whom this unique Treasure of both earth and
heaven has been taken by violence. I, on the contrary, who believe, can at every moment converse
with Him. When I pronounce His name, an echo
within makes reply. Someone has heard me and has
understood me. It is He. In the midst of the icy
indifference of men, He alone has come to me and
remained near me. In the hour of temptation, He
has appeared to me walking on the waves and holding out His hand to rescue me. In hours of enthusiasm for the good, the true, and the beautiful, I
have felt myself uplifted to Him, for truth, goodness, and beauty culminate in Him. In hours of
darkness, a ray of light has always pierced the
gloom; it was a ray from His countenance. In
days of difficulties and trials, He has come to take
away the thorns and thistles from the path before
me. In the hour of the unfolding of my holiest
thoughts, what is it but the breath from heaven
that has nourished them? And now, at the end of
my exile, when, old and travel-worn, I think of the
fair country of my soul awaiting me, who is it that
awakens in me those indescribable yearnings of
prayer and desire, that make me cry out: "Father!
Abba! Father!" It is His Spirit: it is He. Remain

then, O my God, my guide and light until the glorious day of the celestial vision, which cannot now be hidden from me long: for old age is its dawn.

CHAPTER
EIGHT

The Gospel—a Torch

I call the Gospel "a torch," and in reality it is the torch, the beacon light of all Christians. Has its light undergone an eclipse during the century I have lived in? It has certainly poured forth its radiance in the midst of great darkness, and the darkness has not comprehended it. But has its own intrinsic brightness failed or even grown fainter? I do not think so. In fact, I believe that just the contrary is the case. I would like to state my impressions on that point—impressions from which my mentality, as a believer, was long ago formed for my entire life. They come to me as distant souvenirs.

Let me think back! I remember Sundays, now so distant, when the saintly priest of our village parish read the Gospel for the day from the pulpit, using for this purpose a large, beautifully gilded volume, ornamented with bookmarks. He then commented on the text, after the custom of the Fathers, keeping the sacred volume open before him, and pronouncing every word of Scripture with an accent of religious authority which made us recognize and revere it as the word of God. I can hear him still. And I, then a little choir boy, used to ask myself: "What is this unusually large and beautiful book the priest incenses at the altar, each word of which is an oracle and before which we are bidden to carry the consecrated candles? I see, also, that everybody rises to hear it read."

I remember, also, long ago, when we boys, pupils of the priests, were obliged, every morning in our grammar classes, to learn, translate, and write at the beginning of our exercises one or two Greek verses from the Gospel of St. Luke. It was a consecration of our work for the day. And I, then a little pupil, used to ponder over the question: "What is this precious essence, the smallest drop of which can thus perfume all that I am to read or write today?"

When the New Testament was given me to read in its entirety, as "the Word of God," I was just graduating from my classical training and about to enter upon other studies which were to be nourished by this divine text. My first impression was one of profound astonishment. How little did this book resemble in form and substance those Greek and Latin writings on which I had hitherto been mentally fed! They had been universally recognized as intellectual works of art, masterpieces of eloquence or poetry, composed, elaborated, and finished for the admiration of centuries. But, from a literary point of view, the book now given me was comparatively rough and unpolished, with an unformed style, of which it was said that "it smacked of the barbarian." Who, then, had written it, and when? Had I not been told that it was a product of the great century, the age of the best writers of Rome? What an anachronism! I was puzzled. Moreover, as regards the substance of the book, the dissimilarity was still greater! These singular writers, although contemporaries of Tacitus, Suetonius, and Petronius did not entertain me, as the others had done, with accounts of politics, brilliant wars, victorious heroes, the Cæsars, the senate, the army, and the empire, still less with the theater, the circus, refined sensual pleasures, and great orgies of flesh and blood. Where, then, had I been suddenly transported? Another world had risen up before me; a kingdom of God, a kingdom of heaven, eternal life, divine love, spirit, and grace. All this was circulating under the rough exterior of those letters, like sap which was rising, overflowing, bursting its old vessels, rending asunder ancient tissues and forms of art, in order to allow the ideal of a perfectly holy life and a perfectly pure truth to flow, like a brimming river, through the world. These were all new writings which spoke a new language through the lips of new men—even rude, simple, obscure, and unlettered men—whom my studies as a humanist had never revealed.

For a moment, I felt out of my element and, if I may say so, (God forgive me!) a little disenchanted. This was due to that same humanist prejudice for which St. Jerome, in a dream, heard himself reproached as follows: "Thou art a Ciceronian, not a Christian." I apologize for it. But, thank God, today the classics—although still endowed with all the honors due their rank—have long since passed into the background of my enthusiasms, while the Gospel has acquired and still holds there the highest place; the place that Jesus Christ Himself will possess in my heart for ever.

The teaching of Scripture was given us in the great seminary by some saintly, white-haired, old men, whose learning drew its inspiration from the best interpreters and commentators of the seventeenth and eighteenth centuries. Their lesson was not one to be despised, even if it did prohibit whatever would have caused us to abandon the sacred path of ecclesiastical tradition. At all events, we—that is, myself and those of my own age—belonged to a period in which the rule that "not a jot or a tittle of the law was to be taken away," made us accept reverently every syllable of Holy Writ. The Spirit of God rested above it in an impenetrable cloud, as over a holy Ark, which cherubim (the leaders of the Church) jealously covered with their wings. It was their duty and our security. Rather than doctrine, the priests bade us seek in the Gospel edification, consolation, food for meditation, and a rule of conduct; in a word, the living Spirit of God to vivify our minds and hearts. The Bible was our inseparable companion; we carried it religiously on our persons, and put our lips to it, as a son does to a dear letter from his father, for it was as precious as this to our piety and faith. Has it still the same value in the eyes of our grand-nephews today?

This was the thoroughly simple, but sincere and elevated education, by which our ideas of the Scripture and particularly of the Holy Gospel were formed; and I am not ashamed to confess that the state of soul which characterized my youth in this respect remains today that of my old age. And I understand perfectly why it is so. It is because my old age is so happy in its possession. How and why is this? What sort of experience has caused it? What certainty of its truth have I received? I must confide this to you, my brother.

It was only after I had left the seminary, that I was brought to a full consciousness of the question then agitating my century in regard to Scripture. I found that the Gospel and even the person of Jesus Christ Himself had become, alas! a subject of contention. The wind was blowing fiercely on the sacred torch, but the wind that extinguishes a little flame, only augments a great one. What happened, my brother? First of all, God be thanked,

the torch was held aloft by powerful hands; I mean
by representatives of Biblical science among both
the clergy and the laity, including authorities of
the highest rank in the Semitic and Oriental languages, who made of their orientalism a stalwart
bulwark for the city of God. One of these intellectual kings was *Baron Eckstein,* known as a "living encyclopedia, the contemporary of all the ages,
a fellow citizen of all nations." Renan, who so
little resembled him, nevertheless wrote of him, the
day after his death, in 1861: "Baron Eckstein was
in touch with all the poles of human thought.
There was no problem laid before mankind that
he did not try to solve. He saw more clearly than
anyone, the fundamental element of the Divine discoverable in humanity. . . . Catholicism was
for him the key to the great apocalypse of history.
He believed in a possible renaissance within the
Church itself, and from this hope he derived an
immense amount of vigor, for it was based on
truths which rose above sectarianism, and not only
nullified the fear of death, but made death seem
desirable." It was, then, the turn of the revered
Silvestre de Sacy, another "encyclopedic man of
immense erudition," as this same Renan called him;
an erudition which included all the ancient languages through which the varied versions of our
sacred books have passed. He was called "the
Orient incarnate," yet all of his vast knowledge

converged finally in this profession of faith: "I declare, before Him from Whose eyes nothing is concealed, that I have always lived in the faith of the Catholic Church, having never doubted the truth and the divinity of the Christian religion, etc." Then came Quatremère de Quincy, also described by Renan, as an "Orientalist of gigantic learning." Quatremère had devoted his last lecture courses at the Collége de France, in 1857, to defending the authenticity of Holy Scripture and its traditional interpretation, and to rejecting the chimerical German theories which the modernistic school of criticism tries today to popularize.

Do not these three eminent men, these three kings of the same science, these three Orientalists, and worshipers of Christ, make you think, my brother, of the three kings of the East who, led by the star, came to lay their treasures at the feet of the divine Child? At the same time, the other auxiliary sciences of history confirmed the utterances of Orientalism. To mention only those of inscriptions and archæology, we had, then, the famous Greek inscription of Autun, which a young scholar who later became Cardinal Pitra, had just discovered and deciphered. In this, the dogma of the Eucharist appeared under its ancient symbols. Later on, the similar Phrygian inscription of St. Abercius, called by De Rossi "the queen of inscriptions," was found. The inscriptions and religious paintings of the Catacombs also form, in themselves alone, an entire dogmatic theology, in which not one of the articles of the Creed is missing. I shall never in my life forget the days in 1862 when, after having been able to visit the cradle of pagan Rome on the Aventine under the guidance of J. J. Ampère, I was permitted to visit, with De Rossi, the cradle of Christian Rome in the cemetery of St. Calixtus and in his museum of the Lateran, then newly established. It was there at Rome that, long before, in the Lenten season of 1835, a young rector of the English college, the future Cardinal Wiseman, already known as one of the foremost scholars of his country, had delivered those celebrated lectures. They were our first introduction to this kind of apologetics which had become more necessary and more opportune than ever. Bunsen, one of his auditors, wrote to him to express his admiration, saying: "They occupy my mind continually, and I believe them destined to produce the most important results."

*   *   *

The most disputed object of controversy, however, was, as always, the Gospel; and on this battle field, the point which it was, above all, necessary to gain was that of the authenticity of the Holy Book, its origin, date, and authorship. To this was linked the problem of its veracity. Around this occurred the great collision of conflicting minds, friendly and hostile. But how the procedure of some of these differed from that of others, and how unlike were their methods, the paths they followed, and the conclusions they reached! It is very instructive to recall them, my brother.

Two very distinct classes of scholars in Europe then occupied themselves with this question of the origin of the Gospel. On one side were the purely speculative minds, the *a priori* philosophers who started out with their own personal and preconceived idea, pursued it to the end, seeing nothing else, referring everything to it, going astray in its search, wandering, floundering, and finally losing themselves in the inanity of their own thoughts. *Evanuerunt in cogitationibus suis;* that is the right expression for it. On the other hand, the positive, conscientious scholars started out without prejudice in search of truth alone, not by the adventurous and personal path of speculation, but by the sure and straightforward way of investigation. They did not fashion for themselves chimeras; they went straight to the facts. They did not build up systems in order to imprison themselves; they made discoveries. Having made their way to the remotest shores of antiquity, they recognized there primitive monuments whose authority their erudition confirmed, determined their date, and assigned to them their historic place. That is the procedure of true science. Now, to what conclusions did those who followed this more excellent way, whether they were Catholics or Protestants, finally come? They arrived ultimately at conclusions practically identical with those of orthodoxy. The doctrine of nearly all of them is completely confirmatory of our own. This we shall soon see. On the contrary, what were the paths pursued by the idealists, the speculative dreamers? And whither have they been led by their preconceived idea that *"the supernatural does not and cannot exist"*? The vast ocean of research traversed by our century is littered with their wrecks. Let us look at some of them, my brother.

Do you—does anyone—still remember the mythical theory conceived by Strauss, that cloud-gathering Jupiter, whose terrible phantom confronted the faith of our youth sixty years ago? For him, since he did not believe in the existence of the supernatural, the miracles wrought or experienced by Jesus were merely myths. The resurrection, ascension, acts of healing, and apparitions of Christ were only figurative, and all the old supernatural world, at last unmasked, was explained away by a clever natural hypothesis. How the whole school of freethinkers rejoiced over this discovery! Edgar Quinet wrote, "Strauss has clearly exposed all the blows which German science has given to Christianity, as Mark Antony, lifting the mantle of Cæsar, exhibited all the wounds which his body had received."

But this delusion did not bear the light of day. After the first dazzling effect, men's eyes were opened. Strauss, beating a retreat, revised his too-imaginative work, without, however, rendering his second attempt any more probable than the first. Then the whole mythical theory crumbled under the learned criticism of Neander's *Life of Jesus*. Finally, there was nothing left of it. Even Littré, the French translator of Strauss, was heard, while dying, to adore this Gospel, of which he said, "Yes, Jesus, Thou hast well said that Thy words shall not pass away. They will not do so, as long as there shall be left one child of Adam to comprehend them." Of the wounds given to Christianity, as well as those inflicted on the resurrected Christ, there remain only those glorious scars before which Thomas, falling on his knees, exclaimed: "My Lord and my God!" Do you also remember—but where are the snows of last year?—the great clamor made about the theory of Baur and the Tübingen school? This theory was a wholly imaginary fiction of a primitive and prolonged conflict between two Christian parties, the Judaizers and the Liberals, a conflict lasting two centuries, and followed finally by a diplomatic compromise, of which the New Testament had been the hybrid memorial. What did they not invent in order to find an historical basis for this dualism and this fusion? It has all crumbled under the weight of dates and facts. "Of all the work of Christian Baur," writes Dr. Adolph Harnack today, "there remains nothing but ruins."

Yet it was from these incongruous ruins that we saw Ernest Renan rear the fragile structure of his *Life of Jesus*. That romance made a fortune for him, though the scandal it aroused was universal. In the world of skeptics the book was received with great applause; in the world of believers with horror; in that of science with disdain. Today, it is no longer taken seriously. It did not collapse with an uproar, like a falling building; but faded away, like a fragile, rainbow-tinted cloud, which evaporates before the sun.

Today, it is modernism that moves about the Gospel with a feline gentleness, in order to salute in it . . . what? Not an historical book, but what they sentimentally call "a mystical, unreal, and purely ideal conception of the legendary Christ which the Christians of the golden age must have created and transfigured." It is not a history, they say, but a poem! Yet hear the historian himself, my brother. The evangelist St. Luke rises solemnly to declare, at the very beginning of his recital, formally, repeatedly, and explicitly the following: "Forasmuch as many have taken in hand to set forth in order a narration of the things that have been accomplished among us, according as they have delivered them unto us, who from the beginning *were eyewitnesses* and ministers of the word, it seemed good to me also, *having diligently attained to all things* from the beginning, to write to thee in order, most excellent Theophilus, that thou mayest know the truth of those words in which thou hast been instructed." Where is to be found in such a narration a place for inventions, poetry, and fantasies? This is actual history, solid history, a temple with a granite foundation and built of hewn stones. Let us enter it and remain there with confidence, my brother!

Let us hear, also St. John: "That which was from the beginning, which we have heard, which we have seen with our eyes, which we have looked upon, and our hands have handled of the Word of life, which was with the Father and hath appeared to us, this we declare unto you."

Now what, on the contrary, do the tardy deniers of a faith of nineteen centuries announce to us? What do they bring in opposition to this firm testimony and to these solemn assertions of the authors themselves? Nothing but hypotheses, scaffoldings, and frail intellectual constructions which speedily collapse on one another. Such were the hypotheses proposed yesterday by Renan—the pretended "hallucinations" of hundreds of witnesses who, sensible and truthful enough when they heard and collected the discourses of Jesus, became deluded

creatures, deceived and deceiving, when they saw
and reported His miracles, which, nevertheless, had
been facts plainly evident to them! Try to comprehend that. Other hypotheses much in favor at
one time were those of successive interpolations,
which, it is claimed, in the course of time—but
when, where, by whom?—slipped into the marvelously unified and compact recital of the Gospel.
These intentionally changed the unique physiog-
nomy of Jesus, so harmonious in its features and
hopelessly inimitable, that Rousseau said of it: "It
is not thus that one invents. Such an inventor
would be greater than the hero."

Of the combined attack of France and Germany
upon the Gospel, whose advent and whose ending
we have seen, what now remains? About as much
as remained of the tower of Babel, after the confusion of languages. Of Christ, the Son of the living God, what do the modernists leave us? Only
a few traces; not much more than the disciples
found in the sepulcher after His resurrection—a
winding sheet and some napkins. From these poor
remnants, the Christian soul goes sorrowfully
away, saying: "They have taken away my Lord,
and I know not where they have laid Him."
Finally, of Christianity itself — the ultimate
product of the evolution of thought and of the
progress of humanity through the turmoil of the
centuries—what is left of that, according to the

modernist theory? About as much as survives the agitation of the sea after a night of storm—a little foam upon the waves.

I come now to true science, to scriptural science, the only serious and decisive one, derived, not from empty theoretical systems, but from the discovery of manuscripts and the revelation of facts. This science, proceeding backward little by little to the farthest limit of the apostolic age, has found there traces of the Gospel. Where the feet of the first disciples of the apostles trod, beautiful footprints have been discovered under the surface of those distant roads, at the end of which is seen the rising light of Christ. Will you follow me there, my brother?

*   *   *

The most distant date at which, in my time, the first trace of the appearance of the Gospels was indicated by tradition was the Apologia of St. Justin Martyr in the reign of Marcus Aurelius. In this, he relates that every Sunday the faithful were accustomed to read in their assemblies the *Memoirs of the Apostles*, written by the disciples of Jesus and their companions; and in the year 138 of the Christian era, Justin spoke of the Gospels as books of apostolic origin, already distributed through the churches. From this point of departure, let us follow the progressive researches of contemporaneous scholarship and their results.

It was our own nineteenth century that deciphered and dated the famous official, canonical catalog of the four Gospels, discovered in the preceding century by Muratori. But Pope Pius I, who formulated that catalog, occupied the chair of St. Peter in the year 142 after the birth of Christ, consequently only about 110 years after our Lord's ascension. This is our first halting place. It was in our century, also, that Dr. Cureton discovered among the numerous Syrian manuscripts of the British Museum the venerable version of the Gospels known as the *Peshito*. This version is recognized by science as the most certain text of all, since it dates from the beginning of the second century, or possibly from the end of the first.

On February 4, 1844, Tischendorf discovered the celebrated manuscript known as the *Codex Sinaiticus*, which reproduces a primitive text of an antiquity more remote than any yet attained. Tischendorf's conclusion about it is as follows: "We believe ourselves justified, therefore, in placing the date, not of the 'composition' of the four Gospels, 'which was anterior to it,' but of their combination into a canonical form, at 'about the end' of the first century." And he added, in the preface of his monumental publication of 1862, "God reserved this discovery until our time, which is so painfully prolific in anti-Christian attacks. He did so, doubtless, that it might be for us a true and satisfactory proof of the written word of God, and might reaffirm to us its authentic character."* Naturally, the defenders of Christianity rejoiced over this discovery as keenly as did the gold seekers of California over the finding of that precious metal. It was also in our century that students of the Church Fathers who were investigating the works of the very earliest ecclesiastical writers of the first and second centuries, found in them, like the scattered fragments of a broken mosaic, a considerable number of Gospel texts, quotations or allusions, from which they reconstructed the original work. One chapter emerges from this process almost completely reëstablished, and it has been said: "The Laocoön issued from the earth less perfectly preserved, than did those pages of the Gospel from the writings of the first and second centuries. Almost nothing is lacking there."

But I am not giving a lesson in history. I will, therefore, merely indicate the latest conclusion reached by these explorers of the nineteenth century. The least suspected of those investigators, a Protestant writer, leader of the German Liberal party, and at present a professor in the University of Berlin, Adolph Harnack, in a recent volume on

---

*Has the following coincidence ever been noticed? The year after the appearance of Tischendorf's work, Renan, writing his *Life of Jesus*, felt himself obliged to place at the beginning of it the following declaration: "On the whole, I admit the four canonical Gospels as authentic. In my opinion all of them go back to the first century, and are pretty nearly the work of the authors to whom they are attributed."

the Gospel of St. Luke, thus fixes the origin of each of the four Gospels: St. Mark between A.D. 65 and 70; St. Matthew between 70 and 85; St. Luke between 78 and 93; and St. John between 80 and 110. All four in the first century! It was, therefore, almost immediately after our Lord's death, only 32 or 37 years after Calvary, that the early Christians began to collect souvenirs of Him Who, having scarcely left the world, "still illumined these apostolic memoirs with the light of His countenance."

I confess that this statement and avowal from the pen of a rationalist gives me a thrill of satisfaction, as does every confirmation of the truth of the history of my Savior; and I think that a brilliant feature would be lacking in the picture I have been drawing of the progress of my time, had I not given to this fact special prominence. Our century, therefore, has not failed to fulfill the mandate which every century receives, to enrich with one more ray the nimbus of the God of the Gospel, and this fact gives to my religion not only light but joy. The early origin of the Holy Book attests its veracity. And it is Thou, Lord Jesus, Whose features I discern more clearly in the light thrown on them by the science of my century, just as Thine own disciples, our predecessors in the faith, pictured Thee in Judea, in Asia Minor, and in Rome!

*   *   *

But is this an unalloyed joy? Is it equivalent to saying that this recognition of the original and true portrait of the divine Christ, drawn by actual eye-witnesses or by men who remembered Him well, consoles me wholly for the traces of that expectoration with which a hate-inspired science had covered His face? Can these discoveries, which form, after all, only the reserved domain of few scholars, make me forget the harm official calumniators and well-paid falsifiers of truth have done to the faith of the masses? Can I see, unmoved, the desertion from our ranks of those who, as they leave, destroy page after page of the Gospel they once adored and preached, and on which they had taken their most solemn oaths? "Woe unto him by whom the scandal cometh," said the Master. Are there not some among them who already have that "millstone" around their necks, with which His justice threatened them? May God spare them from sinking irredeemably into the depths!

St. Leo the Great once conceived a plan of universal evangelization—a scheme "to impregnate the entire world with the Gospel of Christ." That would assuredly be the great and only remedy for the world's present degeneracy, the oil and wine necessary for its mortal wounds. For the Gospel is able to work miracles of grace. One such miracle was its conversion of the well-known French

writer, François Coppée, who gives this touching
testimony to its power in his beautiful book, *La
Bonne Souffrance*: "During the weeks and months
passed in my bed and in my room, I practically
lived with the Gospel till, little by little, every line
of the Holy Book became imbued with life for me.
I saw the truth shine through its pages like a star,
and felt it pulsate in me like a throbbing heart.
Why should I not henceforth believe in miracles,
after the miracle which the Gospel had just
wrought in me? My soul was formerly blind to
the light of faith; it now beholds that light in all
its splendor. It was once deaf to the Word of God;
today it hears distinctly its persuasive tones. It was
once paralyzed by indifference; at present, it
mounts heavenward with the eagerness of ardent
love, while the vile demons that possessed it, have
been driven out of it forever."

What, then, is this marvelous and unique Book,
which I have never closed without finding that it
has changed my doubts into assurances, my weakness into strength, my sadness into joy? It calls
itself the Gospel of God, and truly its contents
convey to us the impression of divinity. Our duty
is not to discuss it, but to listen to it and read it.
It comes from heaven and speaks the language of
eternity. It is also the torch of history, lighting
up the past, the present, and the future. The great
events of the world still gravitate around it,

illumined by its splendor. To my soul, it is like
the first ray of the rising sun, which drew from
the colossal statue of Memnon, seated on the The-
ban plain, a musical response of welcome, reverence, and love."

CHAPTER
NINE

The Church Authority

Do you remember, my brother, the words which the great ʼhistorian, Augustin Thierry, in his last days spoke to Father Gratry? "I am," he said, "tired of being a rationalist; I wish to enter the Catholic Church, to the authority of which I submit." Weary of rationalism and of reasonings, weary of doubts, hypotheses, and endless disputations, he felt the need of some superior, superhuman, decisive authority, which can judge, decide, pronounce upon, and terminate a matter in dispute. He, consequently, recognized the duty of submission to that authority, through docile faith, for the sake of "the inexpressible and incomparable boon of peace in mind and heart." Finally, he joined the Catholic Church, which is at once the temple and the school of God. How many of earth's noblest souls do we not find there whose entry has been caused by weariness, spiritual need, and urgent duty!

But many do not know this Church, this highest of all schools. They fear it, as a prison; whereas it is a palace; they find the door through which they must enter it too low; in reality it is sublime. And the Master, Who says to them with open arms: "Come, come to Me, all you who labor and you shall find rest unto your souls!" They do not even know Him.

But *we* know Him, my brother. In the words of Andrew, "We have found the Messiah." Let us lead others to Him and to that Catholic Church, which is still He; and in submission to her authortiy, which is that of God, let us recognize the security, the dignity, and finally the happiness of man. My brother, for you and for me only one conception of the Church is true and possible. *De jure* and *de facto,* that Church is Jesus Christ Himself, continued and perpetuated on earth in her doctrine, her action, and her history. From this source are derived all her rights over us and all our duties toward her; for she is, above all else, Jesus Christ continued, in her authority.

What, then, is this mighty voice which, for nearly two thousand years, has made itself heard in every century; a voice, authoritative and imperative, which, in the name of God, the Creator and Savior, brings to the entire world not only His teachings, but also His commands concerning what man must believe and do? If need be, also, it can declare an anathema against those who refuse to listen and obey. It is the certain, faithful echo of the voice of Him, Who said to His Church, "Who-soever heareth you, heareth Me; and whosoever de-spiseth you, despiseth Me." Those who listened to Jesus said of Him, "Never man spoke like this man," for He did not discuss; He said: "Verily, verily, I say unto you." Men also hear the Church today, and her official word is likewise an affirma-tion, a definition, a promulgation. Those who listened to Jesus said of Him, "He teacheth not like the scribes and Pharisees." So, also, it can be said of the Church that her words are not like those of the philosophers who say, "This is what we *think*," but resemble the words of Jesus, Who said: "Verily, I know whereof I affirm. I speak to you of My Father, because I know Him."

It was declared of Jesus that He taught as one having authority; that is, His own authority, the sovereign authority of the divine Word. Of the Church, too, it can be said that she teaches by vir-tue of a mission and a doctrine, which she receives, not from men, but from God. It is from that celestial height that her words soar above all human speech.

Finally, Jesus was called upon to prove His mis-sion and to exhibit His vouchers for it; in reply, He pointed to His works: "If ye believe not the words that I speak to you, believe at least the works that I do." Those works were three years of mira-cles, such as the world had never known. The

Church also presents to the world her works, two thousand years of them—achievements, miracles, and benefactions—which testify to her divine origin. But those whom she has healed—her deaf who hear, her blind who see, her lame who walk, and her dead who are brought to life again—are not only individuals; they were, and are, peoples and empires!

*   *   *

This view of the Church as Jesus Christ not only imposes submission but also glorifies it. It invests that submission with dignity and holy pride. When I see all the poor mendicants pitifully begging for this bread of truth at the various doors of public opinion, while I, the son of the house, find it at my Father's table, should I not feel honored? It is this feeling which made Paul Lamache exclaim one day at a meeting of the Brothers of St. Vincent de Paul, "Look you! There are times when I am so proud of being a Catholic, that I am afraid I shall have to confess it to a priest."

It is this view of Jesus, as still teaching in His teaching Church, that explains the wholly supernatural means of her instruction. This was the cause of the superb disdain which St. Paul had for the fine language of human eloquence and the reasonings of philosophy. "The efficacy of our preaching," he said, "is not in the wisdom of man, but in

the power of God," working in men's souls. And
this Church, taught by Christ, I find as in the days
of the Gospel. Of course, I should like to see its
entire flock of sheep and lambs united in one fold
under the crosier of the one Shepherd; but I recognize it still in the "little flock" of today and in
the little band of the friends of God, who, sometimes seem well-nigh lost amid the countless hosts
of His enemies. Hence I am not astonished nor
scandalized at seeing, in our churches and about
our pulpits, not the learned and the powerful of
the world, but women, children, and the simple
and lowly of heart. Did not the Master say that
to them, and not to the proud, are revealed the
mysteries of the kingdom of heaven?

The Russian novelist, Tolstoi, wrote a book on a
question applicable to all places and all times,
namely: "What, then, must we do?" But this sup-
poses another question: "What, then, must we believe?" In that volume, the author introduces a
workman, Sutaief, who, in all the sincerity of his
soul, exclaims: "Ah! If someone would only teach
me in what respect I am in error, and at what point
I depart from the truth! I would serve that man to
my dying day, and I know not what I would give
him!" Well, this Someone, this Teacher, Whom
every uneasy and uncertain mind is instinctively
yearning for, has come. He said of Himself, "I am
the Truth." And, having come, He has not gone

away again completely. "Behold!" He says; "I am with you always till the consummation of the world." He still has His dwelling place on earth, and this dwelling place is His Church. Where the Church is, there is Christ.

Oh, let us, who are in its fold, remain in it! Enter it also, artists, philosophers, and poets, who still linger in its courtyard and claim to be able to judge it from that standpoint. You do not yet see the real Church from there. Enter it, and I assure you that you will find it infinitely more beautiful within, than without. Such was the experience of the convert Augustin Thierry, who described it under this beautiful metaphor: "Between Christianity seen from within and Christianity seen from without, there is the same difference as between the painted glass windows of a Cathedral, looked at from one side or from the other. Seen from without, they resemble dark-gray stains, separated from one another by dull leaden lines; seen from within, they are beautiful figures, glowing with light."

The interior of Christianity is Catholicism; there is truly "the abode of God with men." There, with the teaching Christ, I have found the truth; and there, with the living Christ, I possess life: the fountain of life, the word of life, the bread of life, and the channels of life in grace and the divine sacraments. It is from the divine altar that this life flows. Protestantism, however, has neither altar nor priesthood. But what, my brother, is a "religion," which has neither sacrifice nor priest? What can it still retain that is, strictly speaking, religious? The Catholic religion, on the contrary, is the most religious of all religions, for there exists a close intimacy between itself and Jesus. It lives with Him in the most familiar, the most tender, and the most uninterrupted communion. It has not lost, like Protestantism, the notion of the supernatural and its association with it. Its creed has not diminished the number of sacraments and eternal truths in order to bring them into conformity with the liberal and unimportant opinions of the children of men. In Catholicism, Jesus Christ still retains all the adorable radiance of His divinity, before which every human head must bow. The Catholic Church has not forgotten the words of absolution which she learned from Him, and which she, every day, lets fall with pity on our troubled consciences and contrite hearts. She has not replaced by a symbolic and empty representation the real presence of Him Who called Himself the "Bread that came down from heaven"; and Who descended thence to give Himself to us substantially and continually. She has not broken the spiritual relations which He opened between this world and the next; and her wonderful doctrine of the Communion of Saints is the vastest and most perfect ideal of a solidarity of all souls, coming from every land, united and bound together in an ineffably helpful community of prayers, merits, hopes, and love, the world has ever known.

In short, the Catholic Church is the one in which Jesus is most ardently and effectively loved. It is, above all, the Church in which this divine love has created and still creates such marvels of virtue, devotion, and self-renunciation, that after 2,000 years of the world's daily observation of them, our century, bad as it is, has been unable to refuse to it its admiration, if not its gratitude. There is the "sacred fire," which Jesus came "to kindle on the earth," as He, Himself, said. The Church is its hearth; and where does it burn more ardently, where does its flame emit more radiance than there?

I think, too, of the beauty of its acts of worship. Philosophers of pure reason, have you, when weary of thinking, never sometimes *felt*? Have you ever been present at some of our imposing and most touching Catholic ceremonies? The Holy Mass, when perfectly understood, naturally leads them all; but have you ever seen, also, a general Communion for men on Easter morning at Notre Dame? Or a departure of young missionaries for foreign lands, accompanied by farewells and the kissing of their hallowed feet? Or the pure and beautiful early ceremony of a First Communion? Or the taking of the veil, or a religious profession, such as moved Racine to tears? Or the last Communion of a dying Christian with the reception of the Viaticum and the last farewell of a husband or wife?

As a priest, I have beheld scenes still more intimate, which are known only to the clergy. They are those which the Savior said caused joy in heaven; those which take place in silence, at the meeting of two hearts which have long been separated and find each other at last; those of the Heavenly Father and the poor prodigal son, falling, as it were, into each other's arms! Or the unspeakably touching sight of sinners weary of sinning, weary of living, weary of human vileness, and weary of themselves, who come to the Church, as to what Huysmans called "The hospital of souls."

"There at least," he adds, "you are received, put to bed, and cared for. There the doctors do not turn their backs upon you, as in the clinic of pessimism, and merely tell you the name of the disease from which you suffer." Huysmans wrote these words in his book entitled, "*En route*," the route which led him finally to the cell of a lay monk in a Benedictine abbey.

*   *   *

It is a common remark today that the Church has outlived its time, and that its authority has become incompatible with our modern, mature, and emancipated democracy. Just the contrary is true. It is an axiom that the more a people has freed itself from political obedience, the more it must make up for this by the inward maintenance of moral obligation. Now this moral obligation, as the sages have always told us, rests upon religion. De Tocqueville makes this the theme of the finest chapter in his *Democracy in America*. He says, "I doubt whether a country can ever at the same time maintain complete religious independence and full political liberty. And I have come to believe that if a country has no religious faith, it must obey; while if it is politically free, it must have faith." The late M. Vandal recently testified to this fact before the French Academy as follows: "We shall not find the foundation of duty outside of that faith which has so long formed the support of the French soul. There is no example of a people without religion ever having remained a free people." And in regard to Catholicism in particular, it is Taine (incredible as it may seem), who, in his *Journey to Italy*, associates the destiny of the Church and that of democracies, ungovernable without her. He writes, "No end to the duration of Catholicism is discernible. The difficulty of governing democracies will always furnish it with partisans; the secret anxiety of sad and tender hearts will always bring it recruits; and the antiquity of its possession will always preserve the faithful to it."

What, then, must be the special duty of democratic governments toward religion? De Tocqueville answers this question and concludes positively,
as follows: "The legislators of democracies, and all
honest and enlightened men who live in them, must
constantly apply themselves to the task of uplifting
souls and keeping them headed for heaven. If, then,
there be found among the opinions of a democratic
people, one of those obnoxious theories which tend
to make mankind believe that everything perishes
with the body, consider those who profess such
doctrines as the natural enemies of that people. . . ." But what if those "natural enemies
of the people," themselves, are its governors?

I will add that the more indispensable religious
authority is to a society which has freed itself from
all notions of superiority of any kind, the more
necessary it is that this religious authority should
keep and show itself strong. Providence has seen to
this. Have you observed, my brother, that, while
temporal sovereignties in the hands of growing
democracies have abdicated more and more, either
voluntarily or by force, the spiritual sovereignty
of the Church, on the contrary, has asserted itself
ever more emphatically and made itself stronger by
continually increasing concentration of authority
in the Apostolic See? This was the necessary coun-
terbalance to the preponderance of the libertarian
element in the equilibrium of the moral world;

which like the physical world, is stable only by the equalization of these two forces.

Running counter to this authoritative conception of the Church, our age has recently become enamored of what is now called the "libertarian" concept of a new kind of church, which is supposed to evolve in the direction of modern liberties and to accommodate its ideas, doctrines, precepts, and institutions to the progress of our century and the present state of society. This is an internal danger to the Church. Liberalism in religious matters has gone far beyond anything that we in our youth ever knew. There are, it is true, shades of opinion in its ranks, as there are degrees in error; but where will this tendency end? We see it sinking rapidly from so-called Liberal Catholicism to a compromise of combined fallacies. Under the generic and collective name of "modernism," it is leading us to some chaos of the spiritual world like that which prevailed in the beginning, when the earth was "without form and void"—before the hand of the Almighty had divided the light from the darkness.

Shall I confess something to you, my brother? It is that I am afraid. There are moments when it seems to me that we are hastening toward what is called "Liberal Christianity," but which is really a natural and logical descent, from the private nothing else than liberal Protestantism, sliding, by judgment of yesterday to the free thought of to-day. It is essentially the same thing and has almost the same name—"Free Christianity." But this is a Christianity, each of whose disciples is free either to reject Christ as God entirely, or to recognize in Him only a kind of superman. In this Christianity, the up-to-date adept may be nothing more than an idealist, a subjectivist, or an atheist; while its doctrines resolve themselves into an impalpable something, which will become for us anything we want, except religion. Yet this, we are told, is to be the religion of the future, and even today it boasts of one advantage: our revolutionaries will not resent it, our radicals will not be offended by it, nor will our Freemasons quarrel with it. On the contrary, they all advance to meet it, as toward an accomplice or an auxiliary. Protestantism is henceforth to extend its hand to all sorts of apos-tasies, its sympathy to all iconoclasms, and its ten-der heart to all weaknesses; it says to them all: "Enter my fold"—I tremble, my brother.

The great duty of us Catholics today is to rally more closely than ever around the Papacy, the cen-ter of the Church's divine authority. During our century we have seen—and it was not one of its least important spectacles—the growth of what may be called the unification of a vast movement, progressively grouping all things Catholic about the Holy Roman See. The pontificate of Pius IX especially enjoyed the glory of this universal centralization, and the Vatican Council by its definitions, was its supreme exponent and glorious coronation. This Council was assuredly not an act of human ambition or merely a lofty, prophetic intuition of human genius. It was an inspiration from Him Whose aid is promised to His Vicar on earth. Foreseeing the formidable attack about to be made upon the Catholic Church, and the necessity of Christian unity for its defense, its supreme Pontiff, Pius IX, called for a general concentration of its forces. And so it happened that when the enemy presented himself to call for the Pope's surrender, a host of Catholic defenders massed themselves about their Chief, whose arm they had strengthened and whose crown they had confirmed.

Two years after the Council, on December 23, 1872, Pius IX declared that this union of minds and hearts was the greatest consolation of his pontificate, then drawing to its close. He said, "Our consolation is to see the episcopate of the Catholic world courageously devoted to the Chair of Peter, fighting for its cause and meeting, by means of a compact, Catholic unity, the assaults of the enemy invading us from all sides." Already this same episcopate had assured him four times that it stood solidly with him and would stand by him "loyally everywhere and forever." Nearly 500 bishops, present in Rome, signed this declaration.

This force of unity is still ours; and if, when the hour of persecution came, the episcopate was found standing firmly behind the rampart, united to its new Chief, taking its orders from him, and inseparable from him, to what was this due? On the one hand, to that original and uninterrupted movement of hierarchical concentration initiated by Pius IX; and on the other, to that Roman discipline which, during the thirty years of the reign of that Pope, had become, among the clergy, a habit and a second nature. In the presence of this "compact unity," schism became impossible, and it was Pius IX who saved us from it.

We should have no differences of opinion in regard to this Pontiff; his name is above all attack. The liberalism of today has no right to abuse him for his previous condemnation of its course, and to set up a claim for its modern liberties above the decrees of that authority and its sovereign sanctions. It should not protest at every opportunity against the Syllabus and the pontifical Encyclical which it embodies, as if they were responsible for all our controversies and present evils. Neither should irony and blame be heaped upon the Pontiffs themselves, nor on the most respectable and meritorious of publicists, whose only fault was that of having served Pius IX in his work of truth and salvation. Nor is it necessary to find wisdom exclusively among his opponents or in those who differ from him in opinion. Is it becoming to carry arrogance so far as to ask whether "Pius IX has always had a correct idea of the true interests of the Church, of its future, and its dangers in modern times," thus attempting to belittle his person and his reign? Finally, we should neither ourselves see, nor make others see, the history of our time with prejudiced and partisan eyes, which disfigure or throw into confusion and error Christians, to whom He brought the true light. That would be to play into the hands of the enemy.

It is, to say the least, rash and always dangerous, to set up the teaching of one Pope in opposition to that of another. Cardinal Lavigerie said, and this was his rule, "It is always necessary to stand firmly with and for the reigning Pontiff." Moreover, experience shows us that our Lord chooses and gives to His Church the Pope most needed for that special period, in order to make his work most useful for that epoch by the means then opportune. Lawfully, Leo XIII could not teach a different doctrine or a different Gospel from that of Pius IX. In fact, his first Encyclical takes up again the latter's teaching by declaring formally that he "reproved what Pius IX reproved and condemned what he had justly condemned." His memorable Encyclicals *Immortale Dei*, 1885, *Libertas*, 1880, and *Sapientiae Christianae*, 1890, retracted nothing from this statement, whatever anyone may say;

the form is different, but the doctrine is identical, and fundamentally it is all one.

Certainly, I can distinguish between the teaching which is *ex cathedra* and the teaching which is not, as I can distinguish between infallibility and impeccability. I find much wisdom in the following protest of the venerable Cardinal Guibert (June 4, 1885) against the opposition of Cardinal Pitra: "This evil habit of criticizing the Pope always originates in an exaggerated self-esteem and in an unrestrained self-confidence. During my long career of 44 years as bishop, including many great events and disturbances, the thought sometimes occurred to me that the Head of the Church should have adopted this or that measure or avoided some other. But God, by His grace, has always made me comprehend that I had not received the personal assistance promised to Peter and his successors; and experience has proved to me that the Popes under whom I have lived have governed the Church wisely, as all the Popes who had preceded them had done for 1,800 years."

We old men have passed our lives under pontificates destined to leave in the history of the Church a long and exalted memory. I have now no fairer recollections than those which give me back the vision of the days when I found myself in the august presence of those representatives of Christ on earth. I see again those distant hours when, on the Feast of Easter, Pius IX, standing in the loggia of St. Peter's, chanted *urbi et orbi,* that solemn benediction to which the trumpets of our army and the cannon of the Castle of St. Angelo replied. Church and country at that moment were interwoven in my heart. I see once more the public audiences of that time, when Pius IX bade us lean only on the arm of God, to have confidence in Him alone, and to defend the papal cause with nothing but the weapons of truth and charity. I see myself again at his knees in those private audiences, when the illustrious prisoner of the Vatican spoke to me of the "Chains of Peter," which I had come to venerate and which I kissed at his feet. I have seen that true saint of God shed tears at the altar during a Mass, which was that of the feast of a great Pope who had "died in exile for having loved justice and hated iniquity."

Moreover, as the founder of our Catholic University of Lille, Pius IX always showed himself particularly its father. Less than two months before his beautiful death, he wrote to it, saying how greatly he had been consoled and pleased to learn with what sentiments of filial piety we never ceased to support him, and with what ardent zeal we were resolved, not only to obey his commands, but also to gain inspiration from his spirit and his desires, taking for our device that celebrated utterance of St. Ambrose: *Romanam Ecclesiam in omnibus sequi cupio.*" These wishes, together with his final benediction, were his last utterances to us. In our university, I was officially one of the executors of his will, and it is a consolation to me to be able to affirm today that, during the twenty years I was at the helm of the university, it was by this beacon light of the Roman Church that I guided our course.

The pontificate and the august personality of Leo XIII also evoke in me the memory alternately of imposing scenes and private interviews. I took part in those pilgrimages of workingmen when thousands of them acclaimed Pope Leo XIII, borne along in his chair, and later seated on his throne. He extended to them his paternal arms saying, "Come unto me, come unto me, all ye who labor!" It was an embrace of the Church and the people. Happy was he who beheld those scenes! Happier still were those who could come very near to that paternity, which was even more imposing than his authority! Happy, therefore, was the humble son who, summoned by him, was admitted more than once to a secret audience. On those silent evenings, after having presided over the prayers of his household and having retired into his private apartments, the great Pope, otherwise quite alone, bade him sit at his feet, near his lamp, and deigned to acquaint him thoroughly with the whole truth of the papal history of our time; and finally left him overwhelmed by so much confidence, and, at the same time, filled with admiration for such wisdom.

My advanced age has made it impossible for me to lay at the feet of the Sovereign Pontiff, Pius X, a similar homage of my obedience and filial piety, but God knows what a place in my heart the person and the work of this Pontiff have always held. Above all, He knows how much and continuously I admire the serene firmness with which, contending against so many iniquities and in the midst of so much opposition, this Pope has never ceased, by word and deed, to affirm the indestructible authority of the Church and the Holy See. In this, the divine aid given him is plainly visible. It is the Spirit of strength that has armed him for the combat; and it is the Spirit of light that illumines his path, enabling him to walk erect and firm in the way of the Gospel, between the pitfalls of his enemies and the illusions of his friends.

CHAPTER
TEN

Bereavements
Consolations

The last years of life are usually years of mourning. The closing part of our journey is made along a road bordered with graves. Our parents were probably the first to leave us, and with their departure, our old age really began. One is no longer young when there is no one at the fireside to say to us, "My child." After that, graves succeed graves along our path. They are those of husbands or wives who have said, for this life, an eternal farewell; they are those of brothers or sisters torn from one another's arms; they are those of children dying under the eyes of their helpless parents. But why enumerate? It is a story of supreme sadness. Do not restrain your tears for them, you who are left—sons, daughters, widowers, widows, brothers, and sisters. Weep freely for your hallowed dead, remembering the tears of Jesus at the tomb of Lazarus. Those divine tears justify our own, as do those shed by St. Augustine over his mother, Monica, and by St. Jerome over the friend of whom he writes, "My friend Nepotienus was

166

also thine, Heliodorus; or better, not ours alone, but Christ's; he has gone from us in our old age, leaving the dagger of his death in our hearts."

Nevertheless, after all such bereavements, we have to begin life again. We do it with difficulty but we must live somehow. Who will teach us how to do so? Who will assist and sustain us? We read in the Gospel that when Mary, weeping over the death of Lazarus, heard her sister say that the Master had come, she rose up quickly and went to Him. But who will call *us* to rise from our mourning and our tears? Who will bring *us* consolation and hope? It is of consolations, human and divine, that I would speak with you today, my brother.

Before the coming of Christianity, great minds, distressed by their bereavements, sought consolation in philosophy. During our classical studies we were given the letter of Sulpicius to Cicero, for translation. The great orator was then mourning the death of his beloved daughter, Tullia. Neither glory, the consulate, nor his love for Rome could console him for her loss. Sulpicius tries to comfort him by relating an impression made upon him in his travels: "While sailing along the coast of Greece," he says, "between Egina and Megara, I saw the ruins of twenty cities, all formerly flourishing, but now lying nameless in the dust. At such a spectacle, I asked myself: 'Ought I to be astonished if the years, which have overturned so many famous structures, also reduce to ruins our own frail existences?' " This was the only balm that eloquent philosophy then found to soften irremediable suffering! Was Cicero, the scholar, consoled by it? We do not know. But Cicero, the father—the father?

St. Paul, however, who also visited Greece and Italy, treats this subject very differently. He does not, like his contemporary, Seneca, address to the afflicted the mournful consolations of the "Letters to Marcia" or of the "Consolation to Helvia." To the Thessalonians, whom he had just evangelized, he gave *the assurance of a life beyond the grave.* His words are a complete disclosure of the Christian hope in God: "I would not have you ignorant, my brethren, concerning them that are asleep, that you may not be sorrowful, as others are, who have no hope. For if, as we believe, Jesus died and rose again, even so will God bring with Him those who have fallen asleep in Jesus. . . . Wherefore, comfort ye one another with these words." His meaning is: Be comforted, therefore, ye fathers, mothers, brothers, sisters, husbands, wives, and friends! Have no anxiety concerning those who slumber in the earth; they will wake again. Do you ask yourselves what they have become? They have become what Jesus Himself has become, for they have been called to rejoin Him. Your own mortal bodies, also, shall one day rejoin their immortal souls, because *"we who are alive and are left shall be taken up together with them to meet Christ, and so shall we be ever with the Lord."* *Forever with God, forever with them!* Everything is contained in those words. They form the charter of our Christian hope. I would like to see them written at the head of every last will and testament, carved on every tombstone, deposited in every coffin.

Yet, at that time, the society of the great rejected this divine consolation. At Athens, the sages of the Areopagus ridiculed Paul, as soon as he touched upon the resurrection of the body. "Enough," they said; "we will hear thee again about this matter." At Cæsarea, also, in the judgment hall of Festus and before King Agrippa, the former stopped the Apostle at the first word that he uttered on that topic, saying, "Paul, thou art beside thyself; much learning doth make thee mad." But all these great personages were among earth's fortunate ones. Those, on the contrary, who were thenceforth to receive the word of God, as the true sons of consolation, were the afflicted, the desolate, slaves, widows, orphans, the old; in fact, all who mourned and whom Jesus called blessed, because they would be comforted.

In the early Christian centuries, therefore, on the one hand, were those who had begged for consolation from philosophers and the poets of anni-

hilation and oblivion, and had received practically
nothing. When they laid away the ashes of their
dead in stately tombs, or placed them side by side
in the funeral urns of their columbaria, they carved
above them illustrious names, pompous epitaphs,
titles, eulogies, and regrets; sometimes, also, the
symbolic figure of a heart, from which escaped a
breath or a flame, representing the last sigh. That
was all. And truly what else could they do? You
have seen, perhaps at Arles, the old Roman tombs
which border a melancholy and suggestive avenue;
and, at Rome, the many sepulchers which line the
Appian Way? Every inscription naturally evokes
the memory of someone or of something from a
vanished past; but nothing makes an appeal to the
survival of the soul or suggests the notion of a
future life. Those who sleep there were only a
part of the mighty multitude whose philosophy
had excluded them from hope.

On the other hand, only a few miles from those
Roman tombs, the Christians were excavating the
catacombs! The mourners who conveyed their
dead to those long, subterranean galleries had not
perused the Tusculan Disputations, the Essays of
Seneca, the Morals of Plutarch, or the Meditations
of Marcus Aurelius. But they had read the Gospels
and the Epistles, in which St. Paul had told their
fathers that the present life would be transformed
into a better one; and that the mortal dust which

they confided to the earth would one day rise again, transfigured into a spiritual and immortal body. They, therefore, symbolized that glorious hope of immortality by emblems of reviving life, such as the palm and the phoenix, portrayed by graphic paintings in which thought and sentiment supplied the want of art. Then, on the walls, or in the little mural cells on either side of the passageways, they wrote their farewells and their *au revoirs,* which shed upon these somber avenues a light from heaven. Have you read, in the catacomb of St. Calixtus, that triple inscription which gives us so much food for thought? I quote from memory and in substance. The first farewell is: "O my Sofronia, live in God!" It is a wish. The second is: "O my Sofronia, my sweet Sofronia, thou shalt live in God." It is a hope. Finally, the last: "O my Sofronia, my good Sofronia, thou livest in God!" This is certitude and a cry of happiness.

During all the generations which have passed since those first centuries, the double mentality of the human race has not essentially changed under the blows which decimate it. On one side there are those who have no hope *(spem non habentes)*; on the other, those whom the same Apostle speaks of as "rejoicing in hope" *(spe gaudentes).* What, then, is needed by the former in order to have hope? *The belief that their dead still live.* "Rachel mourneth for her children and refuseth to be com-

forted," saith the Scripture, "because they are not."
In order to be comforted, it was necessary for her
to be assured that they still lived and that she would
one day find them again. The Rachel of our days,
therefore, will not carry her grief to professors of
annihilation and ask them for a remedy; they
would not understand her, nor would she understand them. They do not believe, as she does, in
the God of Abraham, Isaac, and Jacob, the God of
the living and the dead. "Our end," they cynically
say, "is the same as that of the beasts." And, on
hearing that, desolate mother, your cries would
make themselves heard with still more poignant
sobs.

Even now, in this generation which is supposed
to stand upon the heights of human wisdom, philosophy can only stammer when it tries to offer
consolation. The pen of the historian Guizot, for
example, was that of an eloquent and sincere
writer. But, although he, himself, was acquainted
with sorrow and had twice been struck to the heart
with anguish, as husband and as father, what had
he learned from his philosophy, wherewith to comfort the grief of others? "Count only on yourself,"
he wrote stoically to one of earth's great sorrowing
souls, his friend, De Rémusat. "Rely on your own
heart! The wound is there; there, also, is the
strength that is needed." What strength? That of
external activity! "Do as I do," he continues, "I

belong now entirely to the outside world. I am like a man who has no longer any home and who henceforth will pass his life in the street." But what does he find there? Forgetfulness? Not at all. He exclaims, "To forget is unworthy of man. The principal cause of my irritation against men and the world is the need they have of oblivion and the ease with which they find it. The true test of a strong soul is the duration of a genuine sorrow." He adds, "Let us make a kind of *real presence* from our memory of the dead which shall replace the reality—absent but not destroyed—for I have need of the real presence of those I love."

Now, the Catholic Church satisfies this need in part by that very real Communion of souls, which it calls the Communion of Saints. But Guizot, being a Protestant, knows nothing of this experimentally, and is reduced to the following vague, doubtful, and plaintive aspiration: "God does not, I think, permit us to have a clear view of the relations which exist between those of us who linger here below and those whom we have loved and lost. But I am sure, in spite of the darkness which separates us, that they are touched by the tender fidelity of our hearts."

The light of Catholic dogma, however, has penetrated that darkness which Guizot laments; and the Church continues our relations with the world beyond the tomb by a mysterious Communion, which forms the beginning of our consolation here, and at the same time stimulates our desire and re-animates our hope of a reunion. It is because he does not know this that Guizot remains in the darkness and cold of the great unknown.

The social world offers no more consolation to our desperate griefs than does philosophy. Among the men of the world, the men of little faith, I consider the frankest to be those who decline to attempt to do this service, because of their acknowledged incompetence and powerlessness. Such is Edmond Rousse, who writes thus to one bereaved, "My old and very dear friends, I am distressed and overwhelmed by the death of your brother. But forgive me, my dear Henry, if I can say to you only 'Courage!' . . . For, after all, what would you have me say? If I wrote more, I should have to resort to commonplaces and the songs which, for so many centuries, have stilled the sorrows of humanity; such as, 'Think of your children; of your wife; of the worthy brother who is left to you; of your friends, and of me, your second brother. . . . Ah, my dear Henry, I am a poor consoler; my hand is too heavy and my heart too tender for this surgery. But I suffer and weep with you. I am with you, heart and soul; and I want to tell you so, before your dear dead shall have left you forever."

That is all that friendship found to offer in the

person of a man of intellect and heart, but who did not yet know how to hope and to pray, and who at last confined himself to this irresolute, wavering glance into the realm of mystery: "Assure your wife that my poor mother has every day prayed for you and for your dear dead to the great Being, whose omnipotence has such impenetrable secrets."

*   *   *

But enough. Let us, my brother, leave the unsatisfying philosophers of the world, the half-believers and the men who pray for a day or for an hour only, and let us seek consolation from the teachings and examples of those who are "Christians all the time." What is their conduct and counsel in hours of bereavement? Consider one of the greatest of them, André Ampère. At the bedside of his dear dying wife, he had found again the faith and piety of his better self, and it was in expiation of his evil life, that he bowed his head beneath the blow that was soon to fall upon him. He writes in his journal, "O my God, I thank Thee for having recalled me from my wanderings to Thyself, and for having forgiven me for them. I feel that it is now Thy will that henceforth my entire existence should be consecrated to Thee. . . . Merciful God, deign to reunite me in heaven to her whom Thou hast permitted me to

love on earth." From innumerable similar examples of love, faith, and trust in the agony of bereavement, I select these words of a father who has
seen pass away before him, in the flower of youth
and hope, his only child, whom her mother had left
behind her to console him.

"More than the half of my heart is already in
heaven. Heavenly Father, may what still remains
of me soon be there also! Meanwhile, wilt Thou
Thyself take in my life the place of my dear lost
ones? Accept and use in Thy service the time and
strength which I should otherwise have devoted to
them. I give myself to Thee unreservedly. The
more Thou hast taken from me, the more I wish
to give Thee, that I may complete my sacrifice
and obtain, by my entire submission, the right to
find in Thee what I have lost!"

Finally, these words from a letter of consolation
written to one who had recently lost by death both
wife and daughter:

"Dear friend, if God has taken from you thus
the strongest ties of affection which He has
implanted in the human heart, it is because He
wished to draw you to Himself. It will no longer
be possible for you to forget the fatherland
of the soul, whither you have sent in advance such
precious hostages. . . . Happy the homes which
have already half of their loved ones in heaven, to

make a bond of union between the temporarily separated, and to extend one day the hands of welcome to those who still remain!"*

---

*But these are Christian commonplaces, the reader will perhaps exclaim. Precisely; and that is why there is no need of quoting more of them. But these suffice to illustrate the enormous difference between the respective attitudes of the Christian believer and the unbeliever in the presence of death. We Christians are as much accustomed to see this consolation, submission, faith, and hope in cases of bereavement, as we are to the sunshine and the air which make life possible. Hence, we can hardly realize what our desolation at such times would be, were we "without hope and without God in the world." (Note by Translator.)

CHAPTER
ELEVEN

Shadows — Mistakes — Regrets

Shadows of regret and disillusionment frequently
fall upon the soul in the evening of the day called
life. They dim the sunset's beauty with their memories of past mistakes and present disenchantments,
give to its joy an ending of discontent and sadness,
and often leave us alone in darkness, remorse, and
fear upon the edge of the abyss to which our wanderings have led us. Maxime du Camp, in his
Crépuscule, writes sadly: "Of all men, even the
happiest and most capable, I do not believe there is
one who can truthfully say that he has reached old
age without having seen many of his projects
crumble into ruins and his hopes vanish into thin
air. For that is what life is. It dissipates the dreams
of youth; it overturns the plans of the mature; it
nullifies the efforts of the old. If this enrages us,
life does not care, but goes its way like a Jugger-
naut, indifferent to the victims whom it crushes.
Those who are killed outright are the most fortunate; the ones to be pitied are the mutilated."

Regrets and disillusionments come from com-
paring our impressions and hopes of yesterday with

our mistakes and disappointments of today. How sadly the voyage of life ends! The start was, nevertheless, joyous, with sails all spread for the great and beautiful life awaiting us, including pleasure, happiness, fortune, power, glory, immortality! That was yesterday. And today? Someone has said that disillusionment is the skeleton of our dreams.

Do you remember the painting by Gleyre, so full of melancholy and eloquent philosophy? A bark*que* is sailing down the river of life. Upon its deck is glory, indicated by the palm; and poetry, symbolized by the harp; joy, too, is there, for hear the songs which are so audible; and love, for see the little winged god who strips his crown of its leaves and drops them one by one into the somber water. The evening has come; the last crescent of the moon rises pallid in the sky. The concert ends. The auditors applaud. An elderly man is seated on the shore; beside him lies a pilgrim's staff. He has finished his journey. He looks and listens. His soul is with the singers; but from the boat not a glance is directed to him and no one gives him a smile, a word, or a sign. In a moment he will be alone; the bark*que* will have passed on. How fast it moves! Beneath this picture, the artist wrote two lines: *"The evening of life. Lost illusions."*

What has caused the loss of these illusions? What has destroyed them? Sometimes, time alone is sufficient to do this; age has withered them. The old man sighs and says, "I have nourished within me those deceptive dreams too long. I have built and rebuilt castles in Spain too many times; I have bought too many tickets in the lottery of fate, which always disappoints me; but I have allowed myself to be deluded by this mirage and have pinned my hope to those fair, golden clouds which vanish quickly in the sky for the last time. Hereafter, I will tell my poor old heart to love and hope no more. Now I have ended the headlong chase. Panting for breath, fatigued and saddened, I have stopped at last. What did you say? 'Forever?' Yes, forever."

What besides time has killed those bright illusions? Perhaps the spectacle of the world. We have been admitted into the wings of its deceptive theater, and have seen there all the stage machinery, painted canvas, masks, grease paint, and disguises. Seated in front of the stage, we have witnessed the play itself, and watched rascality and hypocrisy concealed beneath the cloak of cleverness, treason lurking under the kiss of friendship, and vice depicted on the shield of honor. When we realize that we are not merely the disgusted spectators of this drama, but also its dupes and victims, can it be expected that a revolution should not take place in our souls, overturning them from top to bottom? "I have been deceived," we exclaim bitterly and add, "but I will be so no more." Then it is that "the heart either breaks or turns to bronze."

*   *   *

Let us consider, first of all, the broken-hearted, the disillusioned, and the discouraged; those who no longer know whom to trust, who refuse to admire anything, dare not undertake anything, and are unwilling to devote themselves to anything or anybody. But let us not be too hasty in our judgment. Does not this painful disappointment come in part from our own mistakes? Have we not expected too much from the world and from life? Was not that charming something which deceived us to the point of blindness, the glittering reflection of our own ambition and pride? Moreover, if we suffer, may it not be from an excessive susceptibility on our part? Is not our skin too sensitive to the stings of evil and the proddings of the wicked? Prévost-Paradol once wrote the following poignant lament, "Against the obstacles with which we have collided, against the blows which have eventually struck us down, we can still make resistance, if we are twenty years of age. But, in advanced life, our poor souls, when beaten back by experience in their upward flight, are nothing more than spent balls which, having lost their elasticity, fall to the ground and lie there flat and motionless in the dust, moved only by some external agent, like the foot of the passer-by."

In the case of others, the complaint is milder. They perceive, too late, that their careers have been a failure. Perhaps their true life would have been that of the family. But to preserve what they considered their independence, they passed by happiness unaware. At sixty years of age, the late Edmond Rousse wrote to a friend: "Here we are, then, arriving at the end of the journey! But you, at least, are marching forward, followed by two generations which have already received from you a torch which can never be extinguished, but is forever quickened by the eternal breath of time! You fondle on your knees the daughter of your own daughter; you will sing her to sleep with the songs that lulled you to rest in your own childhood; you will recount to her the stories which your mother told you. You are actually the head of a family, the chief of a tribe; a grandfather, an ancestor! But while you propagate your race and while your line takes root in our old, mutilated country, I have ceased to ripen and must rot away like an old, withered fruit tree, without having even a twig to form a branch. Ah, my old friend, paternity doubtless has its cares; but if you only knew how sad and frightful is this prospect of dreary solitude and of the void which I shall leave behind me!"

Other causes of disillusionment are the sudden misfortunes of life, the unlooked-for transformations of destiny, such as are now so common in these days of social revolutions and unstable governments. O Chrysostom, were you alive today, how often you would repeat your eloquent *Vanitas vanitatum*," in view of so much vanished grandeur and the ruins of so many fortunes! For example, like a ship that has sprung a leak and tomorrow will be a wreck, a family, wealthy yesterday, is today ruined. The father was about to retire from a life of toil, to enjoy repose and happiness. Now it will be necessary for him to begin the struggle all over again; yet the evening of life has come, the night is at hand!

"I thought I stood where rest was now secure;
   'Twas but the doorway of a house sublime;
In answer to my prayers, God said: 'Endure,'
   And showed great stairways that I still must
     climb."

Alas, if that were all! But there are many cases far more tragic. A prodigal son, a dismembered home, a blot on a respected name, a torch extinguished in an acrid smoke, hereditary honor lost forever! Confiding in me, as a priest, two aged parents of a wayward son told me of their mental anguish one day. It was necessary for them usually to conceal their tears throughout the day, till they were free to shed them in the solitude of night. Before society they still had to smile and feign enjoyment with the unsuspecting world. They must participate in its festivities, go out, receive, while all the time repressing in their hearts the burning flood of grief, soon to consume them. Those are the hearts that break.

Less touching, but more bitter, is the haughty disillusionment of hearts that thereby turn to bronze. They are the hearts of the stoics, the pessimists and skeptics, who sneer at all that ordinary humanity respects, admires, and adores. Sarcasm is on their lips; irony is their favorite form of speech. They mock at everything. Are they not above "all that folly?" Read the hundred posthumous pages left by Challemel-Lacour, entitled, *Reflections of a Pessimist*. They contain the most cutting denunciation conceivable of his epoch and his country, which, nevertheless, that blasé cynic had himself aided in making precisely what he there condemns.

Another disillusionment is caused by hope deferred. Man was called by the ancients: "A mind full of troubles and anxious about the future." (*Animus calamitosus, futuri anxius.*) This type of man is illustrated in the *Agamemnon* of Æschylus by the slave, stationed on the roof of the palace of Argos, in order to discern from there the first sign of the returning ships from Troy. He sings to console himself for his long vigils; but the hours go by, the stars sink below the horizon, and the blazing torch on the deck of the first coming vessel does not flame out its joyful tidings. When, after many years, its tardy light appears above the waves, the slave is stooping under the weight of time. He can do nothing more than die; and the Greek chorus chants to him: "An old man is a shadow, wandering and vacillating for a day."

*   *   *

Such are the disillusioned of humanity. What, then, distinguishes the disappointed Christian from the disappointed unbeliever? For true believers there is no fundamental mistake possible, because they have not centered their affections on the things of a world, "the fashion of which passeth away." Life has not kept all its promises to them either, but *they have not made their lives dependent on those promises;* and as they were not wholly devoted to their earthly possessions, so, too, they have not shown themselves dismayed or astonished when they lost them. Need we say that the souls, which thus voluntarily detach themselves from the frail and finite, are the loftiest of all, and that this sentiment is proportionate to their greatness? Since they measure everything by its relation to God, is it surprising that they find the things of this world small and inferior to their sublime conceptions and their heavenly desires? Out of the ruins of their shattered past and their unrealized hopes, the genuine Christians of our century have reared in their hearts an altar in which they enshrine Him Who alone never can deceive. Detached from life's accidents and instability, they remain more closely united with the Eternal. Let us note a few such souls, my brother.

When I was a youth, no one in Europe enjoyed greater popularity than Silvio Pellico after the publication of his famous book, *My Prisons*. His dream had been the liberation of his country; but he had awakened from it under the "leads" of Venice and behind the bolts of the Spielberg in Austria. His popularity came later with his literary fame. But what was such glory to that great Christian then, after nine years of prison life had put into his heart the supreme love of God? He did not now regret, but blessed, the sufferings he had undergone. To a friend, he wrote, on March 12, 1840: "My youth till then had been a mixture of pride, vain philosophy, and a foolish medley of worldly notions. Ten years in a living tomb were necessary to bring me to God; but in that frightful silence of the dungeon, I heard at last the voice of truth and saw its divine beauty. I can never sufficiently thank God for that experience. His apparent anger was only love."

On January 31, 1854, the old patriot, feeling himself near death, sent for his confessor and received him, smiling. "My father," he said, "I feel that I am going. In a few hours I shall be, I trust, in Paradise. . . . When I wrote *My Prisons*, I had, for some time, the vanity to believe myself a great man, which was not true; and I have repented of that all my life." Then, with a serene countenance, and more cheerful than he had been for a long time, he asked his confessor to read aloud to him the Church's beautiful prayers for the dying. When the priest had finished reading, he looked at Silvio; he had breathed his last.

In 1876, one of the most brilliant novelists of the time, Paul Féval, lost his entire fortune, at an age when it is hardly possible to make another. Ruin for himself and family seemed certain. "But," exclaimed his devout and noble wife, "God at least is left to us." "What!" replied her despairing husband, "do you mean that God can still love and care for *me?*" Yet through that shock and its attendant sorrows, Paul Féval, the once notoriously frivolous novelist, lived and wrote thereafter only in the service of God. Instead of a pagan writer, he became a Christian one. Truly, God often captures a spiritual citadel by passing through a breach in a shattered wall.

Another cause of regret in old age is that occasioned by uncompleted work. This may be due to enforced retirement from public service in Church or State. Montalembert was never consoled for having been removed from the political arena, where, for twenty years, he had fought so valiantly for God and liberty. Lacordaire, who had, himself, voluntarily descended from the pulpit of Notre Dame, and knew where peace of mind, combined with a life of honor, could be found, wrote to Montalembert as follows:

"Cicero, writing the peaceful pages of his philosophy in retirement at Tusculum, far from Rome and the tumults of the Forum, has always seemed to me one of the noblest figures of antiquity. But we Christians have in our solitude something that Cicero did not possess—the strength of will and power for good which exist in a soul not unacquainted with the evil of the world, yet united to God. You can hardly believe how thankful I am to Him for having given me the inclination for retirement. What an unhappy man I should be today, if I did not love the tranquil glory of obscurity!"

Finally, there is the regret inspired by undertakings which have failed. Lacordaire testifies to this sorrow, also, from his own experience. He writes, "When one has spent his life in a disinterested work, and, at the end of a long career, sees evil triumph over all his efforts, the soul, even though it does not really detach itself from the good, feels, nevertheless, the bitterness of a sacrifice which has not been recompensed; and it turns toward God with a sadness which may be blameworthy, but which divine goodness will assuredly forgive."

But, my brother, I know a sorrow of old age more poignant than regret for days that have been lost and enterprises that have failed. It is the sorrow for *lost causes;* for the defeats of the *principles* of truth and virtue, of which we priests are frequently the powerless and repulsed defenders. Listen to Father Gratry, when he says: "O God, to know that one possesses the truth and upholds virtue, and yet to see them crushed and trampled under feet, and feel at the same time that the forces of the soul—although increased tenfold by indignation and a courage unto death—are, nevertheless, impotent! That is indeed the crown of sorrows, the supreme temptation to despair." Yet that is precisely the sorrow of the present day, the agony of our own old age.

But, after all, let us remember that these are God's defeats. He permits them. Let us not vex His patience by our complaints, for He is eternal. It is true, they are also our defeats. But recollect that God, Who has granted us the honor of fighting for His cause, has never promised us the happiness of victory; and the purest victory—because the most unselfish—is that which enables us to prepare for other triumphs we shall never know. As for success in this life, only one thing is important: it is that duty should be done and conscience saved from blame. All may be lost, save honor!

The shadows which the errors and regrets of life

cast on old age are like the fogs of late autumnal days, which come at times to enshroud this valley. Yesterday, while walking in the country, I saw their huge, gray masses rolling inward and enfolding, first the lowlands, then the humbler hills, and finally the entire landscape in an overwhelming veil of moisture and melancholy. Trees, leaves, and even blades of grass wept silently; and I, myself, in sympathy with nature, saw the whole vista through a mist of tears. But, thank God, these autumnal fogs soon disappear, and the country has far different symbolisms to offer us. Let us speak of them, my brother; let us dream of a retirement in our old age to its green fields, its peaceful rest, its remedial benefits, its lessons, and its duties. This, too, is a theme appropriate to the evening of life.

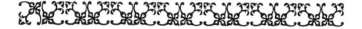

CHAPTER TWELVE

Retirement
Repose — The Fields

Who that has reached the threshold of old age does not long secretly for rest, tranquillity, and retirement? The Psalmist exclaims, "Let me be refreshed, before I go hence and be no more"; and again in that grand and beautiful evening hymn, "Fear and trembling are come upon me, and darkness has covered me. And I said: Who will give me wings like a dove, and I will fly away and be at rest. Lo, I have gone far away . . . for I have seen iniquity and contradiction in the city." (Ps. liv.) "To retire from what?" it may be asked. From business, government, service, conflicts, bustle, crowds, and noise; from the heat of the day, the furnace of passions, the fire of disputes, the fever of ambition, the canker of envy, the scandals of vice, and the allurements of the world. And the reward? Solitude and the unfettered upward flight of the soul, freed from the confines of the merely intellectual and the emotional.

But is retirement accessible to all? Between it and the majority of mankind rise many barriers, difficulties, and entangling family ties. "Where the goat is tethered, there it must browse," says the proverb. Hindrances, also, are life's chains of duty, the burden of affairs, long-standing engagements, and the inexorable interlocking of the wheels of life. Lastly, there are the heavy fetters of poverty. The evening has come, but the day's wages have not yet been paid. Poor, indigent old man! To the lengthy labor of your day of life must now be added the long hours of its evening. When can ever come to you the moment for retreat? The will of God gives the signal to each of us. The first warning is usually that of failing health. When one can no longer walk, one must sit down. Often, also, our consciences tell us that we can no longer do our work well, and that we should yield our places and tools to those who will do it better. This is the official notice that we are reduced to the ranks of the unemployed, and it is usually a stunning blow. All these and similar premonitions are so many voices from heaven, which, together or separately, make us hear in our hearts the same imperative words: *God wills it!*

One of the specialties of political revolutions is to force the retirement from office of many men who had not asked for it, because the retiring age had not been reached. The wisest are those who quietly submit to it, as to a dispensation of Providence. The letters of Guizot, after 1848, are admirable in this respect. In one of them he writes, "Here I am again in my country home; but I did not return to it without a great mingling of joy and sadness. Still, the Revolution has not disarranged either my trees, my fountain, or my books. That is something. Moreover, I am now at liberty. I have paid my debt to all that world of other days, including parties and persons. That past will suffice to fill my soul.   .   .   ."

I find the same sentiments in another great defeated politician, Royer-Collard, the distinguished philosopher and statesman of the Restoration. Having retired in 1830, he wrote to Alexis de Tocqueville from his retreat in Châteauvieux: "I find again, to my great joy, in the perfect solitude in which I now live, the same thoughts and tastes which have characterized my whole life; and they are as keen as if their end were not so near. Far from being saddened by the fact that there is no more future for me here, I accustom myself to the idea with pleasure, as to a hope. The very small part that I have taken in the affairs of my time has been sufficient for my activity, or, if you like, my ambition. It was not in my vocation to undertake more."

After these illustrious politicians, I wish to call forth from the obscurity into which time has cast him, one of the world's most beautiful literary figures at the beginning of the nineteenth century.

He is the poet Ducis, of whom it has been written that "he had even more poetry in his soul than he put into his verses, and more heroism in his life than he had exhibited in his dramas." Heroic, indeed, were the refusals which the pride of this poor man made to the favors offered him by Napoleon I. Of these he could say, "Even though the men of my time consider me a fool, my natural pride is not the less satisfied with the emphatic *no's* which I have uttered in my life. Some people would like to see me other than I am. Let them blame for this the potter who molded my clay!"

In 1806, this poet thus described his retired life to his friend De la Tour, "Dear and good friend, have no anxiety about my future. My income, modest as it is, is sufficient for the expenses of a man for whom the needs of a conventional mode of living no longer exist. Reassure yourself. I need so little and for so short a time! . . . I am surrounded here by my consolers—old trees, a beautiful view, and quiet walks. I work innocently and with pleasure, like a woodcutter, who sings in the forest, as he gathers his fagots. I take care of the health of both my body and my soul and try to make them go on well together. . . . Provided my real self lives, there is another self that I shall willingly abandon. The air of this globe is not the pure air I desire; nor is our sun the right luminary for me. I expect something better.

Meanwhile, I project my soul into the future and try to lift myself so high, by a contempt for all that is *not* all, that terrestrial grandeurs seem to me no more than a vanishing point. . . . I learned from my mother the great lesson for a man and Christian—that of suffering in silence; and I have put my trust in my mother's God. Moreover, I ask Him never to let me lose this profound faith and that He permit me to die, as she did, under the blessing of heaven." Eight years later, the empire of Napoleon I crumbled into ruin. The lonely octogenarian himself had then only two more years to live. To the end, his life was totally devoted to God, and his last, and perhaps most beautiful verses were in praise of "happy solitude, the only blessedness." It was a solitude which kept him near to God.

* * *

In considering retirement, I say to myself: It will, first of all, liberate me and enable me to become acquainted with my soul. In that outer world, I have not been myself; I have not even belonged to myself; I belonged there to everything except myself: to my official functions, to my political party, to the prevailing fads, to visits, to the news of the day, to pressing business, to the wind which whirls about and passes on. I had no time for application to anything, no orderly

sequence in anything. It was all a waste and scattering of my faculties and time. Hereafter, I shall
be able to collect myself and to introspect in that
necessary intellectual and spiritual concentration,
to which is given the religious name of holy contemplation. At last, I shall be my own master!

Retirement, I tell myself also, will renew me.
In the desert, I shall shed my old skin, as the serpent leaves his outworn scales in the bushes or in
a crevice of a rock. I shall rid myself of that old
past, so full of prejudices, habits, attachments, and
dust-covered manuscripts; in a word, I shall dis-
card the impediments of all sorts, that now encum-
ber and retard my progress by turning it from its
true end. Is not this to create within me "the new
man," of which the Apostle speaks? That is another blessing that I shall owe to solitude and
silence.

The retirement which withdraws me from places
and things, will also withdraw me from men. Not
from all, of course, but from the mass of men;
from those who would bring me only their passions
and tiresome chatter, largely made up of vanity,
envy, self-interest, and folly. These are the men
by whom old Horace rejoiced to be forgotten in
his little Tibur: *oblitusque vivis, obliviscendus et
illis.* But those who love me for myself will come
to me, since I can no longer go to them. They will
be welcome, not only if they have need of me, but

also if they merely wish to see me again, to have a *tête-à-tête* as formerly, to recall old times, to read together, and even to become once more a pair of laughing boys. Besides these good and faithful friends, and in default of others whom I can well dispense with, I have some excellent and assiduous visitors whom you do not perhaps know. That is what I replied recently to someone who was good-naturedly pitying my isolation in this little village —"No one to see; always alone?" Oh, no! And I reminded him first of the divine visit, with which the holy Liturgy provides me every day; the visit of a Friend Whom it wishes me to receive with incense, candles, and hymns. From morning till evening, I am wholly devoted to this revered Guest in varied forms. He may come to me sometimes as a poor man, sometimes as a wealthy one; sometimes as a youth, sometimes an aged man; or a holy woman, a Sister of Mercy, a priest, a soldier; all good people, the flower of humanity. They confess their past life to me, which often makes me very much ashamed of mine. They tell me of the happiness of their spiritual life, which inspires me with the desire and hope of sharing it with them. I ask them the way to it, and we converse together, pray together, and sing together. My day is consecrated to them in heartfelt happiness, and in the evening, I say farewell to them: "Adieu Peter, or Paul, John, Marie, Joseph, as the case may be:

good-by till perhaps next year at this time. Au revoir." No; they are not alone, of whom it is written: "their conversation is in heaven."

In retiring from the world, I have also retired from noise. That is not the least of my gains. Noise is peculiarly obnoxious to the old. I shall shut it out, not only from my ears, but still more from my mind and heart. I shall defend them both from the tumultuous assaults of political controversies, personal scandals, quarrels, and the hollow resonance of worldly disputes; and I shall reserve what still remains to me of strength and life for the defense of solidly established truths. The silence of my nights is, of course, sacred. Sleep has a sovereign right over those healing and restorative hours during which the Spirit of God, floating above the lawless chaos of our thoughts, prepares to restore to them order and discipline with His *Fiat lux,* which will soon bring to us the welcome dawn. But it often happens that, in the case of old people, insomnia claims many hours for itself. I do not complain of this unreservedly. Those hours are not lost, any more than the heavenly blessing of the dew is lost for plants and flowers during the fruitful mystery of night. I do not mean, of course, the torturing insomnia of sickness, and still less the exhausting sleeplessness that follows dissipation. But when an old man has good health, and sleep has already taken its needful and rightful share of rest, then the nocturnal vigil which succeeds it is a draught of strength and sweetness. Then, screened by darkness from the outer world, the mind, rejuvenated and refreshed by a preliminary slumber, finds that its regained faculties are keener and their power increased. And suddenly there often appear flashes of inspirations, ideas, and forms of expression, by which the whole work of the coming day will be illumined. "The night brings counsel," says the proverb, and what a counselor it has been to me! I have confided to it not only my mental work; it has been my habit then to reflect on what I have been, on what I am, and especially on what I ought to be. . . . In those blessed hours I have conceived and made my most serious determinations and then, with my mind at peace, have with the returning light performed the best acts of my life. Above all, it has been in those religious and mysterious silences, that I have poured out my heart and my tears to Thee, my Savior! *Benedicite, noctes, Domino!*

*   *   *

A very practical question now arises: To where shall we retire? Where shall we old men shelter our last years? Can there be a question or a doubt on this point? "In the country," reply alike the voices of the soul, of nature, of wisdom, of poetry, and of religion. Are not the words *"retirement"* and *"the country"* almost synonymous? "The country is the tranquil refuge of souls which are weary or vanquished," writes Hippolyte Rigauld. "The dew which, in the evening, falls upon the plants fatigued by the heat of the day is not more salutary than the inward peace diffused by nature over souls which contact with the world has wounded. When we have watched the weaving of contemporaneous history in a great capital for a long time, we note it has not always threads of gold or silk in its composition. How refreshing it is, then, to go where one can see the trees budding and unfolding their leaves; to draw between ourselves and the world of facts a curtain of verdure; and wrapped in peaceful shade, to wait and to forget."

Do you not find, my brother, that nature herself invites us there by her serene indifference to our little troubles? What do our agitations and our revolutions matter to her? The sun rises every morning behind my hedge, and every evening sets behind my trees, just as if the burden of four billions in taxes had not been added to the back of France. The nightingale sings his song and the lark soars skyward with joyous trills, having apparently no suspicion that Freemasonry threatens the crosses on our steeples while the minister Viviani boasts that he has extinguished the lights of heaven.

In his country residence, Guizot drank deep draughts of oblivion from the revolutions which had caused his political downfall. He writes from there: "The more one becomes a mere spectator of the affairs of this world, the more one needs to have something beautiful to look at. I live much in my study, where I read and write; but I love unspeakably, on lifting my eyes, to behold a cloudless sky and a smiling landscape. I yield to the invitation of the sun; I go out and take a leisurely walk, sitting down, now and then, on the benches which command different views of my valley. I live much with my children, much also in the past, and I go over it again in memory, waiting until I go to form a part of it. It is very beautiful here; my trees are green, my flower-beds are in bloom, my orchard is full of fruit. I take delight in little things, while thinking of great ones."

That is well; but is that all? Alas! for most people it is. They see only the exterior of nature, its face, its body, if I may call it so. But what about its soul?

The soul of nature is the atmosphere derived from it which communicates to our own feelings of pleasure, love, peace, sometimes even fear. Nature itself weeps, laughs, and trembles. One day it breathes out happiness, the next sadness and mourning; and the sentiments which it diffuses arouse reciprocal feelings. It is the blending of its

202 THE EVENING OF LIFE

soul with ours. Who has not experienced this; not, of course, in the midst of noise, but in silence; not in the crowds of cities, but in the solitude of the fields? And how much more is this felt in an old age blessed with peace and contemplation! Yes, nature does not merely live, it *speaks* and preaches. It is, by its symbolism, a sort of Gospel, expressing itself in parables. There is the morning and the evening lesson, the message of the dawn and the message of sunset. Each season has its own voice, and together or in turn what do these voices say? They tell us of the universal law of life and death, the law of evolution and decay; also the law of transformation and resurrection, which presides over our future, and already fills us with a sublime hope. Is not old age the time when the chrysalis begins to enter into its sleep? It will awake again.

Not only does nature speak, it also prays and causes man to pray. Springing spontaneously from it, is a spirit of admiration, thanksgiving, and adoration. Mere contemplation has something in it eminently religious, but how much more inspiring is a thorough comprehension of the work of the Creator, which a broad survey of it suggests to the thought of the philosopher and to the meditation of the Christian! The genius of Greece called this divine work, order (*cosmos*); the Latins styled it beauty (*mundus*); we call it the universe, or unity in variety. The latter is the name which best conveys an idea of this gigantic system, in which nothing is isolated, and where all of its creatures, united in constant relations of dependence and service, from the least to the greatest, form that marvelous reciprocity, the sight of which amazes mind and heart.

Do you see, my brother, this little seed, a thousand of which would not fill my hand? We scarcely recognize in that a child of the sun; but the father of it makes no mistake. I plant that little seed in a tiny piece of earth. The sun has seen it. "Rise," he says to some drops of water from the Mediterranean or the Atlantic! "Rise, and on the wings of the wind, go and moisten the cradle of my child!" At the same time, a ray of light and life leaves the paternal bosom, traverses millions of miles, and awakens the embryo and its nurse, the earth. And soon a brilliant plant emerges from the soil, salutes the daily rising of its father, opens to him its bosom, nourishes itself with his warmth, follows him in his diurnal course; and when he disappears below the horizon, closes its petals and waits for his return in the immobility of sadness! These, my brother, are some of the things which the gardens and fields reveal to us every year. Do the cities and their theaters ever offer spectacles of greater beauty?

*   *   *

My brother, if you take my advice, you will make your home in the country. There are places where, the *Imitation of Christ* says, "the air is purer, heaven nearer, and God closer to us." It is such a place that you will choose for your rural retreat. What does it matter if your dwelling be a modest one, provided that its site be broad and free, and the perspectives open to it extensive? Such a site, selected on a somewhat isolated hill, will put you into the possession and continual enjoyment of all that you behold: the valley, its river, and its woods; and, a little further, the vast plain with its harvests, its distant church spires, and its blue horizons—the only limits to your visual domain. Beyond them lies for you, perhaps, an unexplored region, suggesting that mysterious unknown and the Infinite, which man always looks for at the end of his perspectives.

What does it matter whether your house is made of stone or brick, provided that within it you possess a treasury of good thoughts, filled with the memories of your childhood and peopled with the forms of those whom you have most revered and loved, including noble figures of the Church and State? Such a home is a sanctuary, consecrated to the religion of memory.

And now I am going to ask you the most serious question of all: Have you come here to live for yourself alone? Look around you at the men who are your neighbors, and whom you must henceforth consider as your friends, your brothers. This is a very different interest than that of nature. That was the garden of God, this is the garden of souls. Let me say a word about this village and its villagers.

Do you remember the day when you were received here? What a welcome, what a festival it was! All the local authorities came at the head of a procession of villagers to meet you. I have never forgotten it. At present, it is not enough for you to be *in* the village; it is necessary for you to be *of* it. What do these fathers, these mothers, these children, these old people who welcomed you that day expect from you? What did you secretly, in your soul, promise to do for them, when you settled here? Was it not to be one of them? I repeat: What do they expect from you? First, respect. You will find here people who labor, and who follow the oldest of all work, that of the soil. They are men and women of brave hearts, content with little and living on next to nothing. They have worthy homes, peopled with children who are, perhaps, among the last remnants that we shall see of the old agricultural population, the ancient, granite-like foundation of our people. Therefore, they are all the more precious.

These villagers are also worthy of your gratitude; for the men whose guests we are have made the village what it is. It was they or their fathers who opened these roads, laid out these paths, dug ditches along the river, built that church and this school, constructed your own house, and planted the very trees which offer you their fruit and shade today. It was your home that they were unconsciously preparing; that pretty nest, of which you say: *In nidulo meo moriar.* To whom are you indebted for its existence?

And you owe them not only respect and gratitude, but service. If, with your social position, education, experience, and acquired skill, you have more than they, you ought to put these possessions gladly and humbly at their service. But when I say humbly, I do not ask you to adopt their rustic habits and modes of life, like certain pretenders of equality who exploit them under this disguise. Do not let your condescension mean the abdication of your personality. I should rather see them little by little brought by you to enjoy that patrimony of delicacy and refinement which your condition and education have given you. If you stoop toward them, let it be with dignity; after the manner of those fine old trees, which keep their noble forms erect, while lowering their branches to the reach of every hand that seeks their fruit. . . .

I wish also that the residence of a true Christian in the village might inaugurate there, not only an era of refinement, but one of religion, virtue, and faith. The old are specially adapted to do this work. It is true, unhappily, that all villages are not alike. Some are no longer villages. Near great industrial centers, they are now nothing more than the extensive suburbs of the neighboring city, which recruits from them its masses of male and female workers, many of whom return home every evening, bringing the infection of bad examples, evil ideas, and corrupt morals. How can we restore the kingdom of God to such hideous, godless places? That is a fearful problem. But we are now considering only a real place of retirement—the genuine country village. It seems a much less difficult task to accomplish something good in a rural community, for that should naturally be more imbued with God's presence. Yet even there, in order to perceive that Divine Presence, it is necessary to have eyes illumined by faith; and alas! the eyes of the people have of late been officially blinded: in the case of children, by the atheistic school, and in the case of the adult, by irreligious or antireligious newspapers, while indifference shuts the eyes of all who do not wish to see. And yet the sensible, practical mind of the peasant, when it has not been led astray by the agnostic teachers of today, understands very well that in his life and labor he is always dependent upon One more powerful than himself. Appeal, therefore, to the good sense of such a villager.

If, when walking together on the road, he speaks to you of the sun and rain, speak to him, in your turn, of the God who sends us both; and if, at that moment, the evening Angelus sounds from the neighboring steeple, you should both simultaneously bare your heads, make the sign of the cross, and pray. Another day, you may speak to his heart; and when, on the same road, he talks to you tenderly of the wife and children whom he loves, remind him of One Who loves him infinitely more and gave His life for him. Then, if you pass a roadside Crucifix, you both should kneel with folded hands at the feet of your Redeemer.

And the village children? Upon them the future depends. From my room I can hear them now, by turns singing, praying, and playing in the school yard. The salutation of those joyous voices, as the priest passes, is the Hosanna to one who has been sent to them by the Lord. Hence, if there is a Christian church in your village, you will be its support, and if there is a Christian community there, you will become a member of it; a head to direct it, a heart to inflame it, or a hand to sustain it.

I do not ask you whether there are any needy poor in your village, for that is a superfluous question. But among those poor, I would recommend especially the old. How great are frequently the needs of both their bodies and their souls! It is impossible to pity the abandoned aged and infirm in the country too profoundly. The old day laborer, the old servant, the old workman, the old housekeeper—all those decrepit derelicts of life, who can no longer work, who have no home, no fire, and no husband, wife, or children able or willing to assist them! How can they live today? How will they die tomorrow?

But the corresponding number of their years and yours, my brother, is precisely a bond of union between you.

"What is your age?" you will ask one of them.

"Eighty years."

"But that is also my age!"

"What was the month of your birth?"

"April."

"That, too, is the same as mine!"

"And the date of your First Communion?"

"What a coincidence! It is also that of mine."

These similarities give rise at first to sympathy and then to friendship. May not this path of souvenirs, by which you both go back to the dear old days of childhood, of youth, of the family, the school, and the Church, enable you to lead the soul of this old comrade back to God? Brothers in age and soul, brothers also in Jesus Christ, you have likewise the same Father, and can with a peculiar sympathy repeat in unison: "Our Father, Who art in heaven!"

But the theme of retirement in the country is not yet exhausted.

CHAPTER
THIRTEEN

Books
Last Pages

For my last labors I desire "the supreme sweetness of twilight hours, passed tranquilly and serenely behind a screen of verdure, not far from a library and very near a church." Yet I do not wish my retirement to be one of idleness. *Otium cum dignitate* is, of course, desirable; but *otium cum labore* is necessary. To do nothing would be to cease living.

Moreover, in releasing me from my professional duties, did God intend that I should give up all activity? On the contrary, did He not wish that I should be the freer to serve Him, when He thus restored me to myself? By this I do not mean a restoration to that which I am most capable of doing, but at least to what I am most inclined to do by choice; and consequently, to what I shall now do "with all my soul, with all my mind, with all my heart, and with all my strength"; the last strength that remains to me.

The supreme occupation of life's last years for many is study, writing, and reading books. "I must return to my dear studies," repeated an old and well-known statesman when he retired, weary of politics, or pretending to be. This was also my excuse to my colleagues when I felt that I must leave them. "Like you," I said, "I shall still work on. When the sword has become too heavy, it surely is not a complete disarmament if I replace it with the pen. There is plenty to do. Everything, for example, has not yet been said and written about our dear Church, its struggles, its achievements, its saints, its inherent, divine strength, and the guarantees and sources of its immortality." I shall, therefore, devote myself to my pen and to the last pages which still remain for me to read or write.

Books naturally form the usual companions of old men. They are a recreation for some, an occupation for others, a delight for all. To some, also, they are a balm for suffering. Goethe, "the Olympian," said that he knew of no vexation which a half hour of reading would not drive away. He was a man of marble.

But at our age, my brother, we do not read as we once did. We read different things in a different way. The books we shall read in our retreat will be few, but they will be well chosen. "Read only the best books," we were told formerly; but it is more necessary to do this now than then, on account of the appalling output of printed volumes at the present time. Moreover, we have become more difficult to please, for we bring to our choice the demands and delicacies of an experience ripened by years. We have seen and compared, our taste has grown more delicate, our aesthetic sense has become finer, our ideals higher, our judgment maturer. All that is below the standard of beauty which one dreams of and admires, all that is bad, common, and inferior has disappeared, like the precipitate, which sinks to the bottom of a jar, taking with it everything foreign and impure. That which remains floating above, purified and clarified, is a perfect, exquisite nectar, fit to be served—as the phrase used to run—"at the table of the gods." I prefer to say "at the table of the old," for they will make it the vivifying stimulant of their last years. From wine that is too new and crude the aged turn away their lips. I remember the remark of Royer-Collard to a candidate for the French Academy when confessing that he had not read his books: "It is," he said, "because at my age, sir, one no longer reads; one *re*reads."

The preference of old age is for classical antiquity. The literature we love might well be called a Muse with white hair. Greece, Rome, and France of the seventeenth century always remain in our eyes the three highest summits that intellectual literary evolution has attained. Yet, on the other hand, we are too much a part of our own time, not to retain a very tender affection for the best literature that the nineteenth century also produced, in and after the noble years of the Restoration, which was indeed a golden age.

When we turn from the works of that period to those of today, what a disappointment awaits us! It is no longer the same language; and I find in this modern dialect much less dignity, distinction, grace, and beauty. We have become a democracy. The sovereign is the people, and language has hastened to pay court to this new master by making itself popular, sometimes even vulgar. This deterioration has been particularly the work of journalism, and I cannot congratulate it on its achievement; the style of the book has followed that of the newspaper, and poetry has fallen into the wake of prose. Can the old style of literature be restored? I doubt it. But at least we will give to it our homage and regret. A book, to please me, must be good and true, but it must also be beautiful. Καλοκάγαθόν, the Greeks called such a work in one word. For me, as for them, beauty in this case signifies not so much brilliancy, as clearness, propriety, sincerity, and simplicity. The last is its supreme charm.

*   *   *

Of all forms of reading, history is the one that most attracts the old man. History is the past, and it is to the past, brother, that we belong; the distant past, toward which history takes us back, is where our regrets and our illusions like to place the virtues and happiness of the golden age. Let it, then, console us for the present by the image or the mirage of what was better.

Yet it is real history, not fiction, that I mean. Today, an attempt is being made to write another kind of history, whose only aim is to make the past lie for the benefit of a present whose errors and mistakes must be justified and pardoned at any cost. That is the kind of history which De Maistre called "a vast conspiracy against truth." You will recognize it at once due to the fact that, being obsessed by fatalism or determinism, it no longer knows anything of God. There is no longer a divine intervention in events, no Providence, no freedom of the will, no moral law, no guiding idea, no sequence of causes; nothing but facts, rough, isolated, necessary, fatal facts, rising from the inexorable, mechanical movement of things. Previously we had not suspected that, under the pretext of remaining objective, the historian had only to register material facts in a disinterested tone and with a soul indifferent to his story; as if, in the events of this continuous narrative, the interests of human souls, of Christ, and of God were not implied.

What, then, is history today? A collection of

documents, a lawyer's brief, instead of being the book of humanity. And the historian? A mere clerk of the court, instead of being the first of judges; an impassible examiner and registrar of events in which the actors are only marionettes, moved by strings hidden in the impenetrable darkness of the cellar. Fundamentally, he is often a skeptic, too, for whom revolutions and the fall of empires are merely the natural game of fatality, and of which one can say with Byron: "On the highway of the centuries, they are relay stations where the destinies change horses."

Poetry, memoirs, and letters are also always liked by the old. Has not someone said that in three quarters of the race a poet can be found? It is true, he usually dies young, stifled by the humdrum occupations of life; but he sometimes comes to life again later, and brings into old age the freshness of his youthful sentiments, like morning breezes which return at evening to cool and caress our heated brows.

There is first the poetry of things; of nature, especially as seen in the autumn or at twilight, the splendor of sunsets, the farewell of day's waning light, and the return of laborers from the fields, when "the curfew tolls the knell of parting day." The old man will take delight in this, provided it is a truthful representation of the soul in its most intimate feelings, passions and griefs, in its loftiest ideals and hopes. The true poets are those who can make the human and the superhuman fiber in us vibrate; and this is more perceptible at eighty than at twenty-five. But rare, very rare, it must be said, are the inspired masters who can stir us in this manner. Do you like modern poetry, brother? I have the sad conviction that, for the last fifty years at least, France has produced no real poets. Is not the materialism of our philosophy, which is the father of literary realism, responsible for this? It is rather among some of our prose writers that great poets are now to be found. Let us read their prose, my brother.

But beware! Will all our prose writers, novelists, or poets prove a company worthy of the dignity of our old years? Contemporary literature is a deep, overgrown, luxuriant forest. It has its majestic trees, but it has also its quagmires and dens of wild beasts. There, too, are many flowery plants whose perfume is a poison. It is not in such shade that our old age should seek repose, my brother. That shade itself is deadly. No age is immune from it.

But if you desire a genuine form of poetry which will elevate you, and a serious literature which will nourish and ennoble, while it charms, there is a new one, scarcely more than born; it is the *poetry of science*. I do not mean by this the technique of the sciences. I mean the revelation they have brought to us of the universe as it is; of its immensity, its energies, its harmonies, its affinities, and the marvels of order, life, and beauty discoverable in the infinitely great and the infinitely little; all presented as luminous and simple truth, which is the only appropriate framework for such grandeur. This language, at the same time scientific, philosophical, and poetical, is already in the making. It will be the language of the future. Let us anticipate it, my brother.

I have spoken of books, but have not yet mentioned that book of books, the Bible. That would be too vast a subject, should I treat it thoroughly. I will say only that it combines at once history, philosophy, poetry, eloquence, and the drama; yet with what sublimity of thought and word! It is especially the book for old men. What figures of old men you will meet there, my brother! The patriarchs, Noah, Job, Abraham, Jacob, Joseph! The judges and the prophets, Samuel, Elijah, Isaiah, Daniel, and many more! Would you not like to see those great and venerable friends of your childhood again and to hear them tell you how one must grow old, how one must meet death? This book of the Old Testament recalls to me the days when my good grandmother read to us a chapter of the Bible in the evening. Then, when the reading was ended, she would close the volume, leaving her spectacles in it as a bookmark, while we, her grandchildren, astonished and affected by those heroes and those narratives, would look at her who seemed to us so old and ask her: "Did you ever see them, grandma?"

*   *   *

All old men read, and some write, in their last years. Some of the latter write for the public, others for the intimate circle of friends. For some this is a duty; for others a satisfaction, a consolation, a reparation, perhaps a necessity. For all it is a pleasant exercise of their faculties and a renewal of their youth. "I asked Michelet one day," recounts Maxime du Camp, "what he did to remain so young under his white hair." He pointed to his inkstand, and in his beautiful, sonorous voice replied: "That is my fountain of youth!"

Writing is, in the first place, a duty of *work;* a duty to which years can raise no objection; a duty which has no other limits than those of power. There are some who abdicate this power only at the last hour. Sophocles composed his *Oedipus at Colonna* when he was eighty years of age; yet it is the most admirable, the most plastic, and the most nobly religious of his tragedies; one which, after more than two thousand years, "has not a wrinkle."

At the age of ninety, Michelangelo presented his model of the Basilica of St. Peter's at Rome to the

Pope. At that time, also, he wrote his last sonnets, some of which might be taken for a free translation of the finest psalms of David. Did not the Lord say: "Work, while it is yet day; for the night cometh, when no man can work."

Writing is also a duty, as well as pleasure, when it means the *completion of work* long since begun. I think of Albert Sorel who, at the end of his masterpiece *Europe and the Revolution,* inscribed the two dates: "1874-1904." They indicated the beginning and the end. Then he wrote to his son, "This is a solemn date in my life. I have just written the last line of my work. *Nunc dimittis servum tuum, Domine!* Now I can depart, and you can send the manuscript to the printer. Such as it is, it embodies thirty years of my life. What a labor it has been! But what a support in times of temptation, of despair over irreparable losses, and of doubt of oneself—that abyss of the soul, which makes one giddy to contemplate, yet into which one is always tempted to peer. Were it only for that reason, it will have been, not only the companion of my life, but the viaticum of my journey. Will it be anything more for others? Perhaps it will mean for them a little more light cast here and there by a few brilliant pages, a little intelligence, a little knowledge of human nature. That is all that the most ambitious man can hope for, even when he has passed his life in studying that nature and impregnating himself with it." Albert Sorel died three years later at the age of sixty-five, and he died a Christian.

Writing is also a duty of remembrance. It is the duty of those who have done or seen things worthy of remaining in the memory of man to record them. Guizot did this by writing his *Memoirs*, to serve as the history of his time; and also his *Meditations* on the Christian religion, in opposition to the rising flood of antagonism to Christianity. He wrote of these: "I continue my *Memoirs* and my *Meditations* at the same time, interweaving thus my souvenirs of earth and the perspectives of heaven. May old age, which follows closely at my heels, leave me strength enough to finish them! That is all I ask of God. For the rest, I am ready to depart."

This letter was written in 1865. He labored nine years longer. Then he wrote: "The days pass so rapidly! I shall come to their end, without having done the fourth part of what I still would like to do. Life is a vase too small for all there is to put into it; for a long time it overflows, then finally breaks. I would like to put into it still many things, and I shall die with my hands full of material. As God wills! I desire that His summons may find me still busy in preparing what I would have done, had He left me longer here."

Writing is also a duty when it has as its object:

to edify one's brethren and to glorify God. That is what Lacordaire did, when, from a bed of suffering, he still found moral strength enough to dictate the first eleven chapters of the history concerning the reëstablishment of the Dominican Order in France. Of these pages, Montalembert says: "Originating in a veritable miracle of moral force and dictated with an unequaled rapidity and certainty during the last struggles of his mortal life, these 150 pages, each of which was preceded or followed by agonizing crises, will remain the most beautiful of his writings. And it would be difficult to cite another example either of such mastery of an intrepid soul over a broken body, or of the splendid power which a virile genius can retain to the last, illumined by that terrible torch which is sometimes lighted for the dying!"

Writing is also a duty of reparation for those who, having amended their lives, feel the need of amending also their former literary works. Paul Féval, Huysmans, and Coppée have recently given magnificent examples in this respect. "What is work? What are books? What is intelligence?" wrote the first of this trio in his *Steps Toward Conversion.* "All these are nothing if they have been misused, as is evident if one retraces and reviews one's past. It is a question now, not so much of believing, as of *doing* something, and of making reparation."

And Augustin Thierry, the historian, although blind and paralyzed, made every effort, under this fearful burden, not only to attain a knowledge of perfect truth, but also to make a public testimony to the fact of his conversion by revising his writings. To Father Gratry he said: "I wish to correct every word that I have ever written against the truth, even though I did so in good faith. I implore God every day and every night to give me the strength and time necessary to finish this work; for it seems to me that, in so doing, I am working for God."

Lastly, writing in old age may be a duty of friendship. The dear and venerated Amédée de Margerie, eight days before his death, was still correcting the last proofs of his biography of the Count de Lambel, his friend for fifty years. On the evening before his death, after his last Communion, he said of this biography, smilingly: "This is a work of which one can say, that it was written by a dying man about a dead one."

Happy is he, whether author or artist, whose pen or brush has been employed finally, before falling from his hand, upon the figure of some sage or saint whom he will meet again, glorified in heaven! Is not the writing of such lives the best way of sanctifying and of ending one's own?

CHAPTER
FOURTEEN

Old Age and the Better Life

"The better life." Of what use would it be for us
to grow old if we did not also grow better? Everything in old age makes it easy to become better
and invites us to do so. First of all, old age has
more solitude; the solitude of which it is written
that "God brings man to it, in order to speak to
his heart." The solitary life of the country, if it
can be obtained, is, no doubt, favorable to spiritual
growth; but more advantageous still is the inward
solitude of a tranquil mind and a heart less bur-
dened by the ties of business, worldly affiliations,
and affections which distract the attention from
God and from oneself.

Formerly, I was one of those of whom it could
be said that "after a long career, they died without
having found time to get acquainted even with
themselves." Today, however, in my old age, the
barriers are down; and even the dust of the arena
has settled. I see both God and myself more clearly;
I begin to feel between my soul and Him those
silent intimacies, of which a great philosopher could
say: "I am never less alone than when alone."

The better life is a life of greater *goodness,* greater *charity,* and greater *purity,* all gained by a more intimate union with God. Let us, my brother, incite each other to such a life; not so much, however, by fine phrases as by useful examples.

The special characteristic of old age should be goodness. Does not one usually speak of a septuagenarian as the "good old man," as if the two adjectives were really only one? We French do the same thing, when we almost invariably speak of God as *Le bon Dieu.* This identification of age and goodness honors us old men greatly. If deserved, it is our chief distinction. Fénélon, in translating Sophocles, has said: "My son, it is only a great heart that knows how much nobility there is in being good!"

But the paramount and divine reason for leading a good life in old age is that which our Lord presents to us in the Gospel: "Be ye, therefore, perfect, even as your Father in heaven is perfect." Ah, my God, I well know that Thy infinite greatness is incommunicable; but there is at least one side by which I can draw near to Thee and wish to do so; it is that of goodness. This will be the star to guide my course; the honor of constantly pressing toward it and of approaching it ever so little, will console me for my despair at never actually reaching it.

Why, then, should old age be called "gloomy and

morose"? It certainly is not. Beyond a doubt it carries with it a certain majesty, and the goodness of the old man will not be without dignity. In years, at least, he is a king, of whom it has been said: "The joy of his countenance makes the life about him radiant, and his benign goodness is like the gentle rain upon the fields at evening." Amiability, kindliness, courtesy, and affability are the traits revealed by his features, which are not so much commanding as they are paternal; attractive rather than awe-inspiring.

The old man has not only a good face, but also a good mind. He thinks well of his fellow men and wishes them well. He is the personification of good will. He tries to see everything in the most favorable light. His optimism is proverbial. It will be said that he is often self-deceived and that he exposes himself to the chance of being duped. Granted; but in any event, he has made his decision which, after all, is that of all good hearts and happy dispositions. How much happier he is than the depressed and gloomy man who everywhere sees only the dark side, whose utterances are always pessimistic! Such a man, being sad himself, saddens everyone about him; and, what is worse, he paralyzes in others all enthusiasm, generosity, and joy in achievement—in a word, everything good. For in order to do good, it is necessary to believe in goodness; and in order to esteem, love, and serve good people, one must believe that good people exist.

Old age must also have charity toward all. It is the age of indulgence and clemency. From the lofty height on which he has found peace, the good old man imparts serenity to all below him, following the example of the Father in heaven, "Who maketh His sun to rise on the evil and on the good, and sendeth rain on the just and on the unjust." "If you have the new life," said St. Paul to the Christians of Corinth, "purge out the old leaven, that you may be a new paste. . . . Let us feast, not with the old leaven, nor with the leaven of malice and wickedness, but with the unleavened bread of sincerity and truth." Thus man progresses toward old age from darkness to light, from anger to gentleness, from sadness to joy, everywhere discovering the beautiful, enjoying the good, silencing blasphemy, and rendering homage to all that is worthy of admiration.

At eventide there is an hour of infinite stillness, when the horizon, though still clear, glows with the colors of the setting sun, while opposite, in the pallid east, the silent moon ascends the heavens from a world in shadow. It is suggestive of the evening of life. Serenity, calmness, the peace of life's sunset, tranquillity of thoughts, feelings, memories, and judgments—these form the atmosphere in which the old man lives. He is content with it. He has known the storms of life; but to-day all those tempests are beneath his feet; and even if he still is troubled by misfortunes and mistakes which he was unable to avert, he no longer allows himself to be distressed by them. His is the state of mind which Guizot describes at the beginning of his *Memoirs*: "I have often contended fiercely in my life," writes the old man; "but age and retirement have now poured over the past the balm of peace. It is now from a perfectly serene sky that I direct my thoughts back toward that far-away horizon, lowering with storms. If I examine my soul carefully, I discover there no sentiment of hate to poison my memories, and where there is no bitterness, there can be much frankness. It is a narrow mind that in its memoirs alters or discredits the truth, and that is why, wishing to write of my epoch and my life, I prefer to do so, while living, from the brink of my grave, rather than, posthumously from its depths. I find it is more dignified for me to do this. I use greater care and delicacy in my choice of words and in the expression of my judgments."

Ours is no longer a suitable age, my brother, for ardent, passionate disputes, still less for violent railing. When the attacks of tongue or pen are furious, I think that truth and justice are as little served as wisdom and virtue; and one may always read with profit the chapter in the *Imitation of*

Christ entitled "Concerning a good peaceable man."

In fact, an old man will, as far as possible, avoid even heated discussions. "Disputation is contrary to my nature," writes Doudan; "I have learned to say quietly what I believe and to speak with moderation of what I do not believe. I also try to understand perfectly the mental attitude of others, in order thus more easily to bring them to an understanding of my own. If I finally yield to the force of numbers, I do so by remaining silent, without, however, on that account admiring more than is necessary the opinions of the majority. I love peace, and accordingly conceal myself under a sheepskin and hurry away the moment I see or hear any sign of a wolf."

*   *   *

All well and good to a certain extent; but if the wolf is one of those spoken of in the Gospel, which enter the sheepfold to ravage, kill, and destroy, what then? Well, if the old man is a guardian and defender of sacred truths and imperiled souls, he will not purchase peace by flight, as a deserter. He owes a better example to those whose eyes are fixed upon him, that they may learn from him to what persons or things they shall say "Yes," and to what persons and things they shall say "No." He, above all, since he is rendered more independent by his advanced age, will utter his "Yes" or "No" boldly, with energy, and will remain to the last unyielding in regard to truth, uncompromising in respect to duty. Then, having reached the limit of his life and labors, he will be able to give that testimony which Cardinal Manning at the age of eighty-two could render, when he said: "I am not conscious of ever having let fall to the ground a stone of the Church or a particle of truth."

Yet this grand old man, so firm in his convictions, was by no means intolerant, but rather nobly generous and just toward those of his compatriots who held different opinions, and he covered with the broad wings of the Church many who were unconsciously her children. Nothing is more instructive in this respect than his manuscript notes, written in 1890, regarding the religious good faith of a very large number of English Protestants. He wrote, "I have known intimately many souls outside of the Church who lived lives of faith, hope, charity, in sanctifying grace; lives also of humility and absolute purity of body and heart. They meditated continually on the Holy Scriptures and were devoted, with complete self-renunciation, to personal work among the poor. In a word, they were revealing lives as saintly as any I have ever known."

*   *   *

I have said that the better life of old age must be characterized by goodness and charity, but it must also be a life of the most delicate purity—purity of body, purity of conscience, and purity of heart. "Who shall deliver me from the body of this death?" cried St. Paul, under the buffets which Satan gave him through what he called the thorn in his flesh. But he reduced that body to servitude until he had not only deadened, but extirpated that "messenger of Satan." It was a conflict to the death, but it is from this death to sin that the life of the spirit is born.

Regarding this new life to which the Gospel invited our old age, let us listen to the evening interview which a great master in Israel had sought with Jesus. "Verily, verily, I say unto thee, unless a man be born again of water and the Holy Ghost, he cannot enter into the kingdom of God," said the divine Master. To be born again of water is to purify oneself, to wash away the impurities of one's life, one's thoughts, and one's heart in a baptism of tears. And to be born again of the Spirit is to take on a new and better spirit, and to create for oneself a new soul, freed from error and cleansed from sin.

But does this concern us who are so old, my brother? Is it really the old man who can and must thus be born again, in order to make himself a new man? This was exactly the objection of

Nicodemus to Jesus: "How can a man be born again *when he is old?*" To which Jesus replied emphatically that it was true, "Verily, verily," and added, "Wonder not that I said to thee: You must be born again."

Since, therefore, this applies to us, let us hasten, while there is still time, to complete within us the final victory of the spiritual over the carnal man. In conformity with that strong, striking maxim of St. Francis de Sales: "We must begin to live here on earth, as if we already had our body in the tomb and our soul in heaven!"

*   *   *

But I have not yet said enough. I have spoken of the *better* life of old age, but I desire also that it should be a *perfect* life, the supernatural source of which is none other than God Himself. Let us strive to reach that height, my brother; the height not merely of the better life, but of the divine life. Let us say not only the "good old man," but also the "saintly old man"; not simply the man of goodness but the man of God.

What, then, is the man of God? He is primarily a man who lives in the presence of God; for a conscience constantly confronted by the thought: "God is here; He sees me," is a spiritual force, invincible against any evil power. How can a soul whose "conversation is in heaven," descend to the commission of a vile act? The old man should be exalted by a life and labor of many years to a lofty purity and dignity, forever guarded by a jealous conscience which fears the very shadow of evil and is indignant at a stain.

In short, my ideal of old age is a state of supreme perfection, a mirror of justice, a flower of delicacy, a vessel of honor. In the course of my life, I have met old men who were enveloped in a sort of divine transparency, which seemed to put a nimbus on their brows. As children, we used to kneel before such men and ask their blessing.

The man of God converses with God, for his is a life of prayer. For many years now, whenever I review the past, the words "old age" and "prayer" have come to be united in my thought, associated with the same venerated and sacred personalities. How does the Gospel represent the three kings of the Orient who hastened to the feet of the Divine Child? As *old men*. And what did they do there? They knelt in prayer and adored Him. And the two worshippers of the Infant Jesus, when He was presented by His parents in the Temple? They, too, were aged: one, the venerable Simeon who then sang his *"Nunc dimittis,"* and the other, Anna, the prophetess who found consolation for her extreme age of eighty-four years, by praying in the Temple day and night.

O God, revive in me in my old age the voice of

prayer! With me, the harp has too long been silent; its chords, alas, have become either broken or unstrung. My days have been without life, my evenings without joy. And yet, who shall pray in the Church, if not the priest? Who shall pray in the village, if not he, from whom the children crave a blessing? And who will pray in the family, if not the father?

Yet, while we speak to God, let us also listen; for He speaks to us. It is still the Divine Word, the Son of God, Who makes Himself heard by every soul in the mystery of prayer. Happy are those who can thus hear Him! Happy are those who daily open their hearts to that personal, secret voice, which responds to every sigh of the suppliant and satisfies every need. If we do not hear His words, it is because we ourselves are not sufficiently silent. The Lord is not in the wind, the tempest, or the lightning, but in the "still, small voice," such as the sound of the Angelus brings to us from the distant spire.

But how, dear Lord, can I find this interior silence, which Thou askest of me, when everything disturbs me by its uproar? My nerves are almost shattered by the noises of my house, my factory, my office, my profession, and my children. That is all true; and yet there have been many servants of God who, in order to obey Him and listen to His voice, have finally acquired that silence of soul, even amid the roar of the ocean, the howling of the tempest, and the thunder of cannon.

The secret of this, as of all true piety, consists in fulfilling the will of God, that is to say, in doing one's duty; and the will of God is easily known, for duty is marked with the sign of His cross which means sacrifice.

Between the Christian and Jesus there has been concluded a sublime contract, characterized by intimate communion and religious tenderness. It resembles the contract in the making of which Jesus, still bearing on His glorified body the scars of Calvary, asked of Peter: "Lovest thou Me? Lovest thou Me? Wilt thou realize in thyself the kingdom of God? Dost thou desire it at any price, in poverty, conflict, and suffering? Will thy love for Me be stronger than the lust of the flesh, the lure of glory, and the pang of death? Dost thou truly love Me?"

For two thousand years an affirmative answer to this question has never been wanting. It is the response of numberless true and faithful disciples, who know, not only how to pray and meditate, but also how, through love, to fight, to suffer, and to die for Christ. It is these hosts of repentant sinners, apostles, virgins, voluntary martyrs, and the humble and oppressed of every age, who, more than all, are able to reply with Peter: "Lord, Thou knowest all things; Thou knowest that I love Thee."

CHAPTER
FIFTEEN

Expiation — Reparation

It is, however, only too true that, beside and beneath such beautiful and saintly specimens of old age, there are many which are unsaintly, tarnished, and godless. If, in some of these, their impiety arises from errors of the mind, in most of them it has its origin in depravity of heart or debauchery of morals. The former suffer from spiritual blindness; the latter from spiritual leprosy. Age brings no remedy for the evil of impurity. Each passing year forges a new link in the captive's ever-lengthening chain, which he is always more powerless to break. It is really a chain, my brother, and the old man who drags it is not only a slave; he is a galley slave, condemned for life, unless he one day becomes the object of God's sovereign grace and mercy.

Under the title of Expiation, I would like to speak with you, my brother, first of this servitude and then of the redemption from it. Some of those captives have accepted the penance of expiation and have performed it; others have rejected it; and of the errors, falsehoods, and misfortunes of these last I must also speak.

It is the duty of our old age to render homage to the justice of God in the punishments which He inflicts, as well as to His mercy which forgives. Nevertheless, it is not without genuine sorrow that I speak of God's judgments upon certain of those men endowed with brilliant talents which I sometimes extravagantly admired, without, however, being led astray by them. In these cases, I shall let other witnesses and judges speak who, as laymen, will not be suspected of bringing against them the retaliation of the Church.

How sad and humiliating, for example, was the old age of Ernest Renan! At that venerable period of his life, what remained in him of the young Christian who, in 1845, sat at the feet of Frédéric Ozanam, of whom he said: "I never go out from one of his lectures without being stronger, more uplifted, more courageous, more resolved to accomplish something great, more eager for the conquest of the future!" What remained, also, of the young philosopher who, at that same period, proclaimed that Christianity was as indestructible as human nature itself, to which the religion of Jesus adapts itself so perfectly? "In my opinion," he said, "it is one of the greatest proofs of the divine origin of Christianity that, in order to demonstrate its truth, it is necessary to analyze what is most profound in the nature of man. That is, its crucial point. If, on the contrary, Christianity were false, analysis would destroy it." And of the serious scholar who wrote the *History of the Semitic Languages,* and of the philosopher who dreamed of a future for science that would make it dominate humanity completely—what was left at the age of sixty-nine, the time of wise conclusions and broad generalizations?

At the end of his life, there remained of the first Renan nothing more than an old, skeptical, blasé Epicurean, who turned to the mocking Mephistopheles as his master. Everything—truth as well as morality—had been dropped by him on the way. He was empty. What is God? "An old and rather heavy word," which has no longer any meaning. And the world? A game of puppets. "Let us enjoy the world as it is made, my poor friend," he makes his *Priest of Nemé* say." "It is not a serious work, it is a farce, the product of a jesting deity." And his century? "Not the greatest, but the most amusing, of centuries. On leaving life, I shall only have to thank the cause of all good for the charming promenade that I have been allowed to make through reality." And life itself? "A joyous exercise in skating on the ice of a single night." His native land? "A prejudice." Humanity? "The soil which covers the globe, the layer necessary for a great man to be born in." And truth? "Anything you like. To abandon oneself according to the mood of the moment to confidence, skepticism, optimism, or irony, is the way to be sure that at least at some time or other one has been in the right."

No more convictions, no more principles, and no more moral sense or moral life. He puts to himself the question: "What can save us?" and replies, "It doesn't really matter. For one it is virtue; for another, love of truth; for another the love of art; for others, ambition, travel, luxury, women, wealth; for the lowest, alcohol and morphine. The virtuous find their recompense in virtue itself; those who are not virtuous have their pleasure."

This is all that this cynic of art can preach to the youth of Paris, when he one day says to them, "Amuse yourselves! Having done very little of that sort of thing when I was young, I like to see others having a good time. Those who take life thus are perhaps the true philosophers. My dear children, it will only make your heads ache to change one error for another. You are twenty years old; amuse yourselves!"

He was, as I have said, empty. Without faith or conscience, compass or anchor, he was no longer a ship; he was only a piece of floating wreckage. And those who saw him drifting over the deep, the plaything of the winds and waves, asked "Who is he?" And the answer came: "He is an apostate; he has thrown God overboard; and God having left him, all is lost." That was the first punishment of Renan in his old age.

The second was the contempt and disgust which
he inspired in those who had this loathsome spectacle before their eyes. Paul Bourget says, "This
man disappoints me. I expected from him an impressive ending, a glorious sunset. He gives me a
sunset behind wine casks." Gabriel de Séailles
writes of him: "The impossibility of making foolish jokes, which this old man encountered, more
and more permitted him, he thought, to say anything that came into his head." And Brunetière
writes: "This rôle of a universal cynic and mocker
was not only accepted by Renan, but was eagerly
sought by him; he did not perceive that people
now laughed no longer at what he said, but at the
man who said it. And because youth is cruel, it
laughed at what was really far more terrible than
laughable—the spectacle of an old man who, under
the waxen mask of Rabelais, polluted all that he
had once adored!" His last days were those of a
poor, helpless paralytic; and he died in a state of
physical deterioration, suggestive of another still
sadder.

In Renan's most intimate circle of friends a
punishment was soon to fall upon another haughty
head, that of Challemel-Lacour, his successor in
the French Academy. He carried that head very
high. First, supplementary professor of philosophy
in the normal school, a brilliant instructor; then
prefect of the Rhône, deputy, senator, minister of

Foreign Affairs, ambassador to London, member of the Academy, vice-president of the Senate, etc., this spoiled child of fortune and of the republic, rose by all these steps to such a paroxysm of pride, that, not content with defying God, he finally came to substitute himself for Him.

This astounding revelation appeared, after his death, in some posthumous pages published under the title: *Reflections of a Pessimist.* The work is one prolonged blasphemy. In it God appears as nothing more than one of the world's meanest, puerile things, which he enumerates contemptuously as "Women and love, toadying to contemporaries, promises of paradisaical brotherhood, God, and a lot of high-sounding promises for the future dependent on that great name, like the gilded fringes of a cloud; prejudices, metaphors, words which softly lull to rest sleepy minds, but which make those who are awake smile bitterly . . . ," etc. He then adds, drawing himself up to his full height: "All of us who come from the school of Voltaire, Hegel, Lavoisier, and Laplace, do not want any more of that old poetry, which vanishes like a mist before the intelligence of the nineteenth century. . . . Little poets thank God for having made the earth so good, and they are weak; great poets have all sung of the nothingness of life, and they are strong."

God having been suppressed, there remains man;

but this man has made himself God! Free thought
has deified him. "More than six thousand years
ago," writes Challemel-Lacour, "thought, under
the form of the serpent, spoke to the first man
thus: 'Give me your life and I will give you a
world, an empire which the centuries will only
enlarge. . . . Do not be discouraged. By my
aid you shall become formidable to the most powerful. Wherever you shall see injustice crowned
with honor, I will create for you societies of sages
and associations of the learned, which shall be indestructible kingdoms of light and liberty. I will
crown you with glory, I will seat you upon a
throne, I will make you a God?' "

But what kind of God? We shall see. To these
unpublished papers of the old man, there was
joined another, a sort of imitation of Rabelais,
that master-sensualist, whom Challemel-Lacour is
pleased to bring back from hell to impart true
wisdom to our century in the language of his own.
And what wisdom, my brother! It recommends
"a kind of life, made gay by pleasures, by copious
draughts of wine, by laughing, singing, and love-
making; fearing nothing, hoping for nothing, and
with no worry about a Providence who amuses
himself up there by playing at skittles with the
world, and thinking nothing about us; all this, in
order to come where I now am, in a place where
it is awfully hot, but where one sees very clearly,

etc." And it is a president of the Senate who writes such stuff!

Yet, like the proud demigods of whom I recently spoke, this jovial old man is also sad. These "Reflections" are well named those of a pessimist. Challemel-Lacour is dissatisfied with everything—except himself. He places these thoughts under the patronage of the gloomy Leopardi, poet of despair; and under that of Heinrich Heine, that facetious monster, ruined body and soul by his long debaucheries. From the latter's work he would suppress only these words at the end: "Yes, I have come back to God like the prodigal son, after having tended swine with the Hegelians." Soon after having written those pages of blasphemy, Challemel-Lacour lost that reason which he had deified and died in dementia.

This, my brother, is not the only example which our epoch has given us of madness inflicted by heaven on the blasphemy and savage impiety which has defied it. A notable instance is that of the Saxon, Nietzsche, the incarnation of brutal, ferocious, and even cruel egoism: "Be not only strong," he writes; "be hard!" I will merely mention his last work, *Antichrist*, which he presented, he expressly said, "as an unreserved attack upon the Crucified One," his personal enemy. But I wish at least to make known to those who are not aware of it, the fact that, four months after this criminal act of defiance (January, 1880), dementia fell on the head of this madman also, whose evil conduct founded a school on both sides of the Rhine.

Woe, likewise, to the old age of him who, to the end, has concealed under an elegant skepticism an entire life of shameless immorality. It is because of this double standard—that of the mind and that of morals—that Sainte-Beuve excluded himself absolutely from the Savior's forgiveness. He had written, paraphrasing the magnificent figure of Lucretius, "It is necessary to receive and hold the heritage of life as a torch. Some have taken it as a wax taper, many as a cigar." He was one of these last; and his was the poor life of an Epicurean, consumed in the voluptuousness of which he had sung; the life of a dilettante, evaporated in the hazy theories of art for art's sake and *mala gaudia mentis.* "I have the reputation of being a skeptic," he said, "and I accept it willingly. Yes, everything amounts to the same in the end." That was his motto.

But the word skeptic is not sufficient to describe the fanatical hatred felt by Sainte-Beuve for God and the Church. Sainte-Beuve is the man of "meat dinners" on Good Friday at his house, with Prince Napoleon, Edmond About, and Flaubert as his guests. He is the man who wrote to the Princess Mathilde: "When will the Emperor and France purge themselves of this clerical leprosy?" And,

referring to the religious Congregations, "When
will these vile vermin be finally drowned for once
and all?"

Nor is the name of "Epicurean," any more than
the word "skeptic" sufficient to describe the debauchery of that low, abandoned life. "He adopts,"
said Veuillot, "the cult of the lewd muses." He
preached the doctrine of free-love to youth, and
himself set a fine example of it. He boasted of being a master of the art of seduction, and under
what pretenses and hypocritical masks! "I learned
a little of the Christian mythology in my day," he
wrote in 1863, six years before his death, "but it
has all evaporated. I used it, as the swan of Leda,
to achieve my purpose." "Why do you not
marry?" Jules Janin asked him one day reproach-
fully. "I am too ugly," he replied. And in fact
he was; but his worst ugliness was not of the body.

Moreover he was easily bribed. At any price he
must have money, honors, good food, popularity,
and he sold himself to obtain them. He sold himself
to the empire, to the Freemasons, and to all the
political parties which knew they could buy him,
and who despised him enough to do so. And so it
was that he was able to die, at the age of sixty-nine,
full of "honors." But at what a cost! I do not
triumph over such examples of miserable ignominy.
But I consider it my duty to warn men of every
age against the ignoble degeneracy which the in-

toxicating cup of Circe prepares for their last days.
An accomplished mind alone is not sufficient to
protect even the strongest, unless supported by
divine aid. And Sainte-Beuve himself furnishes the
proof of it in his private journal where he has revealed the degradation of his life. "When literature
does not render those who follow it absolutely better," he wrote, "it makes them worse. . . ."
"The blind indulgence for men of talent," remarks
Hippolyte Rigault, "is one of the evils of our
country."

But for all, whether writers, poets, or philosophers, there comes an hour when God will be for
them either an Avenger or a Redeemer. We recall
the lines of Shakespeare in the play of "Julius
Cæsar."

The night has come. The lyre lies silent in the
relaxed fingers of the weary slave.

BRUTUS. "How ill this taper burns! Ha! Who
    comes here?
    I think it is the weakness of mine eyes
    That shapes this monstrous apparition.
    It comes upon me. Art thou anything?
    Art thou some god, some angel or some devil,
    That makes my blood cold and my hair to
    stare?
    Speak to me what thou art.
GHOST. Thy evil spirit, Brutus.
BRUTUS. Why comest thou?

GHOST. To tell thee thou shalt see me at Philippi.
BRUTUS. Well, then I shall see thee again?
GHOST. Aye, at Philippi.
BRUTUS. Why, I will see thee at Philippi, then."
    The spirit vanishes.
Similarly, the threatening phantom which the
ingrates see at evening gliding into their darkened
room, is the divine figure of Him Whom they have
assailed with many blows. He comes to warn them
that the avenging hour has sounded, that tomorrow will be the day of the supreme and decisive
battle. They will see Him again at death!

*   *   *

But let us now, my brother, turn from these
horrors and utter the words which Dante wrote, on
coming out of his *Inferno*: "Let us leave behind us
such a cruel sea and hoist the sails of our bark, to
plow through better waters. I will sing of a kingdom where the soul is purified and becomes worthy
of ascending to heaven." It is the terrestrial purga-
tory of old age that we must visit.

One sees at first, upon its threshold, aspirants
who all their life have intended sometimes to become reconciled with the Church. But rather than
go to her at once and beg for her pardon and benediction, they have waited till they should reach a
certain age, or till some event should take place, or
till an hour should sound, which for them never

came. I know a striking example of this. Maxime du Camp, by turns a Saint-Simonian, a Garibaldian, a journalist, a romantic poet, and novelist, had passed through all the questionable paths of life, but seemed to have abandoned them when he wrote these lines: "A great cleft was made in my life when I was about forty years old. When, by study, one has touched the very limit of experience, has comprehended the weakness of all things human and the nothingness of hopes, he feels an imperious need to look beyond this world, to seek the support of a remunerative power, to have faith in the destiny of the immortal soul, and to think with the author of *Ecclesiastes* that if the dust returns to dust, the spirit returns to God Who gave it."

Subsequently, he took another step toward Christian belief and hope. He wished to bring his soul to the Church that she might lead it to God. He wished to ask of her absolution and Communion, the happiness of which he anticipates. He writes, "When the hour of death shall sound for me, one of the priests of this Church, which I shall have perhaps forgotten, will open my door softly and say to me: 'It was I who welcomed you in your cradle, and now I am going to conduct you to your tomb. What have you done since the day when we met for the first time? How have you kept the vows which you made in confirmation? I have kept all my promises, but you have not kept

yours. Yet every time you have come back to me,
you have found my mouth full of gentle chidings,
my hands full of indulgence, my heart filled with
pity. Now you have suffered; you are about to
die, you weep, you are filled with dread, you
repent. I pardon you! Go to rejoin in eternity
those whom you have loved and who await you.
Meanwhile, commend to me those whom you love,
that they, too, may go to rejoin you in the bosom
of God. You will find again after death whatever
of your past deserves to survive. Let your soul
make a supreme effort, let it make a great bound
into death, in order to reach those heights to which
God will deign to descend to help you rise to Him!
Pray with all your heart. If you have forgotten
the prayers of your childhood, repeat those which
I am going to say to you; they are always the same.
Upon your forehead, which I marked formerly
with the sign of baptism to protect you in this
world, I am going to mark a new sign in the same
place, which will obtain entrance for you into the
other world. Sinner, twice redeemed, sleep in the
peace of the Lord; and when, thanks to us, you
shall be in the presence of your divine Master, pray
to Him in your turn for us who are sinners like
yourself.' "

These words are beautiful. Beautiful, also, were
his words when, in 1885, he wrote his excellent
book on *The Private Charity in Paris*. He laments

there, it is true, that he has not the faith, but he
admires it and envies it: "Happy is he who possesses it!" Who stopped him on this road to Da-
mascus, of which he speaks? Maxime du Camp had
emerged from the darkness, but was he not drag-
ging along behind, in some old, evil, and well-
beaten path? I have not tried to penetrate this
mystery. I remark only that his last book, *Crépuscule*, (1891) is not a Christian book. It is a reversion to liberal skepticism, nothing more.

But, at least, he loves the poor. At the asylum of
Villepinte, of which he was one of the founders,
he said: "Pray much for me; I am growing old."
At Baden, where he was taken as a sick man, he
asked the Curé for a Mass, but wished it to be kept
a secret. Why this secrecy? Whom could he fear?
"A person who exercised a pernicious influence
over him," relates a witness of his last days, "constantly tried to turn him from the sacraments.
Owing to her, the door of the dying man's home
remained closed to the priest, and finally opened
only after the man, in a dying state, had lost consciousness and the power of speech. It was on
February 18, 1894, and he was seventy-two years
of age."

*   *   *

Those who have betrayed, blasphemed, and
stifled the voice of truth within them, seldom come

back to the faith. But some do. I will mention
again that great and good scientist, Littré. He was
one of our illustrious old men who had to make a
long journey back to the Church. He had been left
totally ignorant of religion in his youth. He had
never been baptized. His father, a Jacobin, had
given him the first name of Robespierre Maximilien. That is significant enough. His mother, too,
was not a Christian. His first reading was the
works of Voltaire and the Encyclopedists. In
respect to religion, he was born blind. Jesus took
compassion on him; and, knowing what he was,
restored his sight as He did that of the man in the
Gospel.

The great thing which made it easier for him to
find the light was the austerity of his private and
domestic life. Pasteur, his successor in the French
Academy, recounts the impression made upon him
by a visit to Littré's modest country house after
his death: "Only the simplest parsonage in the
poorest village can give an idea of that house,
where everything reveals a life of solitude and dis-
interestedness. Littré had the cult of austerity. I
saw his desk covered with opened books and scattered notes; the little table where his wife and
daughter worked beside him; and above that table
an image of Christ." Pasteur concluded his discourse to the Academy with these words: "I have
often pictured him to myself seated there near his

wife; he, looking upon the world with tender compassion for those who suffer; she, a fervent Catholic, her eyes lifted toward heaven; he, inspired
by all the questions pertaining to earth; she, by all
the grandeurs of the divine life; she, a Christian
saint; he, a saintly layman, as all those who knew
him called him."

I have already spoken of his charity, his devoted,
gratuitous services as a physician, day and night,
to the poor of his village; and you know, my
brother, there is no virtue which appeals more
strongly than this to the heart of Him Who said:
"Blessed are the merciful, for they shall obtain
mercy." Yet, at the end of Littré's life, it was no
longer merely to the poor that he gave his aid, but
also to the persecuted victims of Freemasonry and
sectarian radicalism. To the nuns of the free
schools in his parish he sent financial assistance, and
in the House of Representatives, he protested
against the odious measures of secularization, which
he called "infamous."

I have described elsewhere his last days; they
were those of a devout Christian. They were the
divinely logical result of his life of charity, integri-
ty, austerity, simplicity, and courage.

On those who are thus healed and who survive
God's pardon, a duty is incumbent. It is that of
reparation after absolution. "Go and sin no more!"
said the Savior; "Rise and walk. Deny thyself.

Take up thy cross and follow Me." This implies two things: reparation and expiation. Such, to the end of their lives, was the work of many celebrated converts of our time: Huysmans, Coppée, Brunetière, Brucker, Hermann, and many more.

I will recall here only one of them of whom I have already spoken, a little more remote than these and now somewhat forgotten, Paul Féval. His old age was an admirable expiation and, also, the most courageous of reparations. The latter consisted in the overwhelming work of revising all his many writings. When some one pitied him for this, he answered: "What is the work, what is the trouble that it costs me? Nothing; when I investigate my life, review my past, and go back over my career. It is not enough to believe or even to lead a Christian life; I must make reparation. Faith is not sufficient; there must be works as well." At this period of his life, it was no more to his former residence in the quarter of the Champs Élysées and the Arch of Triumph that one went to visit the repentant novelist. He had gone to bury himself alive behind Montmartre in a little workingman's house, in the shadow of a tiny garden. The workman there was Féval himself, bound to the feverish labor of pruning or, as he said, of "sacking" his romances, at the risk of perishing at the task. "But God does not ask you to kill yourself," a friend said to him. "God," he replied, "does not ask me to live, but to do my duty." From this little house, it was an ascent of a quarter of an hour for him to reach his beloved chapel of the Sacred Heart, and he was old and short of breath. "Yes," he said, "at my age the road is a hard one, but less hard than was the ascent to Calvary. It is an all-too-feeble expiation due to my God by the author of such deplorable writings. All those pages, all of them, must disappear! God will let me live long enough to convert them, as I myself have been converted by Him."

The rest of his life was spent in prayer and charity. He gave, and he forgave. To a visitor who took leave of him, astonished, deeply moved, and almost frightened, Féval, perceiving his emotion, exclaimed, "I know well that everybody cannot become a hermit, as I have done. But listen: You, yourself, ought also to be converted. I assure you that God loves you. Adieu! But an adieu in two words—À Dieu!"

After the death of his wife, having retired to the "House of the Brothers of St. John the Divine," cared for by one of his daughters, a Sister of Charity, Paul Féval passed away piously in his seventieth year (1887). As Veuillot said of him, "The shipwrecked man had had time to repair his bark and float again, then to cast anchor in the Port of Peace."

CHAPTER
SIXTEEN

Immortality — Hope

In the realm of thought, the idea of immortality is queen. It reigns over all our thoughts. It commands our entire life and confers upon it whatever elevation, dignity, and beauty it possesses. Let us speak of it, my brother, and of the hope which it inspires.

I remember well the time the notion of immortality first dawned upon me. When I was a child, my mother, seeing my delight at the sight of myriad stars sparkling in the firmament, inspired this hope within me, as she told me that higher still extended another and a more beautiful heaven, where, if I were good, I should one day go and live for ever. Thus began my first instruction concerning another life.

The same dear voice also gave me consoling lessons when, by the deathbed of those whom I mourned in childhood, she dried my eyes and bade me look upward, saying: "Do not weep! They are with the good God in heaven." I recollect, also, the time when, in our college classes, we were told to admire the ideas of immortality contained in the

Elysian Fields of Vergil, the *Dream of Scipio* by Cicero, and the *Phaedo* of Plato, which Lamartine had freely translated in his *Death of Socrates*.

The "Immortality of the Soul" was the subject of my dissertation after completing my studies in philosophy, and this, whatever else it may have lacked, certainly overflowed with an enthusiasm that came directly from my heart. It was the hope of heaven, too, which I, as a priest, by means of the parish catechism class, revealed to the children —Jesus said, concerning them, that of such is the kingdom of heaven. After this, I made them sing the hymn "Heaven Is My Home," which in spirit transported them there. What beautiful days those were!

To my older auditors, when I commented by preference on the eight Beatitudes of the Sermon on the Mount, it was still *the hope of heaven* that always came, like a refrain, in each of the stanzas of that sublime chant. I compared it to a great tree planted in the garden of the Church, whose roots, I pointed out, were found in the heart of man, in the Gospel, and in the testimony of the ages; and I spoke then of its fruits: morality, virtue, sacrifice, consolation, peace, and happiness. It was, indeed, the tree of life.

Today I find that, for the old especially, there is something still more pleasing to the soul than memory; it is *hope*. Someone has said, "Old age is

like a traveler by night from whom the earth is
hidden, but to whom the sublimity of the starry
heavens is revealed."

But the principal thing that attaches me to this
lofty virtue is, not the powerful attraction which it
exercises on my heart, but the necessary support
that it—and it alone—gives to my moral consciousness. I hold as incontestable that no moral
law is efficacious which does not have behind it the
notion of a superhuman Authority and Its eternal
sanctions. The following avowal, which I borrow
from one of the great masters of contemporaneous
skepticism, is more convincing than any demon-
stration. Scherer wrote in 1884: "Let us look at
things as they are. True morality has need of the
Absolute; it finds its point of support only in God.
Conscience is like the heart; it must have, to explain and justify it, a *Beyond.* Duty means nothing
if its origin is not from above; and life becomes
trivial unless it implies eternal relations." The same
writer said, at the risk of contradicting all his skepticism, that "the supernatural was the natural
sphere of the soul."

Another unbeliever, the English positivist Huxley, bitterest denier of the supernatural, nevertheless recognizes the fact that a moral code, supported by a hope of heaven, has a moral efficacy which
is lacking in his own halting, self-constituted code.
He writes sadly, "I understand how an upward

glance of hope toward heaven may be an encouragement to an act of virtue. It is thus that the woodcutter gains renewed courage in his work when, through an opening in the forest, he perceives the little home, where, his day's work ended, he will find in the bosom of his family a well-earned rest." Finally, he concludes thus: "If such a faith could rest on a solid foundation, the human race would cling to it as tenaciously as the drowning sailor clutches a lifebuoy."

Today the man who has been robbed of his faith is like that drowning sailor. Only he knows not what to grasp in this irremediable wreck. The ship that carried him had neither compass nor ballast. It had struck on all the reefs and was leaking everywhere. By the term "independent moral code" the poor passengers had understood "freedom from all duty"; and since their teachers boasted of having taught them to do without God, but had not taught them to do without happiness, they sought for happiness in unrestrained license, trampling under foot the ruins of every virtue and all faith. Who will now save them from perdition?

Science, in desperation, seeks now to build up a secular moral code; but all its systems crumble away, despite its efforts, through lack of an immutable and eternal foundation, which is found only in God. Let us hasten to these shipwrecked souls! But we shall not urge them to cling to a floating buoy. We have something better than that. It is a ship that can never sink. Its course is laid for the home of souls. Upon its flag are the words: Hope and Salvation. It is bound for the port of immortality.

*   *   *

The immortality of the soul is not, with us, an empty phrase. It means that the soul actually survives the death of the body for a destiny which time is powerless to change. Let no one flatter himself that he can cheat us with some shadow or semblance of immortality, which has nothing of it but its name. That illusive substitute for it, now in vogue, is the great falsehood of the philosophy of our times.

Sixty years ago, in our philosophical studies, we were made to read a memorable discourse pronounced by a great master, Jouffroy, a short time before his death, at an impressive function in the college of Louis le Grand. He concluded thus: "Young men, never let anything extinguish in your souls that hope which we have nourished in you here, that torch which faith and philosophy have kindled, and which the dawn of an immortal life makes visible beyond the shadows of earth's final shore." That was the Credo of the spiritual or non-materialistic school.

Let us now turn, for contrast, to the lofty mystification at present offered in its place. Twenty

years ago, in August, 1890, in connection with a
distribution of prizes at a general university contest, the minister of public instruction, Léon Bourgeois, addressed the youthful assembly before him
on the subject of hope and immortality. But in his
discourse these two words were only hollow sounds.
After having spoken very forcibly about boundless
progress, universal activity, and the humanity of
the future, the grand master stated what each
man's final reward for his work would be, as follows: "Gentlemen, be useful! Let your efforts be
associated with the efforts of all! The part of yourself that you shall give to the service of eternal
evolution will be your part of immortality." This
is the Credo of evolutionism.

But how small is this part, and how insignificant
such an immortality! I fancy I hear a manufacturer paying one of his workmen in this small ver-
bal coin: "You have worked; you have associated
your efforts with those of your comrades of yesterday and the day before. Nothing of all that will
be lost. That is well; and let this noble thought
constitute your salary. You will get no other. You
will share justly in the honor of this collective
work, after having had the toil of producing it;
but it is the factory that will receive the fruit of it.
You will have contributed to the welfare of society; what matters then your own? The individual
is nothing; collective humanity is everything. Let

humanity's immortality console you for the annihilation and oblivion which await you. What
nobler fate could you desire, poor atom that you
are?"

Do you think, my brother, that a workman thus
addressed would be very unreasonable if he were
dissatisfied with this glorious payment? But you,
yourself, are this workman, and I think that you,
also, would consider yourself to have been deceived
and insulted by such words. "What a cruel mock-
ery!" you would exclaim; "and what a strange
and wretched 'immortal' you make of me! Is the
minister making a fool of us?"

That is substantially the poor moral code of
social interest which the manuals of the primary
schools today teach to our little ones. But these
little ones will presently become great ones, and
when they have reached manhood, I can hear them
say: I do not see why I should trouble myself,
deny myself, and sacrifice myself for the welfare
of this abstract collectivity, called "society." I do
not see by what right I should be ordered to prac-
tice self-denial, unselfishness, devotion, chastity,
honesty, all the commandments of God, and all the
virtues of the saints, because you tell us there is
no longer any God, no longer any saints, and no
longer any heaven. You say: "Each for all"; but
I say: Each for himself! Live from one day to
the next. Try to be stronger than the rest. Refuse

yourself nothing. There are no such things as good
or evil. Do what you please. Take anything that
tempts you. Overturn every obstacle, without
scruples or remorse. Scruples are for simpletons.
Intelligent people have none. See how our masters
act!

That is the Epicurean moral code. Let us now
glance at that of Stoicism; stricter but not wiser.
"Man," writes Ernest Bersot, "is not born to be
happy. He is born to be a man, with a man's risks
and perils. We must go forward into life, as one
goes into the firing line, without asking ourselves
how we shall come out of it again. How shall we?
The reply is simple. We shall come out of it, if at
all, either victors or vanquished; we shall have been
fortunate or unfortunate there. But in either case,
if we have done our duty, we shall be recompensed
for it, and we shall receive the prize. That is necessary justice. Only, we must wait until we have
left the battlefield and returned home, before we
get it. Rewards and happiness are not usually given
in this world. There is little happiness here even
for the good and brave; and for all it is rare. The
reason for it is this, says St. Theresa very aptly:
"God is a Father Who does not pay His children
by the day, as workingmen and women are paid.
He reserves to Himself the right to pay them all
at once, when they shall be in His kingdom, the
happiness of which they shall then share with
Him."

*   *   *

In the doctrine of materialism there is no immortality; the soul perishes with the body. Of the matter, common to both, disintegrated by death, the chemist Büchner with brutal frankness writes: "The best and most useful thing that man can leave in dying, is the greatest possible amount of phosphate, chalk, and rare, fruitful salts, to form a richer combination of molecules, in order to fertilize our earth and increase our sum of prosperity and pleasure."

For man, thus understood, there is only one duty left. It is to give himself up hopelessly and without a murmur, to the laws of indifferent, omnipotent nature. When Monsignor d'Hulst visited Taine, who was already fatally ill, and tried to make him see, beyond that "reign of necessity," a higher law of love, the philosopher replied: "It may be that such a law exists, but I do not see it. I perceive only a beautiful goddess who seems to be neither good nor bad. With her robe she sweeps the sand and overthrows the tiny structures that the ants have built upon it. My life is one of those frail dwellings. I am one of those ants. Can I believe that the goddess is going to lift her robe in order to spare me?"

Man, an ant? Perhaps, if one considers only our "corpuscule," as the Church expresses itself in its Office for the Dead; and materialism wishes to see

in man nothing more. But is there nothing else?
Is man merely an ant—man, whose power of comprehension embraces this world and others? He is,
at all events, an ant that thinks, an ant that cal-
culates the depths of space, that discovers and de-
termines the laws of the universe, masters the elements, changes the face of the globe, searches into
the remotest centuries of the past, and into the
ultimate recesses of intelligence and life! An ant
that has called itself Moses, Plato, Aristotle, Alexander, Cæsar, St. Paul, St. Augustine, St. Ambrose,
Descartes, Newton, Bossuet, Jeanne d'Arc, St.
Vincent de Paul, Pasteur, and thousands more!
An ant of which it has been said: "A man is greater
than a world; and in creating a mind, God achieved
more than when He lighted a star in the firmament
of heaven!"

But do the materialists, in their insolence, believe
that? Do they at heart possess their boasted stoical
and desperate resignation? Paul Bourget says,
"No!" From Assisi, by the tomb of St. Francis,
he wrote these lines: "It is of no use to multiply
sophisms to prove that the true rôle of man is that
of cold resignation to a blind nature. Such an
attitude is only a pretense, against which the really
sincere soul protests. It is a proud and rebellious
hardening of our will. The need of immortality
subsists in the depths of our being."

How well we know those depths of our being!

They form the essentially religious basis of a soul which, dominated by the idea of another life, devoured by the need of it and of that highest good for which it feels itself to have been made, cries, prompted by good desires: *"It must be"*; with all its acts of volition: *"I wish it to be"*; and in all its convictions: *"It is."* I believe it. Without it, abandoned to the finite, the imperfect, and the incomplete, I no longer live as I feel I ought to live; I miss the end and aim of my existence. I am uneasy, complaining, agonized; I torment myself, longing for the whole truth, for complete perfection, and for the supreme happiness which is not given me here and which this mortal life can never give. I, therefore, ask it from an immortality which I cannot doubt, for this thirst is the pledge of its existence.

This thirst for it is also instinctive. The learned entomologist, H. Fabre, whom Darwin considered a faultless observer, presents this argument: "For every naturalist, it is an evident truth that the instinct of even the humblest animal is infallible. Now we, and we alone, among all creatures possess the superb instinct of the Beyond. There is in us an invincible faith in a survival after this life, with an insurmountable repugnance to the thought that all will end with the tomb. Shall we not listen to the modest but certain voice of the insect, which says to us, 'Have confidence! Instinct has

never failed to keep its promises!' " Thereupon the
eminent observer becomes justly indignant at modern materialism, which is at once so insolent and so
abject. He exclaims, " 'No, enough of that!' Man,
the offspring of a monkey; duty, an imbecile
prejudice; conscience, a bait for simpletons; genius,
neurasthenia; love of country, chauvinism; the
soul, a chemical resultant of cellular energies; God,
a puerile myth. . . .' Enough and more than
enough of that! The fad will pass away and the
facts will remain, to bring us back to the good old
notions of the soul and its immortal destinies."

The miserable philosophy which obstinately sees
in this sublime desire of the soul for a future life
only an aimless labor and an endless unrest is, therefore, contrary to nature. So, also, is the philosophy
which makes of man an unfinished and abortive
being, whose noblest faculty soars to such a height
only to lose itself in darkness and in nothingness.
Unnatural, too, is the philosophy which makes God
not a father, but a monster Who, having implanted
this hunger and thirst in the hearts of His children,
lets them die of starvation at the empty table to
which He has invited them.

I will confess, my brother, there are times when,
if I think of the many unhappy men and women
who know nothing, or feign to know nothing, of
their souls, I ask myself—God forgive me—
whether there are not by nature two different

kinds of humanity, represented by these two types of men who present such a contrast to each other. On the one hand are the immortals; and on the other, those who are not immortal, at least so far as it is possible for them not to be so. The former are those of whom a poet has said that they carry their heads high, with their gaze fixed on the heavens; and whom the Apostle calls *"Coelestis homo, spiritualis homo."* The latter, far below them, advance continually bent over toward the earth, through which they drag themselves or wallow; *"Terrenus homo, animalis homo."*

Upward then! *Sursum!* It is heaven that we must seek. And everything in me does seek it— instinct, intelligence, suffering, and love; and I believe in the immortal soul, as I do in a just and eternal God. God does not tell me a falsehood, nor does my heart deceive me; love will not be eternally defrauded of its own; the good will not be always in the wrong; there exists a city of the true, the just, the beautiful, and it will finally be the city of happiness, the reward of virtue.

*   *   *

But alas! It is at present hidden from our gaze. That is my chief cause of sadness. To me, in my old age, there come hours of impatience and fatigue, when, weary of marching for so many years in the desert, I would like to catch at least

a glimpse of the hills of the Promised Land. I long
to have the clouds part a little and reveal to me
the far-away walls of the heavenly Jerusalem resplendent in eternal light. But what am I saying,
madman that I am? Would my frail, mortal body
be able to endure for even a moment the vision of
that splendor without being instantly crushed and
annihilated? Mine was the request of a child, and
I was still almost a child when I was told to read
the answer to such a question in the following
page: "I remember," relates a traveler, "that when
I arrived in France on a vessel which was returning
from the Indies, as soon as the sailors had distinguished clearly the outline of their homeland, they
became for the most part incapable of working the
ship. Some gazed upon their country, wholly
unable to turn their eyes from it; others put on
their finest clothes, as if they were about to go
ashore; some also spoke in subdued tones, while
others wept. As we approached the coast, their
agitation increased; and when the vessel entered
the port, and they saw on the wharf their fathers,
mothers, wives, children, and friends, holding out
their arms to them and weeping for joy, it was
impossible to keep a single man of the crew on
board. All leaped into boats and hastened to the
shore; and, according to the custom of that port,
the work on the ship had to be done thereafter by
another crew."

"How would it be, therefore," asks the same writer, "if we obtained a vision of that heavenly home, where all we have loved most dearly are living? The sight would throw us into a state of ecstasy or stupefaction, which would immediately cause a cessation of all earthly occupations."

But from that other world which none of us has yet approached, Some One greater than we has descended to give us news of it, and has illumined the darkness of the tomb with the lamp of life. That lamp of life is hope; it is the torch of the Gospel, by which we read: "No man hath ascended into heaven, but He that descended from heaven, the Son of man Who is in heaven. . . . I say to thee that we speak what we know, and testify of what we have seen."

In fact, during the three years of Christ's teaching, He spoke of little else than the heaven from which He came, and to which He was to return. In the Sermon on the Mount, He exclaims: "Rejoice and be exceeding glad, for great is your reward in heaven." The words "kingdom of heaven" are to be found fifty-eight times in the four Gospels; "eternal life" forty-five times. The farewell discourse of Jesus to His disciples after the Last Supper points continually to a meeting again in heaven. "I go to My Father; but let not your hearts be troubled; I go to prepare a place for you, that where I am, there ye may be also."

And what He promised, Jesus performed. It is written that forty days after His resurrection, the Son of God, having assembled His disciples on a mountain near Jerusalem, rose heavenward, body and soul, until a cloud concealed Him from their sight. The disciples standing on that height lingered, unable to remove their gaze from the cloud which had just taken from them their divine Master. Moreover, ever since that day, the generations of humanity which have succeeded those eyewitnesses have also not ceased to gaze upward, unable to detach their eyes from the heavens into which once passed the Savior, Who left us, only to draw us to Himself.

Two things are worthy of mention here. First, that after the revelation made by Jesus, after the testimony brought to us by Him as an eyewitness, and after His resurrection, His ascension, and His parting words at the Last Supper, faith and hope in immortality—so indistinct and wavering in ancient philosophy and so weak and cold even in Judaism—shone forth with sudden splendor, turning with unexpected and unheard-of eagerness toward an eternal life, previously obscured by clouds. This is because Jesus, victorious over death, pierced and passed through those clouds, glorified them in so doing, just as in the Transfiguration, *a bright cloud* overshadowed Him. Thereafter the way was clear and open; a direct and certain guidance was given to all souls who wish to follow Him by the same path of love and sacrifice. Secondly, not only is the aim of Christian hope made clearly definite by the teaching and example of Jesus, but the object of that hope is the divine Person, Jesus Christ, to be eternally possessed and loved in heaven.

St. Paul exclaims: "For me, to live is Christ, and to die is gain." His mortal body encumbers him: "Who shall deliver me from it, that *I may go to Christ?*" As his death draws near, he writes: "I desire my dissolution, in order *to be with Christ.*"

This was the sentiment and the inspiration also of the martyrs. St. Ignatius of Antioch longed to hasten the moment of his martyrdom, "The sword, the cross, broken bones, the teeth of lions, limbs sawed asunder, and the body torn apart; let any or all of these tortures come to me, provided I obtain Jesus Christ!" And when the friends of the martyrs placed their relics in their humble tombs, they wrote above them these three words which signified at once their hope and their desire: "*Vivas in Christo!*" Mayst thou live in Christ! That to them was heaven. Nor is this strange; for listen to St. John at Patmos. Heaven was there opened to him, and he introduces us, in the Apocalypse, into the very home of immortality. *Everything there is Jesus.* He is the *alpha and omega,* the beginning and the end; the King of earth and heaven; the Light of the city of God. He is the Lamb slain on the altar, but also the Lamb crowned and seated upon the throne, at the foot of which chant the angels and the saints.

Let us, then, my brother, make our preparations for our journey, like the wise men of the Orient, setting out to find the King of Kings. Like them, let us also take with us our treasures—gold, frankincense, and myrrh—that is to say, the virtues which these presents symbolize. The hour is at hand. The signal for our departure is given us by the star which has appeared to us in the firmament. It foretells the coming call of God.

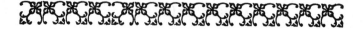

CHAPTER
SEVENTEEN

Preparation — The End

It is, then, with a firm belief in immortality and
in the ultimate departure of the soul to a better
world, to be with Christ, that Christians see the
inevitable approach of death; inevitable, of course,
to all, but to the old inevitably near. Let us not
listen credulously, my brother, to those amiable
flatterers who consider it their duty to prevent
their fellow mortals from thinking of death, and
suppose that they are doing us old people a service,
when they tell us with apparent seriousness that we
poor trembling reeds are still as vigorous as oaks.
Often, alas, our vanity makes itself the accomplice
of these blandishments and thus, though really
old and more or less infirm, we let ourselves be
lulled into the illusion that death is still remote
from us, till we are suddenly overtaken by it, without having had a suspicion that the end was immi-
nent. Is this desirable?

The truth is, that not only must we old men die,
but we must die soon. The average span of life is
less than forty years, and we have passed that mile-
stone long, long ago! Why should we, like the

ostrich, thrust our heads into the sand and refuse
to look death squarely in the face? Is man too weak
and cowardly a creature to do it? On the contrary,
is not this courageous, highly gifted being the only
one that knows how to die, and can die consciously
with equanimity?

Personally, for some time I have noticed a certain slackening of my formerly brisk movements;
also some dimness of vision, hardness of hearing,
and general lethargy. The besieging forces of my
bodily enemies are evidently closing in upon me.
The circumference of my life's circle is contract-
ing; it will soon become merely a point; and that
point—a tomb! My head still holds out bravely.
It is the citadel that refuses to surrender. But what
will this "intelligence served by organs" be able to
do when all its servants refuse to work? I am conscious already of some ominous indications of re-
bellion. It was to be expected; for, after all, what
is our life but a mortal malady? Are we not all
condemned to death, subject to an indefinite number of reprieves? We may not know, and cannot
know, as a rule, the manner of our death beforehand. It is best, therefore, to banish that subject
from our thoughts; but it is not so easy to dismiss
the apprehension that the end of life will be accompanied by suffering. It is true, the separation of
the soul from the body is occasionally marked by
long and painful struggles; for death, which is

called the "ransom for sin," makes some of us pay dearly for it. Yet it is equally true that usually the passing of the soul is not attended by such anguish. Death may resemble a sorrowful separation, but is rarely a violent rupture.

A priest who has written much and well on this subject gives this testimony: "If the common opinion of mankind considers the exit from life as the climax of human suffering, I must declare, on the contrary, that neither the texts of Holy Scripture, the teachings of the Church, nor the observations of science support this theory. I have often watched the 'departure of the Christian soul,' as the Church expresses it, and I do not remember ever having seen any of those desperate conflicts with which imagination frequently surrounds the fatal hour. Such deaths are rare. In the state of exhaustion to which sickness has usually reduced the patient, such vehement struggles could not be endured. Biological science furnishes convincing reasons for this, and experience confirms them. The majority of deaths are marked by an almost imperceptible and tranquil lessening of respiration till the end, so that, in many instances, the bystanders ask one another in uncertainty: 'Is it all over?' "

Such a death is practically falling asleep, according to the beautiful language of the Gospel and the Church. Here, also, God is good to us. The last words of Dr. Cullen, one of the most celebrated physicians of England, were: "I wish it were possible for me to continue to write and to teach, that I might make known to all how easy it is to die."*

Yet "easy" deaths are not desired by all. It may depend upon the cause for which one dies. If I were asked, "What is the most beautiful of deaths?" I should have to answer: I do not know. I once heard an old man, an octogenarian priest and my childhood teacher, say, as he nodded toward his helpless, crippled arms: "What am I doing with the remnant of blood that stagnates in my veins? Ah! Fifty years ago, during the Reign of Terror, our predecessors shed their blood freely for Christ. They were more fortunate than we!" For him, certainly, the most beautiful death would have been that of a martyr; and he was worthy of martyrdom.

But shall we, on the other hand, desire our death to be a sudden and unexpected one, such as Cæsar wished for and many modern pagans crave? The choice does not show courage. A friend of mine, when on his deathbed, heard someone near him say that the death most to be envied is one which comes unheralded. "No, no!" exclaimed the dying man,

---

*Bacon wrote: "It is as natural to die as to be born," and Oliver Wendell Holmes said, "Nature supplies her own anaesthetic." The vast majority of persons pass from life to death in a state of unconsciousness. "Every time we fall asleep, we practically 'die.'" (Footnote of Translator.)

"I have always wanted to know what duty I had to perform." The Church, which reserves treasures of mercy for her children in their final hour, bids us pray to the Master of life to preserve us from a sudden and unforeseen death. But it should be borne in mind that sudden death is an evil only when there has been no preparation for it. Its suddenness is no longer a surprise, when it comes to one who is ready to receive it at any moment and in any way.

Elie de Beaumont, the famous geologist, fell dead suddenly in the courtyard of his ancestral castle, on September 24, 1874, the evening before his seventy-sixth birthday, for the celebration of which his children and grandchildren had assembled there. But this eminent Christian scholar was not unprepared. The scientist, Jean Baptiste Dumas, speaking of him in the French Academy soon after his death, could say: "The day of joy became unexpectedly a day of mourning. But Elie de Beaumont had performed all his Christian duties and was always ready for the summons. If the wing of the angel of death touched him without warning, he was not taken by surprise. He was one of those men whose spiritual debts are always paid, and his pure, immortal soul could, without anxiety, leave this earth whose splendors he had done so much to reveal and whose harmonies he had caused so many to admire."

On this point of being always ready to depart, Montaigne is often quoted. In his essays he wrote: "It is uncertain where death will overtake us. Let us, then, look for it everywhere. As far as it is possible for me to be so, I am prepared for it at any hour; booted and ready to start, and in such a state, thank God, that I can vacate my lodging without regret whenever it shall please Him to require it. I have freed myself of everything and have taken farewell of everyone except myself."

This condition of mind need not be a gloomy one. "The thought of death," writes Angot de Rotours, "is a serious companion, but a beneficent one. It raises us above considerations of visible nature, bringing us the notion of the invisible God and the true meaning of our destiny. It lifts us out of our infatuation with terrestrial things, frees us from spiritual pride, shows the brief duration of life's petty sorrows and the trivial importance of its little joys. It also cools our hatreds, dispels anger, awakens pity, softens selfishness, incites to heroism and magnanimity, and puts us all at last upon a common level—that of the grave. The day we are able to face this phantom fearlessly will be the dawn of a new era of man's liberty and happiness."

Two of my friends bear witness to the truth of these sentiments. One, the illustrious Le Play, wrote: "I have seen the close approach of eternity, but it did not impress me, as it has many others, with the nothingness of human life; on the contrary, it made me realize still more life's importance. The present life is the post where we are stationed to acquire our *spiritual classification in the future life.* We ought, therefore, to be glad to remain here and to do our duty." The other friend wrote: "Flee from the phantom of death, and it will pursue you; advance courageously toward it, and it will vanish." In its place you will discover grand horizons opening before you, which your heart instantly longs to explore. Do you wish to know my remedy for all the dangers, disappointments, and sorrows of this life? It is *the thought of death.* When something happens to disturb and vex me greatly, I read the Office for the Dead and especially the Mass for the Dead. I might say rather that I recite them; for, having read them so often, I know them by heart. After reading them, one has no longer any other desire than to "fall asleep," as St. Paul says; "to return to one's country," as the prophet writes; or to wait, with Job, until "the transforming change shall come."

To learn how nobly multitudes of true Christians are continually dying, we have only to read some of the numberless descriptions of the last moments of the followers of Jesus, if, indeed, personal experience has not rendered that testimony needless. Bend over their beds of suffering and piously receive their parting words. But do so in silence.

Put your ear close to their trembling lips, for those last words are scarcely more than whispered sighs, faint murmurs to an invisible Being, Whose name they lovingly invoke.

Listen to Lacordaire: "Open to me, O my God, open to me!" And with these words the great monk closed forever those lips from which such floods of eloquence had poured. Or to Père Ravignan: "To die is happiness, and what happiness! I have desired it perhaps too much; but God knows it was not in order to escape more suffering, but to go to Him in heaven." The last words of Donoso Cortez, the great Spanish orator, when dying at the age of forty-five, were: "My God, Thou hast said: 'I will draw all men unto Me.' Draw me, dear Lord; take me!" Listen to Cardinal Newman: "I end my long life declaring that God has never failed me." He then asked to have Father Faber's hymn "The Eternal Years" sung to him. "It is like a reflection from the eternal light," he said. "Blessed vision of peace!" Or finally to Cardinal Manning: "My soul is already filled with the beauty of the world beyond! How I understand now the desire of St. Paul to depart! Let us go!"

There is another kind of preparation for departure from this earth which is both religious and philosophical. It consists of a gradual, voluntary detachment from a world, the fashion of which is passing away and leaves no regret. The best way gradually to take leave of it is to follow the counsel of St. Francis de Sales, who says: "We must disengage, one by one, our affections from created things. Trees which the wind tears up from the earth are not fit to be transplanted, because their roots still remain in the ground; but whoever wishes to convey a tree to another soil, must little by little and very skillfully free all its roots from the earth. And since we are to be transplanted to the land of the immortals, it is necessary similarly to get rid of our attachments to this world."

This gradual separation from persons and things can, however, be made amiably. Father Gratry compares such a supreme farewell to the "goodnight" of a child, who, before going to bed, takes leave of all the company in turn, presenting his forehead to be kissed by each. It can also be made solemnly and nobly. "Never," says his biographer, "did Michelangelo's genius appear grander than in the closing period of his life; not as a painter, sculptor, and architect, but as a man of God, who considered it his greatest honor to humiliate himself before Him. . . . The last sonnet which he sent to Vasari—his swan song—was a solemn farewell to art, which he reproached himself with having idolized. 'All is vanity,' he wrote, 'including sculpture and painting; things incapable of fully satisfying a soul which has once become enamored of the love divine. Everything is vanity, except the happiness of loving God and the honor of serving Him!' "

Let us come down to our own time. "The world is leaving us, my friend," wrote venerable Auguste Nicolas; "happy are those who have wings to fly away. Our generation is vanishing and we, who still remain, are like the dead leaves at the top of a tree, which the first wind will blow away. At our age, everything is an omen of departure for us. Announcements of the deaths of my friends knock continually at my door, or are thrust beneath it. Let us forestall the future by so fully occupying ourselves with the eternal life, that when death really comes, it will find us . . . 'gone!' "

In 1891, Monsignor Gay, a septuagenarian, wrote: "Old age is no longer on the way to me; it has arrived, and with it a train of infirmities. My loved ones do not wish me to believe that these are warnings of departure, but in my heart I know that I am like a bird upon the branch. No second call will be necessary for me to take my flight. . . . It is evening, and the Master is not far away. Would that He might come! Neither you nor I, dear friend, will make Him wait, before opening the door."

Among the first words spoken by our risen Lord were these: "I ascend unto My Father and to your Father, and to My God and your God." Such, also, is the farewell that I wish to utter to this world

from which His divine will is preparing to call me.
I am ready to go. For what should I still do here,
my brother? I feel myself more and more solitary
and a stranger. The century of which I formed
a part lies buried now beneath my feet, and already
I am nothing but a shadow wandering among the
living. It is time for me to depart. Moreover, I
can truly say that I go to my Father, for to whom
has God been a Father, if not to me? This life
which I am leaving was His gift, and He has made
it sweeter, happier, more honored, and finally
longer than the lives of most of my contemporaries. During this protracted journey, how helpful, how indulgent, how tender, and how merciful
He has been to me! I wish to bless Him for it once
more before leaving.

And when the final hour shall arrive, His Church
—and mine—will not forsake me. Beautiful and
comforting are her parting words to each of her
dying children: "Go forth, O Christian soul, from
this world in the name of God the Father Almighty
Who created thee; in the name of Jesus Christ, the
Son of the living God, Who suffered for thee; and
in the name of the Holy Ghost Who sanctified thee.
. . . I commend thee, dear brother, to the
Almighty God, Whose creature thou art, that,
when thou shalt have paid the debt of all mankind
to death, thou mayst return to thy Maker. . . .
When thy soul shall depart from the body, may

the resplendent multitude of angels meet thee, may the court of the Apostles receive thee; may the triumphant army of white-robed martyrs come out to welcome thee; may the glorious company of the illustrious confessors encircle thee. . . . May Jesus Christ Himself appear to thee with mild and cheerful countenance, and may He award thee a place among them who stand before Him forever! . . . May He place thee within the ever-verdant gardens of His paradise, and may He, the true Shepherd, acknowledge thee for one of His flock . . . and thus among the companies of the blessed mayst thou enjoy the sweetness of the contemplation of thy God forever and ever! Amen." These and other equally beautiful, precious, and comforting words fall on the ear of the dying Catholic, as his soul is about to leave this world. Incomparable privilege! Ineffable consolation!

It is significant that the concluding lines of the Revelation contain alternate words of prophecy and invitation in the form of a solemn dialogue between the soul and Christ—a prelude to their everlasting union in heaven. Jesus Himself is speaking, and He says: "The Spirit and the bride say *Come*; and let him that heareth say *Come*; and let him that thirsteth *come*; and whosoever will, let him take the water of life freely." Then He adds the startling declaration:

"Surely I come quickly."
And the soul replies:
"Even so, come, Lord Jesus!"

With this last interchange of promise and petition, and with the name of the Lord Jesus, the New Testament ends.

May that Divine Name also be the last to leave my lips, when the moment of my departure shall have come!

FINIS

BIBLIOGRAPHY

A

ABOUT, EDMOND. French novelist and journalist, author of many works. Born in Lorraine, 1828; died at Paris, 1885.

ÆSCHYLUS. The earliest of the three great Greek tragic poets. Born at Eleusis, 525 B.C.; died in Sicily, 456 B.C. He fought against the Persians at Marathon, Artemisium, Salamis, and Plataea. He wrote ninety plays, seven of which are extant in their entirety.

AGNES, SAINT. Roman Christian virgin and martyr who, at the age of thirteen, was beheaded during the persecution of the Church by Diocletian (A.D. 303-315), after having been exposed to the vilest outrage. She was canonized, and her feast day is celebrated on January 21.

AICARD, JEAN. French poet and dramatist. Born at Toulon in 1848; died in 1921.

ALCIBIADES. Athenian statesman and general, and a favorite pupil of Socrates, who saved his life in battle. Born at Athens, 450 B.C. Assassinated in Phrygia, 404 B.C.

AMBROSE, SAINT. Church Father distinguished as a statesman, scholar, and philosopher, as well as a great theologian. Born at Trèves about A.D. 340; died at Milan, A.D. 397. He is the patron saint of Milan.

AMPÈRE, ANDRÉ. Renowned French physicist, mathematician, and electrician. Born at Polémieux, near Lyons, in 1775; died at Marseilles in 1836. Noted for his development of electromagnetism.

AMPÈRE, JEAN JACQUES. French philologist and historian, only son of the preceding. Professor at the Collège de France and a member of the Academy. Born at Lyons in 1800; died at Pau in 1864.

ARAGO, DOMINIQUE FRANÇOIS. French astronomer and physicist. Born at Estagel, Perpignan, in 1786; died at Paris in 1853. He was professor of analytical geometry in the École Polytechnique, a member of the Institute, and a director of the Observatory in Paris.

AUGUSTINE, SAINT. Latin Church Father; converted to a holy life through the influence and prayers of his mother, Monica. Born at Tagaste, in Numidia, North Africa, A.D. 354; died at Hippo, near the present Tunis, A.D. 430. His voluminous theological and philosophical writings have exerted an immense influence on the Christian world. The best known of them are *The City of God* and his *Confessions*.

B

BANKS, SIR JOSEPH. English naturalist and explorer; president of the Royal Society for forty-one years. Born in London, 1743; died in 1820. His herbarium and library are in the British Museum.

BANVILLE, THÉODORE DE. French poet and author. Born at Moulins in 1823; died in Paris, 1891. His most successful play *Gringoire* was translated into English and acted in England and America.

BAUR, FERDINAND CHRISTIAN. German Biblical critic, professor of theology at the University of Tübingen, and the leader of the Tübingen School of New Testament exegesis. Strauss was one of his pupils. Born in 1792, near Canstatt; died in Tübingen, 1860.

BERNARD, CLAUDE. French physiologist, member of the Institute; held the chair of physiology at the Sorbonne. Born at Saint-Julien in 1813; died in Paris, 1878.

BERT, PAUL. French physiologist and politician. He was professor of physiology at Paris, and a member of the Academy of Sciences. Under the administration of Gambetta, he was minister of pubic instruction and displayed the utmost hostility to the Catholic Church and all religious education. Born at Auxerre in 1833; died, 1886, at Hanoi, where he had been sent as resident-general.

BERTHELOT, MARCELLIN. French chemist and statesman. Wrote voluminously on chemistry; and was also minister of public instruction, minister of foreign affairs, professor of organic chemistry at the Collège de France, and perpetual secretary of the Academy of Sciences in succession to Pasteur. Born in Paris, 1827; died in Paris, 1907.

BERTRAND, JOSEPH. French mathematician, and member of the Institute and Academy of Sciences; taught at the Collège de France. Author of several noted mathematical books. Born at Paris in 1822; died there in 1900.

BIOT, JEAN BAPTISTE. French physicist, professor at the Collège de France. Aided Arago in measuring an arc of the meridian. The Rumford medal was awarded to him for his researches into polarized light. Born in Paris, 1774; died there, 1862.

BOSCOVICH, RUGGIERO. Jesuit mathematician and astronomer. Was professor at the Roman College; also taught in the University of Pavia. Born, an Italian, at Ragusa in 1711; died, 1787.

BOSSUET, JACQUES BÉNIGNE. Preacher, historian, orator, and controversial writer of the Church in France. He was for a time—1670 to 1681—tutor to the Dauphin, subsequently Louis XV. His funeral orations are regarded as French classics and have scarcely if ever been surpassed in the literature of French prose. Born in Dijon, 1627; died, 1704.

BOURGEOIS, LÉON. French statesman; minister of the exterior and president of the senate; the first French delegate at the Hague conference. Awarded Nobel Peace Prize in 1920. Born in Paris, 1851; died in 1925.

BOURGET, PAUL. One of the most productive and successful of modern French novelists and critics, and in later years a writer of several books of travel. He became a member of the French Academy in 1894. Born in Amiens, 1852.

BRAHE, TYCHO. Danish astronomer. The Danish king built and equipped an observatory for him on a little island north of Copenhagen. Subsequently he carried on his astronomical labors in Prague. There he had for an associate the celebrated astronomer Kepler. Born at Knudstrup, 1546; died in Prague, 1601.

BRUCKER, JOHANN. German historian and philosopher; author of many learned works. Born at Augsburg in 1696; died in 1770.

BRUNETIÈRE, FERDINAND. French writer and literary critic, member of the French Academy, and editor of the *Revue des Deux Mondes.* Born at Toulon in 1849; died, 1906.

BÜCHNER, LUDWIG. German physician and scientific philosopher. Lecturer in the University of Tübingen. He was noted as a popularizer of Darwinism. Born at Darmstadt in 1824; died, 1899.

BUNSEN, CHRISTIAN, BARON VON. Prussian diplomatist and scholar. Secretary to the Prussian embassy; ambassador to Rome, and later, to England and Switzerland. Born in Waldeck, 1791; died in 1860.

C

CALIXTUS I., SAINT. Pope from 217 to 222. Martyred A.D. 222. Constructor of the catacombs which bear his name on the Appian Way at Rome.

CAUCHY, AUGUSTIN. French mathematician, professor at the Collège de France and the University of Turin, and a member of the Institute. Recipient of the *grand prix* of the Institute and author of many important works; twenty-seven volumes of which were published. Born in Paris, 1789; died at Sceaux in 1857.

CHALLEMEL-LACOUR, PAUL. French statesman, journalist, professor of philosophy, prefect of the Rhone, senator, ambassador to Berne and London, minister of foreign affairs, and president of the senate. Born at Avranches, 1827; died in Paris, 1896.

CHRYSOSTOM, SAINT JOHN. One of the Greek Fathers of the Church. In A.D. 398 he was appointed bishop of Constantinople. He lived extremely frugally and denounced from the pulpit fearlessly the luxury and immorality of the age. This made him many enemies and he was deposed and twice exiled from the city. He was at last banished to the very extremity of the desert and compelled to go there on foot. He died on the way in 407. His sermons, commentaries, and epistles are of great value to the Church. He was known for his eloquent oratory, and his name in Greek signifies "the golden-mouthed." Born at Antioch about A.D. 345; died, A.D. 407.

CICERO, MARCUS TULLIUS. Probably the greatest orator of the ancient world, whose forensic powers were a great political force in Roman history. His orations, philosophical essays, and letters to Atticus, his "second self," are models of perfect Latin. Born at Arpinum, 106 B.C.; assassinated near Formiae, 43 B.C.

CIRCE. Greek mythological sorceress who lived on the island Æsa, and gave travelers a beverage which transformed them into animals. Supposed to have changed Odysseus' companions into swine.

COCHIN, PIERRE AUGUSTIN. French writer; author of many religious, pedagogical, and sociological works. Member of the Academy of Sciences. Born at Paris in 1823; died at Versailles in 1872.

COMTE, AUGUSTE. French philosopher of positivism. In 1830 he began the publication of his *Course of Positive Philosophy*, the sixth and last volume of which appeared in 1842. Straitened circumstances forced him to seek financial aid from John Stuart Mill, Grote, and others. He was regarded by many as the founder of a new religion, that of Humanity. Born at Montpellier, 1798; died in 1857.

COPERNICUS, NIKOLAUS The founder of modern astronomy. His great work on the revolution of the heavenly bodies was completed in 1530, but not published till thirteen years later. Its cardinal truth was that the sun is the center of our system and the earth and planets revolve around it. Born at Thorn, in Prussian Poland, 1473; died, at Frauenburg, Prussia, 1543.

COPPÉE, FRANÇOIS. French poet and novelist; member of the French Academy. Known as the poet of the common people because of his subject choice. Born in Paris, 1842; died in Paris, 1908.

CROMPTON, SAMUEL. Englishman, inventor of the "spinning jenny," which was brought into use about 1779. Born in Lancashire in 1753; died at Bolton in 1827.

CULLEN, DR. WILLIAM. Scottish physician and chemist. Born at Hamilton, Scotland, in 1710; died near Edinburgh, 1790. Lectured extensively in Glasgow and Edinburgh; author of several valuable medical works.

CURETON, WILLIAM. English orientalist, noted for his knowledge of Syriac and Arabic languages, and an expert in ancient manuscripts. He was the assistant keeper of the British Museum manuscripts. Born at Westbury in 1808; died in 1864.

CUVIER, GEORGES. French naturalist, whose great book on the *Animal Kingdom* was for many years the standard book on zoölogy. He was made a Baron by Louis Philippe. Born at Montbéliard in 1769; died in Paris, 1832.

D

DARWIN, CHARLES. Founder of Darwinism and author of the *Origin of Species*, *The Descent of Man*, etc. Born at Schrewsbury, 1809; died in 1882, and was buried in Westminster Abbey.

DESCARTES, RENÉ. French philosopher and scientist whose speculative thought and mathematical work exerted an immense influence. Although born at La Haye, in Touraine (1596), he resided principally in Holland, and died at Stockholm, Sweden, in 1650, where he had been invited by Queen Christina.

DIOCLETIAN, GAIUS VALERIUS. Roman emperor (284-305). Until A.D. 303 Diocletian had protected the Christians, but Galerius, one of his administrative coadjutors, then persuaded him to issue an edict against them. The persecution was severe. In A.D. 305 Diocletian abdicated in favor of Galerius and retired to his palace at Salona on the Dalmatian coast, where he devoted himself to gardening. Born at Dioclea, Dalmatia (whence his name Diocletian), A.D. 245; died at Salona, A.D. 313.

DONOSO CORTÉS, JUAN. Spanish politician, diplomat, and writer. An eloquent defender of the Christian religion and the Catholic Church. Descendant of Hernando Cortés, the *conquistador*. Officer of the Legion of Honor. Born in Estremadura, 1809; died at Paris in 1853.

DU CAMP, MAXIME. French author and traveler. His *Souvenirs Littéraires* in two volumes contain much information about contemporary writers. Born in Paris, 1822; died in Paris, 1894.

DUCIS, JEAN FRANÇOIS. French dramatic poet. He adapted Hamlet and other Shakespearean plays to the French stage; member of the French Academy. Born at Versailles in 1733; died there in 1816.

DUFAURE, JULES ARMAND. French orator and statesman. He was minister of the interior, minister of justice, member of the French Academy, and senator. Born at Saujon in 1798; died at Paris in 1881.

DUMAS, JEAN BAPTISTE. French chemist, perpetual secretary of the Academy of Sciences, member of the Senate and French Academy. He was a prolific writer; the author of many important works, and organizer in France of an admirable system of agricultural instruction. Born at Alais in 1800; died at Cannes in 1884.

E

ECKSTEIN, FERDINAND, BARON DE. French publicist and philosopher of Danish origin. Born at Altona in 1790; died at Paris in 1861. A convert to Catholicism and a talented author of numerous works, some of which are: *Des Jésuites, De l'Europe,* and *De l'Espagne.*

ELIE DE BEAUMONT, JEAN-BAPTISTE. French geologist, professor at the Collége de France, and secretary of the Academy of Sciences; officer of the Legion of Honor. Born at Canon in 1798; died in 1874. Author of several volumes on geology.

EULER, LEONHARD. Swiss mathematician and author of many works on this subject. The Empress Catherine I of Russia invited him in 1727 to St. Petersburg, where he became professor of physics in 1730. During the latter part of his life, he became wholly blind, but made his elaborate calculations mentally. Born at Basel, 1707; died at St. Petersburg, 1783.

F

FABER, FREDERICK WILLIAM. An English priest and author of some of the most beautiful hymns in the English language. He was at first an Anglican rector, but in 1845 went over, as Newman had done, into the Catholic Church. He founded a religious community named Wilfridians, which was ultimately merged into the Oratory of St. Philip Neri with Newman as superior. He himself was superior of the branch at Brompton. Born in Calverly, 1814; died at Brompton, 1863.

FABRE, JEAN HENRI. French entomologist, born at Aveyron in 1823. Lived an extremely secluded life, devoted to studying the history, habits, and instincts of insects. Due to his researches, he was an opponent of the theory of evolution. A member of the Institute and author of several books concerning his studies. Died at Sérignan in 1915.

FAYE, HERVÉ AUGUSTE. French astronomer. Discovered, in 1843, a new comet, which was named after him. Born in 1814; died in 1902.

FÉNELON, FRANÇOIS. French archbishop, orator, and writer, favorite disciple of Bossuet. Wrote *Télémaque*, also: *Treatise on the Education of Girls*, which guided French thought on this question all through the eighteenth century. Born in Périgord, 1651; died at Cambrai, 1715.

FÉVAL, PAUL. French novelist and dramatist. Became a convert to the Catholic Church and defended it vigorously in *Les Jésuites, Pas de Divorce*, etc. His complete works fill many volumes. Born at Rennes in 1817; died at Paris, 1887.

FLAUBERT, GUSTAVE. French novelist and stylist. Born at Rouen, in 1821; died near Rouen, 1880. Traveled extensively with his friend Maxime du Camp in the Orient. At one time he was indicted for an offense against morals following the publishing of *Madame Bovary*.

FLOURENS, PIERRE. French physiologist and author, perpetual secretary of the Academy of Sciences, and a member of the French Academy. His best known book is on *Human Longevity* (1854) which enjoyed great popularity. Born near Béziers, 1794; died near Paris in 1867.

FRANCIS, SAINT, OF ASSISI. Founder of the Franciscan Order of mendicant Friars. One of the holiest examples of self-renunciation; received the Stigmata. Scores of biographies have been written of this "Cavalier of Christ," and further mention of him here is needless. He was canonized by Pope Gregory IX in 1228, two years after his death. Born in Assisi about 1182; died at Assisi in 1226.

FRANCIS, SAINT, DE SALES. Doctor of the Church and bishop; devotional writer and preacher in the Catholic Church. Founded the "Order of the Visitation." His chief work, *Introduction to the Devout Life*, is known throughout all Christendom. Canonized in 1665. Born near Annécy in 1567; died at Lyons in 1622.

G

GALILEO, GALILEI. Italian astronomer and physicist. Incurred the censure of the Pope because of his attempts to conform the Copernican theory with Scripture. Born at Pisa in 1564; died near Florence, 1642.

GERDIL, HYACINTHE. French cardinal and philosophical writer. Born in Savoy, France, in 1718; died at Rome in 1802.

GLEYRE, CHARLES. Swiss artist. His two most famous works are "Le Soir" or "Lost Illusions," now in the Louvre, and "The Separation of the Apostles." Born at Chevilly, in 1808; died at Paris in 1874. In 1840, his painting entitled "St. John, inspired by the apocalyptic vision" created a sensation in artistic circles.

GRATRY, AUGUSTE ALPHONSE, ABBÉ. French Catholic theologian and writer. Born at Lille in 1805; died at Montreux, Switzerland, in 1872. Professor of moral philosophy at the Sorbonne, and a member of the French Academy.

GUIBERT, JOSEPH. French Catholic prelate; bishop of Viviers, Archbishop of Tours, Archbishop of Paris, and finally created a Cardinal by Pope Pius IX in 1873. He was the author of several religious and pastoral books and was responsible for the erection of a basilica at Montmartre as well as founder of a free university for Catholics at Paris. Born at Aix in 1802; died at Paris in 1886.

GUIZOT, FRANÇOIS PIERRE. French historian and statesman. Professor of modern history at the Sorbonne. He was secretary-general under Louis XVIII, minister of public instruction, and prime minister under Louis Philippe. The revolution of 1848 ended his political career. He wrote many volumes of history and memoirs. Born at Nîmes in 1787; died in Normandy, 1874.

H

HAECKEL, ERNST. German biologist; professor of comparative anatomy and director of zoölogy at the University of Jena. A final summary of his speculative views of man's position in the scale of being and of the evolution of organic life is contained in his *Riddle of the Universe.* (English translation, 1900.) Born at Potsdam in 1834; died at Jena in 1919.

HANNO. Carthaginian navigator, who about 500 B.C. sailed through the Straits of Gibraltar to the west coast of Africa and published an account of his voyage, which is still extant in a Greek translation.

HARNACK, ADOLF VON. One of the greatest living Protestant theological writers and Biblical critics. Born in Dorpat, 1851.

HEGEL, GEORG WILHELM. German philosopher; professor at Erlangen, Berlin, and Heidelberg. A great lover of the classics and author of several philosophical works; famous as the inventor of the Hegelian system of philosophy and noted for his lectures on aesthetics. Born at Stuttgart in 1770; died in 1831.

HEINE, HEINRICH. German lyric poet, born of Jewish parents, whose songs are among the sweetest ever written, and whose *Travel Pictures* have perennial charm. In wit and satire he is unsurpassed. He was blind, and his last years were of great suffering. Born at Düsseldorf in 1797; died in Paris, 1856. He renounced his infidelity before his death.

HERMANN, CHARLES. German philosopher. Born at Frankfurt on the ·Main in 1804; died at Goettingen in 1855. Interested in both philosophy and history, and combined these two in his methods of writing. Greek and Latin antiquity were his first interests.

HERMANN, JOHANN. German philosopher. Born at Leipzig in 1772; died there in 1848. Studied at Leipzig and Jena. Member of the French Academy. Author of many works on polemics, mythology, metrics, and grammar; also edited the tragedies of Aeschylus.

HIPPARCHUS. Greek astronomer and mathematician; labored in Rhodes. He invented trigonometry, discovered the precession of the equinoxes, the eccentricity of the solar orbit, the inequalities of the moon's motion, and made a catalogue of 1800 stars. Born at Nicaea in Bithynia about 146; lived to 126 B.C.

HIPPOCRATES. Renowned physician of antiquity. A contemporary of Socrates and Plato. Born on the island of Cos, 460 B.C. Died at Larissa, at a very advanced age, living, according to some writers, more than a hundred years.

HOUSSAYE, HENRY. French historian and critic; member of the French Academy. His history of Napoleon's last campaigns, *1814* and *1815*, are works of great value. Born at Paris, 1848; died there in 1911.

HUMBOLDT, ALEXANDER, BARON VON. German naturalist, traveler, and explorer, especially in South America. Born at Berlin in 1769; died in 1859. In 1808 he settled in Paris, and for 21 years occupied himself with studying and describing the scientific results of his travels. Subsequently he wrote his famous *Kosmos*, a physical description of the universe.

HUXLEY, THOMAS HENRY. English biologist tending strongly toward an evolutionistic view of life. Liberated the English anatomical school from the deductive method of reasoning in biology by his final disposition of the "archetype." Born at Ealing in 1825; died, 1895.

I

IBSEN, HENRIK. Norwegian poet, satirist, and dramatist of the extreme realistic school, whose plays—*A Doll's House, Hedda Gabler,* and *Peer Gynt,* to name a few—have excited much controversy, but have had no lack of admirers and defenders. Born at Skien in 1828. Through the influence of the violinist, Ole Bull, he became director of the theater in Bergen. Lived chiefly in Rome, Dresden, and Munich, but finally returned to Christiania, where he died in 1906.

IGNATIUS OF LOYOLA, SAINT. Founder of the Society of Jesus. Served as a Spanish soldier, and while recovering from a wound received at the siege of Pampeluna in 1521, became converted to a higher life. In 1534, he established the Jesuit Society, confirmed by Pope Paul III in 1540. If Ignatius had never founded the Society of Jesus, he would still be remembered universally for his contribution to the world's literature in his work *The Spiritual Exercises*, completed in 1548. Born at the castle of Loyola in Spain, 1491; died at Rome in 1556.

J

JANIN, JULES French dramatic critic of the *Journal des Débuts* for nearly forty years; member of the French Academy. Renowned for his sparkling and witty style. Born at St. Etienne in 1804; died near Paris, 1874.

JEROME, SAINT. One of Latin Church Fathers. Born at Strido, near the frontiers of Dalmatia, about A.D. 340. Educated at Rome. Visited the Orient and became an ascetic, living in the desert near Antioch, where he learned Hebrew from a converted Jew. Returning in A.D. 382 to Rome, he undertook the revision of the old Latin version of the Bible. In A.D. 385 he left Rome and founded a monastery in Bethlehem, where he labored for 34 years and made a translation of the whole Bible, known as the Vulgate. He died at Bethlehem in A.D. 420.

JOERGENSEN, JENS. Danish writer, whose books, especially since his conversion to Catholicism and his residence in Assisi, have been very popular and translated into many languages. Born in 1866. Author of *Lourdes*, considered to be the best authenticated book extant on the subject.

JOUBERT, JOSEPH. French moralist and critic. Born at Montignac in 1754; died at Paris in 1824. His *Thoughts* (*Pensées*) has been extensively translated and quoted.

JOUFFROY, THÉODORE. French philosopher at the Collège de France and librarian of the University of Paris. Born at Pontets (Jura) in 1796; died at Paris, 1842.

JUSTIN, MARTYR. Christian apologist; born of pagan parents at Neapolis, in Palestine, about A.D. 100. His first *Apology* for the Christians he addressed to the Roman Emperor Antoninus Pius; his second to Marcus Aurelius, pleading for a more humane treatment of them. He himself suffered martyrdom at Rome about A.D. 163.

K

KEPLER, JOHANN. One of the chief founders of modern astronomy. Born at Württemberg, Germany, in 1571. In 1601, having gone to Prague as an assistant to Tycho Brahe, he succeeded him, upon his death, as imperial astronomer. In 1609 he promulgated the first of his three famous "Laws" that the planets travel in ellipses about the sun, whose center is a focus. The other two "Laws" were discovered shortly after. It was Kepler who, as he discovered these modes of planetary motion, exclaimed reverently: "My God, I think Thy laws after Thee." Died at Ratisbon in 1630.

L

LA BRUYÈRE, JEAN. French moralist and essayist; famous for his literary style and the composition of maxims and reflections (*Les Caractères*). Elected to the French Academy in 1693. Born at Paris in 1645; died in 1696.

LACORDAIRE, JEAN BAPTISTE. French pulpit orator and the restorer of the old Order of Dominicans. He preached for several years in Notre Dame, Paris, drawing immense crowds by his extraordinary eloquence and fervent piety. In 1860, he became a member of the French Academy, where Guizot received him. A complete edition of his works fills six volumes. Many biographies of him have been written. Born in Côte d' Or in 1802; died at Sorrèze, 1861.

LAMARTINE, ALPHONSE. One of the greatest of French poets, as well as an historian and statesman; a member of the French Academy. At the outbreak of the revolution in 1848, he was one of the commanding figures. Born at Mâcon in 1790; died in 1869.

LAPLACE, PIERRE, MARQUIS DE. French mathematician, and one of the world's greatest astronomers; author of the *Mécanique Céleste* and promoter of the famous nebular hypothesis. Laplace's *Equation* in connection with the theory of attractions and other discoveries gave him undying fame. He was made a peer by Louis XVIII and marquis in 1817; for years was president of the Academy of Sciences. Born in Normandy in 1749; died at Paris in 1827.

LAVOISIER, ANTOINE. French chemist and member of the Academy of Sciences; one of the principal founders of modern chemistry. He perished by the guillotine in the reign of terror. His request for a reprieve of a few days that he might finish some important experiments was refused. Born at Paris in 1743; died in 1794.

LEIBNITZ, GOTTFRIED WILHELM. German philosopher, mathematician, and inventor of the *Differential and Integral Calculus* published in 1684. He was for many years counsellor and librarian to the Duke of Brunswick at Hanover, and during that period of his life, wrote the philosophical works which have profoundly affected the thought of his posterity. Born at Leipzig in 1646; died at Hanover in 1716.

LEO I, SAINT, SURNAMED THE GREAT. With his pontificate (A. D. 440-461) began the promulgation of papal encyclicals and decrees. He induced the invader Attila, "the Scourge of God," in 452 to spare the city of Rome.

LEO XIII, POPE. A pontiff (1878-1903) of great piety, sagacity, and literary accomplishments. Was nuncio to Brussels, Belgium, Archbishop of Perugia, and Cardinal-priest, and was finally elected to the Papacy in 1878. Born at Carpineto in 1810; died at Rome in 1903.

LEOPARDI, GIACOMO, COUNT. Italian writer, brilliant scholar, and poet, but a cripple rendered extremely melancholy by his sufferings and poverty. He was a profound pessimist. His works have been published in six volumes and his poems have been translated into various languages. Born at Recanati, Italy, in 1798; died at Naples in 1837.

LE PLAY, PIERRE. French economist and engineer; appointed by Napoleon to organize the Exhibition of 1855; prominently connected with the London Exhibition of 1862, and that of Paris in 1867. While editor of the fortnightly review, *La Réforme Sociale*, he became the originator of one of the main schools of sociology. Born in southern France in 1806; died at Paris in 1882.

LEVERRIER, URBAIN. French astronomer; the planet Neptune was discovered through his calculations (1846). Member of the Academy of Sciences, and director of the Paris Observatory. Born at St. Lô in Normandy, 1811; died at Paris in 1877.

L'HERMITE, FRANÇOIS. French poet and dramatist, with the nom de plume Tristan. Member of the French Academy. Born in La Marche, 1601; died, 1655. Author of *Mariamne*, whose success was said to equal that of Corneille's *Cid*.

LITTRÉ, MAXIMILIEN. French lexicographer, physician, and philosopher. Born in Paris, 1801; died in Paris, 1881. He was for many years a great admirer of Auguste Comte, the founder of positivism, and after Comte's death was the head of the positivist school. His greatest work is his well-known *Dictionary of the French Language*. He made several translations, among which were *The works of Hippocrates* and Strauss' *Life of Jesus*. He was also a famous scientist and linguist, and a member of the French Academy. Shortly before he died, he was baptized in the Catholic Church; and at death buried with her rites.

LUCRETIUS. Roman poet. Little is known of his life, but a doubtful tradition tells us that he was insane and committed suicide at the age of forty-three. His great work *De Rerum Natura*, (On the Nature of Things), is a poem of more than 7,000 hexameters, expounding the philosophy of Epicurus. Born at Rome, about 98 B.C.; died in 55 B.C.

M

MAETERLINCK, MAURICE. Belgian dramatist and poet. Born at Ghent in 1862. Inclined toward mysticism. *The Blue Bird* is one of his best known plays.

MAISTRE, COUNT JOSEPH DE. A political, philosophical, and theological French writer, born at Chambéry in 1754. He left France for Turin and became ambassador from the King of Sardinia to St. Petersburg, and subsequently a minister of State. Died at Turin in 1821. *Du Pape* and *Soirées de St. Pétersbourg* are considered his masterpieces.

MALEBRANCHE, NICOLAS. French philosopher of the Cartesian school. Born at Paris in 1638. After studying theology at the Sorbonne, he became a Catholic priest. Honorary member of the Academy of Sciences. Died in Paris, 1715. His principle work was his *Search for Truth*, an attempt to harmonize Descartes' philosophy with revealed religion.

MANNING, CARDINAL, HENRY EDWARD. English Cardinal. He was for more than fifteen years a clergyman of the Church of England, the Archdeacon of Chichester, and a leader of the High Church party. In 1850 he left the Anglican Church, and in the following year was ordained a Catholic priest. In 1865 he became Archbishop of Westminster, and was made a cardinal in 1875. Born at Totteridge in 1808; died in London, 1892.

MARCUS AURELIUS. Roman Emperor and Stoic philosopher; during his reign he was consistently hostile to Christianity. His great literary work, written in Greek, was the well-known *Meditations of Marcus Aurelius*. Born at Rome, A.D. 121; died in Pannonia, near the present Vienna, A.D. 180.

MICHELET, JULES. French historian. Under Louis Philippe he was appointed chief of the historical division of the National Archives. After the Coup d' État of Napoleon III in 1851, he was removed from his position in the Archives and from his professorial chair. On account of his brilliant style, as well as his erudition, his *Histoire de France* (19 vols.), and also his book on the *Revolution* (7 vols.), enjoyed great popularity. His complete works fill forty volumes. Born at Paris in 1798; died at Hyères in 1874.

MILTON, JOHN. The eminent English poet, author of *Paradise Lost, Ode on the Nativity*, and others, as well as a polemical and political prose-writer and defender of liberty. He needs no other mention here except the bare facts that he was born in London in 1608; was educated at Christ's College, Cambridge; became totally blind in 1652; was imprisoned under Charles II; was neglected by his daughters; and died in London, 1674.

MONICA, SAINT. The mother of St. Augustine, famous for her piety and devotion to her son, having converted him from a dissolute life after seventeen years of prayer for him. Born at Tagaste, N. Africa, in 333; died at Ostia in 387. Her feast day is May 4.

MONTAIGNE, MICHEL DE. French essayist. His well-known *Essays* have been translated into all languages and exerted a profound and generally beneficial influence on the literary world. Born at Dordogne in 1533; died in 1592.

MONTALEMBERT, CHARLES, COMTE DE. French historian and statesman, and brilliant champion of the Catholic Church. His great and monumental work, *The Monks of the West*, is a classic. He was a member of the Legislative Assembly and of the French Academy. Born at London in 1810; died at Paris in 1870.

MORE, SIR THOMAS. English statesman. Born at London in 1478. Speaker of the House of Commons and, after the fall of Wolsey, became Lord Chancellor of England, the first layman to hold this office. Acquired the enmity of Henry VIII on account of his opposition to the former's ideas concerning the royal supremacy of kings to the Church and divorce; committed to the Tower, accused of high treason, and beheaded in 1535. *Utopia* is his famous literary work.

MURATORI, LUDOVICO. Italian scholar and historian. Born at Vignola, Italy, 1672; died in 1750. Ordained priest in 1695. Was Prefect of the Ambrosian library at Milan and librarian at Modena; also wrote the history of Italy from the birth of Christ to 1750. Published in 1740 a *Summary of the Canonical Books of the New Testament*, which was written probably in the time of Marcus Aurelius.

N

NERI, PHILIP, SAINT. The "Apostle of Rome"; Italian Catholic churchman who devoted himself in Rome especially to the relief of the poor and sick; also to the teaching of children. In 1575 he founded an order known as the Congregation, or Fathers, of the Oratory, composed of secular priests whose only common bond was charity. He was the first to introduce the musical selections known as "oratorios," because performed in an oratory. He was canonized in 1622. Born at Florence, 1515; died at Rome in 1595.

NEWMAN, JOHN HENRY, CARDINAL. English cardinal. His departure from the Church of England and entry into the Catholic Church in 1845 was an epoch-making event, requiring no comment here. He established the Oratory near Birmingham as well as the London Oratory. Created a Cardinal by Leo XIII in 1879. He was the author of the world-famous classic, *Apologia Pro Vita Sua* (1864), *Idea of a University*, the *Grammar of Assent*, *Loss and Gain*, *Tracts for the Times*, and several hymns, including *Lead, Kindly Light*, and poems of rare merit. Born in London, 1801; died at Edgbaston in 1890.

NEWTON, SIR ISAAC. An intellectual giant in mathematical astronomy and optics. Born at Woolsthorpe, England, in 1642; died at Kensington in 1727. The discoverer of the law of universal gravitation. He was knighted by Queen Anne in 1705, and was president of the Royal Society from 1703 until his death. He is buried in Westminster Abbey.

NICOLAS, AUGUSTE. French apologist and judge. His best known work is *Philosophical Studies on Christianity* in four volumes, which is still highly esteemed. Born at Bordeaux in 1807; died in 1888.

NIETZSCHE, FRIEDRICH. German philosopher of considerable influence on modern thought. He was violently anti-Christian, a hater of the idea of Christian humility, and an advocate of the superman in the struggle for existence. He became insane eleven years before his death. Born, near Lützen in 1844; died in 1900.

P

PASCAL, BLAISE. French mathematician, philosopher, and writer on moral and theological subjects. Author of the *Lettres provinciales* and *Pensées*. He entered the monastery of Port Royal, where he became allied with the Jansenist cause as opposed to the Jesuits. Born at Clermont-Ferrand in 1623; died at Paris in 1662.

PASTEUR, LOUIS. Illustrious French chemist and physicist, whose fame is universal. He was the founder of the Pasteur Institute. Details of his achievements and character have been given in the foregoing pages. Born at Dôle in 1822; died near St. Cloud in 1895.

PELLICO, SILVIO. Italian dramatist who was imprisoned for his liberal and revolutionary views, first in Venice and then in the fortress of Spielberg in Austria, from 1820 to 1830. On his release, he wrote his famous *My Prisons*, an Italian classic (English translation), and the play *Francesca da Rimini*. Born at Saluzzo in 1788; died at Turin in 1854.

PETRONIUS, (PETRONIUS ARBITER). Roman satirist of the court of Nero, famous for his wit, elegant manners, and lavish extravagance. He was, however, made consul and governed the province of Bithynia wisely and well. He was accused by Nero's favorite, Tigellinus, of conspiracy and committed suicide by opening his veins about A.D. 66. He is supposed to have been the author of the licentious work, known as the *Satirae*, depicting the vices of Roman life.

PITRA, JEAN BAPTISTE. Made French Cardinal by Pius IX. Author of the Hymnography of the Greek Church, etc. Born in 1812; died in 1889.

PIUS I. Pope from about A.D. 142 to 156. Now a canonized saint. Born about A.D. 90.

PIUS IX. The well-known "Pio Nono." He was obliged to flee to Gaeta at the outbreak of the revolutionary movements in Italy in 1848. A French force restored him to Rome and defended him there till 1870, when the army of Victor Emanuel took the city. In 1854, Pius IX promulgated the doctrine of the Immaculate Conception of the Blessed Virgin, and in 1870 the doctrine of Papal infallibility in matters of faith and morals. Born near Ancona in 1792; died at Rome in 1878. Pope from 1846 to 1878.

PLATO. Ancient Greek philosopher, pupil of Socrates. Born about 427 B.C., died at Athens about 347 B.C. Author of the *Dialogues*, the *Republic*, *Phaedo*, and other works.

PLUTARCH. Greek biographer, whose *Parallel Lives*, of 46 famous Greeks and Romans forms a gallery of literary portraits of immense value. He wrote also 60 other works grouped under the name of *Morals*. Born at Chaeronea, about A.D. 46; died in A.D. 120.

POINCARÉ, JULES HENRI. French mathematician and physicist. Born at Nancy in 1854; died in 1912. Professor at the University of Paris.

PRÉVOST-PARADOL, LUCIEN. French writer, orator, and politician; editor of the *Journal des Débats* and member of the French Academy. Author of several volumes on literary subjects; one of the best known is his *La France Nouvelle*. In 1870 he was appointed French minister to Washington, and committed suicide there a month after his arrival. Born at Paris in 1829; died in 1870.

PROMETHEUS. Greek legendary hero, friend and benefactor of mankind, who stole fire from heaven, in punishment for which he was chained by Zeus to a rock. An eagle came there every day to gnaw his liver, which was restored every night. Hercules finally killed the eagle and released him. Aeschylus and Shelley wrote dramas on the subject.

PTOLEMY. Founder of the Ptolemaic system of the universe, which prevailed for 1400 years, until replaced by that of Copernicus. He was also a geographer and mathematician of great ability. Born at Ptolemais Hermü, at Alexandria, where he made astronomical observations from A.D. 127 to 151.

PYTHAGORAS. Greek philosopher of the sixth century B.C. He was born probably in Samos. He left behind him no writings, but his philosophy has been more or less imperfectly handed down to us. Inventor of the Pythagorean theory in geometry. He is thought to have lived from about 570 to 500 B.C. and is said to have starved himself to death at Metapontium in Italy.

Q

QUATREMÈRE DE QUINCY, ANTOINE. French archaeologist and art critic. His principal work was a *Dictionary of Architecture*. During the French Revolution, he was condemned as a royalist, but escaped. He was director of arts and public monuments, and perpetual secretary of the Academy of Fine Arts. Born in 1755; died at Paris in 1849.

QUINET, EDGAR. Indefatigable French writer on philosophical and historical subjects. At the age of 24, he came into notice by his translation from the German of Herder's *Philosophy of History* (1827). He was sent by the government on a special mission to Greece; became professor of foreign literature in the University at Lyons and later at the Collège de France in Paris. He was exiled from France by Napoleon III, whom he had opposed, returning only after the fall of the empire. His complete works fill 28 volumes. Born at Bourg in 1803; died at Versailles in 1875.

R

RABELAIS, FRANÇOIS. French author. In his youth he became a monk, but left the monastic life; studied medicine and took his doctor's degree. He published in several volumes his famous satirical works *Gargantua* and *Pantagruel*, the sale of which was for a time forbidden. Under a mask of coarse buffoonery, he displayed profound learning and deep thought. Born in Touraine, about 1483 (some say 1495); died in Paris in 1553.

RACINE, JEAN BAPTISTE. French tragic dramatist and poet; friend of Molière and La Fontaine, and a member of the French Academy. Author of the drama, *Andromaque*, considered his masterpiece. Born at La Ferté-Milon in 1693; died, a devout Catholic, at Paris in 1699.

RAVIGNAN, de GUSTAVE FRANÇOIS. French Jesuit and a distinguished pulpit orator. Preached in Notre Dame for ten years. Born at Bayonne in 1795; died at Paris in 1858.

RÉMUSAT, CHARLES, COMTE DE. French writer and statesman. Secretary of the interior and minister of foreign affairs under Thiers. Wrote on philosophy and history. Born at Paris in 1797; died there in 1875.

RENAN, ERNEST. French historian, philologist, philosopher, and critic of the Gospels, much of whose work and character has been referred to in the foregoing pages. He was a member of the French Academy. Born at Tréguier, Brittany, in 1823; died at Paris in 1892.

RIGAULT, ANGE-HIPPOLYTE. French writer, historian, and critic. Editor of the *Journal des Débats*. Professor at the Collège de France. Born at St. Germain in 1821; died at Evereux in 1858.

ROBESPIERRE, MAXIMILIEN. One of the leading revolutionists in the French reign of terror. A sincere, but pitiless, fanatic. Born at Arras in 1758; perished on the guillotine in 1794.

ROLAND, MADAME. A gifted and highly educated French revolutionist, who, herself, died on the guillotine. Her salon was the headquarters of the Girondists. Her *Mémoires* was first printed in 1820. Born at Paris in 1754; died at Paris in 1793.

ROSSI, JEAN-BAPTISTE DE. Italian archæologist, who made many important discoveries in the Roman catacombs and forum and wrote books on the subject. Born at Paris in 1822; died at Castelgandolfo in 1894.

ROUSSEAU, JEAN JACQUES. French philosopher, born at Geneva, whose influence upon the world has been incalculably great, first by the revolutionary ideas of education which he promulgated, and secondly by the simple, clear, and wonderfully effective style in which he expressed them. Author of *La Nouvelle Héloïse, Émile, Confessions*, and others. Born at Geneva in 1712; died near Paris in 1778.

ROYER-COLLARD, PIERRE. French statesman and philosopher. Professor of philosophy at the Sorbonne; president of the commission of public instruction, and president of the chamber of deputies. He was also a member of the French Academy. Born at Sompuis in 1763; died at Châteauvieux in 1845. His last words were, "There is nothing solid or substantial in the world except religious ideas."

RUYSCH, FREDERICK. Famous Dutch surgeon, and professor of anatomy at Amsterdam. He discovered a way to mumify dead bodies and kept it a secret; also discovered *membrane of Ruysch*, named after him. Peter the Great purchased his anatomical collection for 30,000 florins. Born at La Haye in 1638; died at Amsterdam in 1731.

S

SACY, DE, ANTOINE SILVESTRE, BARON. French Orientalist and linguist; professor of Persian in the Collège de France and founder of the Société Asiatique and of the study of Oriental languages in Europe. Translated the New Testament into Syriac, and many Arabic and Persian works into French. Became a member of the Chamber of Peers, and perpetual secretary of the Academy of Inscriptions. Born at Paris in 1758; died at Paris in 1838.

SAINTE-BEUVE, CHARLES. French critic; author of *Causeries* in the *Constitutionnel*; also articles in the *Revue des Deux Mondes* and other periodicals. He was a member of the French Academy, professor of French literature at Liège and of Latin poetry at the Collège de France. His studies or essays on famous personages number more than two hundred. His power of analysis, insight into character, and brilliant style made him one of the first *littérateurs* of the nineteenth century. Born at Boulogne-sur-Mer in 1804; died at Paris in 1869.

SAINT-PIERRE, BERNARDIN DE. French naturalist and writer. A government official at Mauritius, in the Isle de France, and author of the famous work *Paul et Virginie*, which has been translated into almost all languages. He was superintendent of the Jardin des Plantes at Paris and a member of the Institute. Born at Havre in 1737; died in 1814.

SCHERER, EDMOND. French theologian, critic, and literary historian.

Began life as a Protestant minister at Strasbourg, and became professor of theology at Geneva. Retired from the church and devoted himself to literature. Became chief literary critic and editor of *Le Temps*, and in 1875, senator. Born at Paris in 1815; died at Versailles in 1889.

SENECA, LUCIUS ANNÆUS. One of the most remarkable men of Roman antiquity; a Stoic philosopher, a famous writer on morals, and a great statesman. He was tutor to the youthful Nero and, during the latter's minority, Seneca with his friend Burrus, governed the empire. He became obnoxious to Nero, who ordered him to end his life. Accordingly, he opened his veins and bled to death. Born at Corduba, Spain, 4 B.C.; died A.D. 65.

SOPHOCLES. The greatest of Athenian dramatists and tragic poets. He was esteemed by his contemporaries as superior even to Aeschylus and Euripides. Author of the *Oedipus*. He wrote more than a hundred tragedies, only a few of which are extant. He was remarkable for personal beauty, and excelled in music and gymnastics. Born at Colonus, near Athens in 495 B.C.; died, 406 B.C.

SOREL, ALBERT. French historian, professor of diplomatic history at Paris, and a member of the French Academy. His principal work is *Europe and the French Revolution* in eight volumes. Born at Honfleur in 1842; died at Paris in 1906.

SPENCER, HERBERT. English philosopher of the new, evolutionary, scientific movement of the latter part of the nineteenth century. Born at Derby in 1820; died in 1903.

SPINOZA, BENEDICTUS. One of the greatest of European philosophers. Of Jewish origin, he was born at Amsterdam in 1632. He made his living by grinding lenses, and studied and wrote his pantheistic philosophy in his leisure hours. Died at the Hague in 1677.

STRAUSS, DAVID FRIEDRICH. German theologian and man of letters, whose *Life of Jesus* and *The Old and New Faith*, in which he propounds the mythical origin of much of the New Testament, are well known. Born at Ludwigsburg in 1808; died there in 1874.

SUETONIUS. Roman historian and biographer, and secretary to the Emperor Hadrian. His great work is his *The Lives of the Cæsars*, but he wrote also the Books of *Famous Orators* and *Famous Scholars* and lives of some of the Roman poets. He was a friend of the younger Pliny and went with him to Bithynia in A.D. 112. Born about A.D. 75; died about A.D. 160.

SULLY-PRUDHOMME, RENÉ. French poet. Born at Paris in 1839; died there in 1907. Elected a member of the French Academy; awarded the Nobel Prize in literature in 1901. His best known works are: *Les Solitudes, Les Destins,* and *Le Bonheur*.

SULPICIUS, PUBLIUS RUFUS. Roman orator and statesman, put to death by the party of Sulla in the Civil Wars. None of his orations are extant. Born 121 B.C.; died, 88 B.C.

T

TACITUS. Roman historian, an eloquent orator, and an intimate friend of Pliny the Younger. His marvelously condensed and forceful style has never been surpassed. His *Annals*, his biography of *Agricola*, and his *Germania* are classics. Born about A.D. 55; died about A.D. 117.

TAINE, HIPPOLYTE. French critic and historian. He was professor of the history of art in Paris and was made a member of the French Academy. Among his numerous works was his *Histoire de la Littérature Anglaise*, known in Great Britain and America, and *Les Origines de la France Contemporaine*. Born at Vouziers in 1828; died at Paris in 1893.

TERESA, SAINT. The great Saint of Spain, and a nun of the Carmelite Order, which she reformed and named Discalced Carmelites. Among her works are her remarkable *Autobiography, Letters, The Way to Perfection*, and *The Castle of the Soul*. Born at Avila in Castile in 1515; died at Alva in 1582.

TERTULLIAN. One of the Latin Fathers of the Church, considered second only to Augustine for his writing; possessed great learning, intellectual gifts, and piety. He wrote many powerful controversial works, chief of which was his *Defence of the Christians against the Nations*. Born at Carthage about A.D. 150. Date of his death unknown.

THIERRY, AUGUSTIN JACQUES. French historian and member of the Academy of Inscriptions. For the last thirty years of his life he was blind and paralyzed, yet continued his work to the last by the aid of secretaries. Born at Blois in 1795; died at Paris in 1856.

TISCHENDORF, FRIEDRICH VON. German Biblical scholar and professor of theology at the University of Leipzig. He traveled extensively in search of ancient manuscripts, and discovered at Mount Sinai the priceless *Codex Sinaiticus*. Born in Saxony in 1815; died at Leipzig in 1874.

TOCQUEVILLE, ALEXIS DE. French author and statesman. In 1831, he visited the United States, and in 1835 published his well-known *Democracy in America* (4 vols.) which had an enormous success. He entered the Chamber of Deputies in 1839 and became a member of the French Academy and the Academy of Sciences, and minister of foreign affairs. Born at Verneuil in 1805; died at Cannes in 1859.

TOLSTOI, COUNT LEO. Russian novelist and moral philosopher. Born at Yasnaya Polyana in 1828; died near his home, from which he had fled, in 1910. *War and Peace, Anna Karenina*, and *Resurrection* are considered his masterpieces.

TULLIA. The daughter of Cicero, dearly loved by him. Born at Rome in 78 B.C.; died at Tusculum in 43 B.C. at the age of 35. Upon her death, Cicero wrote his essay on *Consolation*.

V

VACHEROT, ÉTIENNE. French philosophical writer and professor of philosophy at the Sorbonne in Paris. This position he lost in 1852, because of his refusal to take the oath of allegiance to Napoleon III. Born at Langres in 1809; died at Paris in 1897.

VASARI, GIORGIO. Italian art-historian, architect, and painter. He wrote biographies of famous painters, sculptors, and architects, which are of great value and universally known. Studied under Michelangelo and Andrea del Sarto. Born at Arezzo in 1511; died at Florence in 1574.

VAUVENARGUES, LUC DE, MARQUIS. French philosopher and moralist; friend of Voltaire. He achieved fame by his first book, *Introduction to the Knowledge of the Mind*; and his *Reflections and Maxims* made him known and are still frequently quoted. Born at Aix in 1715; died at Paris in 1747, at the age of 32.

VEUILLOT, LOUIS. French journalist and author; editor of the *Univers*, and an ardent champion of the Catholic Church. The *Univers* was suppressed from 1860 to 1867 owing to its attacks on Napoleon III. Born at Boynes in 1813; died at Paris in 1883.

VIGNY, ALFRED DE, COUNT. French poet and dramatist. He was made a member of the French Academy in 1845. His complete works fill eight volumes. Born at Loches in 1799; died at Paris in 1863.

VINCENT DE PAUL, SAINT. French priest and founder of the Daughters of Charity. He devoted himself especially to the condition, physical and spiritual, of the convicts in the galleys. He organized and founded also the Congregation of Mission Priests; known as the Society of the Lazarists, and established two foundling hospitals in Paris. He was canonized in 1737. Born at Pouy in 1576; died at Paris in 1660. (The Society of St. Vincent de Paul was founded in 1833 by Frédéric Ozanam.)

VIRCHOW, RUDOLF. German pathologist, politician, and a professor of anatomy at Würzburg and Berlin. His great work was on *Cellular Pathology* (1858), but his writings were voluminous and treated almost every department of medicine. Born in Pomerania in 1821; died in 1902.

VOLTA, ALESSANDRO, COUNT. Italian physicist alluded to at some length in the preceding pages. The volt is named after him. He was director of the philosophy faculty at Padua. Born in Como in 1745; died at Como in 1827.

VOLTAIRE, FRANÇOIS AROUET DE. French dramatist, poet, satirist, and wit. The story of his checkered career, his visit to the Prussian Court of Frederic the Great, his life at Ferney, near Geneva, his hatred of the Catholic Church and clergy, his burial in 1791 in the Pantheon, and the subsequent disappearance of his body, are too familiar to be more than mentioned here. Born at Paris in 1694; died at Paris in 1778.

W

WALPOLE, HORACE. Fourth Earl of Oxford. An English author, *littérateur*, art collector, and member of parliament. In his villa near Twickenham, he gathered an immense and valuable collection of pictures, engravings, curiosities, and works of art. There, also, he established his own printing press, and the first book which he printed was Gray's *Odes.* His *Memoirs* of the Courts of the Georges and his inimitably graceful and witty letters are still consulted and admired. Born in London, 1717; died in London, 1797.

WATT, JAMES. Scottish engineer, inventor, and chemist; even in youth a profound student of mechanics and experimental sciences. He earned his living at first as mathematical-instrument maker for the University of Glasgow. While there, in 1760, he was employed to repair a crude model of a Newcomen steam-engine, and at once began to improve upon it. One invention followed another till he become a manufacturer of the forerunner of our modern locomotives. He also made important chemical discoveries, especially that of the composition of water. Born at Greenock in 1736; died near Birmingham in 1819.

WISEMAN, NICHOLAS PATRICK, CARDINAL. English cardinal of Irish descent, born at Seville, Spain, in 1802. He was appointed Vicar-apostolic of the Catholic Church in London. In 1850, he was made Archbishop of Westminster, and Cardinal. He was an eloquent lecturer and preacher, and the author of *Fabiola, or Christian Life in the Catacombs.* Died in London, 1865.

CPSIA information can be obtained
at www.ICGtesting.com
Printed in the USA
LVOW13s1629040318
568596LV00034B/712/P